INDUSTRY MATTERS

Englisch für Industriekaufleute

von Fritz Michler und Silvia Welt

Cornelsen

Industry Matters wurde geplant und entwickelt von der Verlagsredaktion der Cornelsen Press GmbH & Co. KG, Berlin

Verfasser/in:	Dr Fritz Michler, Garbsen Silvia Welt, Hamburg
Berater:	Manfred Thönicke, Hamburg Dr Horst-Ralf Steinbach, Halle/Westf.
Projektleitung:	Jim Austin
Verlagsredaktion:	Janan Barksdale
Außenredaktion:	Dr Steve Williams, Rachel Wood
Redaktionelle Mitarbeit:	Eleanor Toal, Fritz Preuss (word lists)
Layout und technische Umsetzung:	Oxford Designers & Illustrators
Bildredaktion:	Uta Hübner
Umschlagfoto:	Corbis/Stock Market/John Madere

Erhältlich sind auch:
Audio-CD
Handbuch für den Unterricht

www.cornelsen.de

Die Internet-Adressen und -Dateien, die in diesem Lehrwerk angegeben sind, wurden vor Drucklegung geprüft (Stand: August 2002). Der Verlag übernimmt keine Gewähr für die Aktualität und den Inhalt dieser Adressen und Dateien oder solcher, die mit ihnen verlinkt sind.

1. Auflage, 4. Druck 2007 / 06

Alle Drucke dieser Auflage sind inhaltlich unverändert und können im Unterricht nebeneinander verwendet werden.

Druck: GRASPO CZ, a. s., Tschechische Republik

ISBN 978-3-8109-6716-9

Inhalt gedruckt auf säurefreiem Papier aus nachhaltiger Forstwirtschaft.

VORWORT

Industry Matters ist ein völlig neu entwickeltes Lehrwerk für Industriekaufleute, die am Berufsschulunterricht oder an betrieblichen Fortbildungsmaßnahmen teilnehmen. Das Werk basiert auf den Lehrplänen der Bundesländer für Berufschulen. Durch die Arbeit mit dem Lehrwerk werden die Lernenden auch auf die KMK-Zertifikate ‚Industriekaufmann/-frau' vorbereitet.

Industry Matters richtet sich an Lernende, deren Englischkenntnisse den Anforderungen eines mittleren Bildungsabschlusses bzw. eines durchschnittlichen gymnasialen Grundkursabschlusses entsprechen. Darüber hinaus enthält jede Unit mit den *Advanced Materials* auch anspruchsvolleren Lernstoff für Lernende mit fortgeschrittenen Englischkenntnissen. Ein Grundwortschatz von ca. 850 Wörtern wird vorausgesetzt. Dieser ist in einem gesonderten Vokabelverzeichnis aufgeführt.

Industry Matters besteht aus zehn Units, von denen jede eine in sich abgeschlossene Handlung enthält. Es ist möglich, einzelne Units auszulassen, jedoch wird empfohlen, wann immer Zeit und Lehrpläne es ermöglichen, die gegebene Reihenfolge einzuhalten, um einen kontinuierlichen Aufbau des Fachvokabulars zu gewährleisten.

Industry Matters ist für einen handlungsorientierten und praxisbezogenen Unterricht konzipiert. In den Units werden die Lernenden aufgefordert, an den dargestellten Handlungen aktiv mitzuwirken, indem sie Aufgaben übernehmen, die im kaufmännischen Betrieb anfallen, z.B. Telefonate entgegennehmen, Buchungen tätigen, Besucher empfangen, Preise und Lieferbedingungen vereinbaren, Faxe und kurze Geschäftsbriefe nach deutschen Vorgaben verfassen u.v.m. Um die Realitätsnähe der einzelnen Handlungsabläufe zu gewährleisten, werden authentische Fälle aus deutschen Firmen den meisten Units zu Grunde gelegt. Die Authentizität der Briefe, Faxe und Dokumente ermöglicht einen durch und durch praxisbezogenen Unterricht.

Industry Matters vermittelt die englischsprachigen Grundlagen, auf denen sicheres Auftreten und korrektes Handeln im kaufmännischen Bereich basieren. Wenn die Lernenden sich dabei mit Vergnügen der englischen Sprache bedienen, hat dieses Werk sein Ziel erreicht.

Dialog bzw. Text auf der CD

CONTENTS

1 A VISIT TO AIRBUS

1 WARM UP

aviation
electronics
iron/steel
ship building
chemicals/textiles
coal
vehicle manufacturing
aluminium

Answer these questions.

1. Can you name the capitals of the federal states?
2. Why are industries located in certain areas?
3. Is there a correlation between industry locations and water?
4. Name the main industries in your state. Why are they there?
5. Where is the aviation industry based in Germany?
6. Do you know how many sites Airbus has in Germany and where they are?

2 2 A VISITOR FROM BRITAIN

Jane Spencer owns a British company which manufactures electronic components. She has an appointment with Daniel Helms of Airbus. Unfortunately, Mr Helms is delayed. Meanwhile Julia Reichel, his personal assistant, takes care of the visitor.

Listen to the dialogue. How does Julia Reichel make her visitor feel at ease?

REICHEL Hello. You must be Ms Spencer from Electronics International. I'm Ms Reichel, Mr Helms' personal assistant.

SPENCER Yes, I'm Jane Spencer. Pleased to meet you.

REICHEL Pleased to meet you too. Mr Helms has just called to say that he will be a quarter of an hour late. I'm sorry about that: the traffic is really heavy right now. Please take a seat ... Can I get you something to drink?

SPENCER Yes, please. A coffee with milk and two sugars would be lovely.

...

REICHEL Is this the first time you've visited Airbus, Ms Spencer?

SPENCER Yes, it is. We do a lot of business with German companies, but we haven't had the opportunity to work with Airbus before.

REICHEL Then let me tell you a little bit about our Hamburg plant.

SPENCER Yes, please do.

REICHEL This plant began operation in 1940, long before Airbus was actually founded. It belonged to Blohm & Voss at that time.

SPENCER I thought that they built ships.

REICHEL That's right, but they diversified into aircraft in the 1930s. Later on they merged with Messerschmitt-Bölkow to form MBB and a year later – in 1970 – the Airbus era began.

SPENCER Right. So what is your contribution here in Hamburg to the Airbus production process?

REICHEL We deliver the largest fuselage section for all Airbus types.

SPENCER I see. Where does the final assembly take place?

REICHEL In Toulouse and in Hamburg. There is a so-called 'air bridge' between the plants of the partner companies and the final assembly sites. It's served by a fleet of special transport aircraft, the 'Beluga'.

SPENCER Oh, yes. I've seen that funny-looking aircraft several times. How many people actually work for Airbus?

REICHEL The company has about 16,800 employees in Germany and 45,000 worldwide.

Beluga transporter

SPENCER And how many aircraft are completed each month?

REICHEL Twenty-seven on average.

SPENCER That adds up to a lot of planes!

REICHEL Yes. To date we've sold about 4,400 aircraft, worth more than 100 billion US dollars.

SPENCER Does that make Airbus the largest aircraft manufacturer in the world?

REICHEL Not quite, but with the new A380, we hope to establish a lead over our main competitor, Boeing.

Read or listen to the dialogue again. What can you say about the following?

1 Airbus' employees
2 Airbus' competitors
3 the 'Beluga'
4 the A380

3 WORKING WITH WORDS

Find the English equivalents of these words in the dialogue.

1 Anlage
2 diversifizieren
3 fusionieren
4 Herstellungsverfahren
5 Montage
6 Konzern
7 Angestellte/r
8 Hersteller

CULTURE

SHAKING HANDS AND FIRST-NAME TERMS

British, North American and Australian business people shake hands the first time they meet, and on meeting again after a period of time (weeks, months or years). They also shake hands on parting if they do not expect to see each other for some time. However, if they meet frequently, most do not shake hands every time.

British and Australian business people usually introduce themselves with their first name and surname. North Americans may even introduce themselves with just their first name.

Most business people from these countries feel more comfortable addressing business associates by their first name. However, they expect German business people to be rather formal, so they may be unsure whether first-name terms are appropriate.

4 PLEASED TO MEET YOU!

Work in groups of three. Use the business cards below to introduce yourself and each other.

George B. Wilson *Head of Sales*
Wilson Exports Inc.
822 Third Avenue
New York, NY 10022
Tel (212) 870-9953 *Fax* (212) 870-9151
gb.wilson@swbell.net

Phil Cartney
Managing Director
Carling Ave. 1274
Ottawa, ON KN1 7K6
Canada
Tel 001-613-559-4748
Fax 001-613-559-2285
cartney@aol.ca
CARTNEY & SONS LTD

Sophy O'Connor
Department Manager Fashion
4, Pembroke Gardens
Dublin 21, Ireland
Tel +35312758387
Fax +35312758145
oconnor@megastore.ie
THE MEGA STORE

KPM OFFICE DESIGN
Daisy Jordan
Director
Product Development
325 Southwest Street
Sydney
New South Wales 2006
Australia
Tel +61-2-3544-2677
Fax +61-2-3544-2866
Jordan@kpm.au

LANGUAGE

INTRODUCTIONS

- **To introduce yourself:**
  formal 'May I introduce myself? / Allow me to introduce myself. My name is Jenny Simpson. I'm from ETS Electronics.'
  informal 'Hello, I'm Jenny Simpson from ETS Electronics.'
- **To introduce somebody else:**
  formal 'May I introduce you to Mrs Wright? She's our accountant.'
  'Mrs Miller, let me introduce you to Mr Evans. Mr Evans, Mrs Miller.'
  informal 'Have you met Dorothy Wright, our accountant?'
  'Judy, I'd like you to meet John Evans. John Evans, Judy Greene.'
- **To respond to an introduction (eg while shaking hands):**
  formal 'How do you do?' – 'How do you do?'
  informal 'Nice/Pleased to meet you.' – 'Nice/Pleased to meet you (too).'

5 A COMPANY BROCHURE

Jane Spencer is still waiting for Mr Helms. Julia Reichel has given her a brochure to look at while she waits. An article attracts her interest.

AIRBUS

Flying into the future

Predictions are for air travel to double within the next ten to fifteen years. Unfortunately, airport and air traffic infrastructures are not expected to keep up with this increase. The result: overcrowding, both in the air and on the ground. Aircraft spend approximately 30,000 hours each year circling over airports, waiting to land. This wastes 100,000 tonnes of fuel – enough fuel for one Airbus to fly around the globe 800 times.

Increased use of current aircraft types obviously cannot solve this problem. One solution could be aircraft with 500 or more seats. A new generation of jetliners offering this capacity is being developed in order to respond to the growth in passenger numbers.

At present, the aircraft with the largest passenger capacity is the American-built Boeing 747-400, with 416 seats and a maximum flight range of 13,570 km – corresponding to the distance Los Angeles–Sydney.

Now Airbus, Boeing's European competitor, is developing a jetliner which can seat as many as 555 passengers (the extended version can even seat 650) and cover a distance of 14,800 km. This new aircraft is the A380. Airbus is also developing an A380 F freighter version with a payload of 150 tonnes and a range of 10,400 km, as the freight market is growing at twice the rate of the passenger market.

Is this new generation of aircraft just a prestige project for the airline industry – or will it really help to solve the air traffic problem? We shall soon see: the first A380s will roll off the production line in 2006.

What do these numbers refer to in the article?

1 650
2 30,000
3 416
4 14,800
5 150
6 10,400

6 WORKING WITH WORDS

Draw this table in your exercise book. Fill in the missing nouns and verbs from the article.

verb	noun(s)
to predict	prediction
... [1]	expectation
to increase	... [2]
to solve	... [3]
... [4]	response

verb	noun(s)
to compete	... [5]
... [6]	development
to grow	... [7]
to produce	... [8]

LANGUAGE

HOW TO SAY AND WRITE NUMBERS

German	English	Written as words
1.200	1,200	one thousand two hundred
155.000	155,000	one hundred and fifty-five thousand
1.000.000	1,000,000	one million
1.000.000.000	1,000,000,000	one billion (*eine Milliarde*)
2,35	2.35	two point three five

- In English, unlike in German, a 'point' is used for decimals and a comma is used to separate blocks of three digits.

7 FINDING OUT THE DETAILS

STUDENT A: Look at the information card on the left below ('Airbus A380'). Complete the card by asking Student B for the information you need.

STUDENT B: Turn to File 6 on page 121. Respond to your partner's questions.

Now swap roles for the card on the right ('Boeing 747-400'). Student A should use File 1 on page 119.

Airbus A380

overall length	______
height	24 m
wingspan	______
number of engines	4
passenger load	555
or (extended version)	650
flight range	______
cruising speed	______
fuel capacity	______
max. takeoff weight	______
first delivery	______

Boeing 747-400

overall length	71 m
height	______
wingspan	64 m
number of engines	______
passenger load	416–524
flight range	______
cruising speed	______
fuel capacity	______
max. takeoff weight	______
first delivery	______

8 MAKING COMPARISONS

Work with your partner to say which aircraft:

1 is bigger
2 can carry more people
3 is heavier
4 can fly further without refuelling
5 has more engines
6 was built first

3

9 GETTING TO KNOW THE COMPANY

At last Daniel Helms arrives. He rushes in to greet Jane Spencer.

1 Listen to the dialogue. Who takes the leading role in the conversation? Why do you think this is?

2 Draw a table with four rows in your exercise book. Then listen to the dialogue again and take notes for each of the companies.

Company organization
Employees
Products
Turnover

LANGUAGE

BUSINESS NAMES

Ltd Limited Company (*GmbH*). These companies are owned privately by up to 50 shareholders.

Plc Public Limited Company (*AG*). These companies sell shares to the public.

Inc or Corp Incorporated. These companies may be 'closed corporations' (*GmbH*) or 'open corporations' (*AG*).

Pty Ltd Proprietary Limited Company. The Australian and South African equivalent of 'Ltd'.

10 PRESENTING YOUR COMPANY

1 Listen to the two dialogues in this chapter again. Write down useful expressions for introducing a company.

EXAMPLE:
The company has about 16,800 employees in Germany and 45,000 worldwide.

2 You are introducing your company to a visitor: what information will you give? Use the word spider below to give you some ideas.

EXAMPLE:
Our company is a manufacturer of office equipment. We have offices in Munich and Berlin and we have subsidiaries in Taiwan and Malaysia. The company has about 500 employees worldwide. Last year our turnover was 150 million euros ...

GRAMMAR

GRAMMAR YOU CAN USE TO ... TALK ABOUT THE PRESENT

1 We **do** a lot of business with German companies.
2 Julia **takes** care of the visitor.
3 The traffic **is** really heavy right now.
4 Predictions **are** for air travel to double.
5 Jane Spencer **is** still **waiting** for Mr Helms.

Simple present

- *Diese Zeitform wird für gleich bleibende Zustände, feststehende Tatsachen und sich wiederholende Handlungen verwendet. (1–4)*
- *Bei* he/she/it *wird in der Regel* -(e)s *an die Grundform des Verbs angehängt. (2)*
- *Das Verb* be *wird zu* am/is/are. *(3, 4)*

Present continuous

- *Diese Zeitform drückt aus, dass eine Handlung andauert und nicht abgeschlossen ist. (5)*
- *Das* present continuous *wird mit* am/is/are *und der* -ing-*Form gebildet. (5)*

11 PRACTICE

Use the words to make complete sentences. Use the simple present or the present continuous as appropriate.

1 people / in meetings / often / business cards / exchange
2 she / not / work / normally / with other firms
3 right now / order / spare parts / I / British company / London
4 he / come / late / always / meeting / new customers
5 competitor / at the moment / new product / develop / our biggest
6 no / car / production line / at the moment / roll off / due to strike
7 my company / goods / produce / Asian market
8 my boss / visit / currently / in Hungary / our subsidiary

Advanced materials

1 INDUSTRIAL COST REDUCTION

Read the article. What are the advantages of the commonality method? Make a list.

AIRBUS COMMONALITY

Right from the start, Airbus developed a system of commonality for airframes, for on-board systems, for cockpits and for training and handling characteristics. This similarity between the different aircraft of the Airbus family reduces training, maintenance and operational costs substantially.

Pilots, engineers and cabin crew only need a minimum of training to transfer from one aircraft type to another. Pilots, for instance, are able to fly different Airbus types with only one qualification, since the cockpit layout is virtually identical between different types.

This 'common design philosophy' was taken further in the mid-80s with the 'fly-by-wire family', which meant that the next product range shared similar on-board systems and almost identical handling characteristics. Thus crew training courses could be reduced from 25 working days to one or two days.

This mobility between aircraft types also leads to greater job satisfaction amongst crew. It offers more balanced workloads due to a wider range of routes and aircraft. Cost savings are achieved through enhanced crew productivity and the ability to schedule different-sized aircraft for the same routes without creating crew scheduling problems.

Finally, significant savings are possible through reducing stocks of spare parts, with common parts accounting for as much as 95 per cent of each aircraft in the single-aisled Airbus family.

2 DISCUSSION

Discuss these questions with your fellow students and/or with colleagues.

1. Commonality is one method of cost reduction. Which other methods are there?
2. Which other industries could benefit from such a commonality approach? Think about the automobile industry, for example: does it use similar strategies?
3. How does your company save costs?

3 A PRESENTATION

Prepare a presentation. Ask people in your company how much money they save through cost-reduction methods. Then present your results and support them with graphs or diagrams.

2 ROLES AND RESPONSIBILITIES AT MEDSET

1 WARM UP

Look at these different places of work. What are the advantages and disadvantages of each of these workplaces? Which one would you prefer?

1

2

3

4

4 2 AN APPOINTMENT

MEDSET Medizintechnik GmbH is a medium-sized company which produces and distributes medical devices. It works in partnership with INNOVISION A/S, a Danish company which has developed Innocor, a new and unique device in cardiology diagnostics. Sven Mortensen of INNOVISION has just arrived at MEDSET for an appointment.

Termin

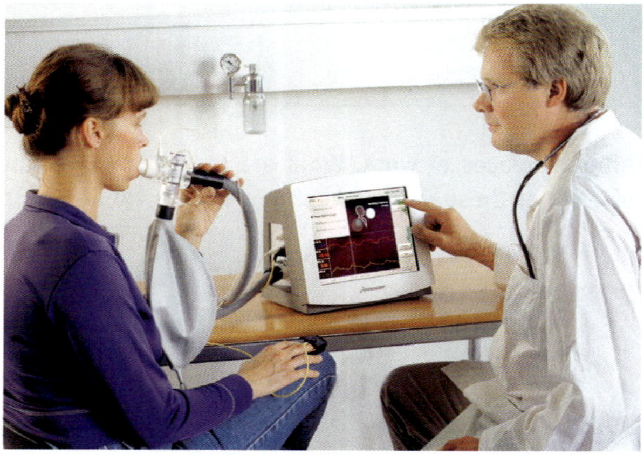

Listen to the receptionist's instructions and find Ms Richter's office on the plan.

Ground floor

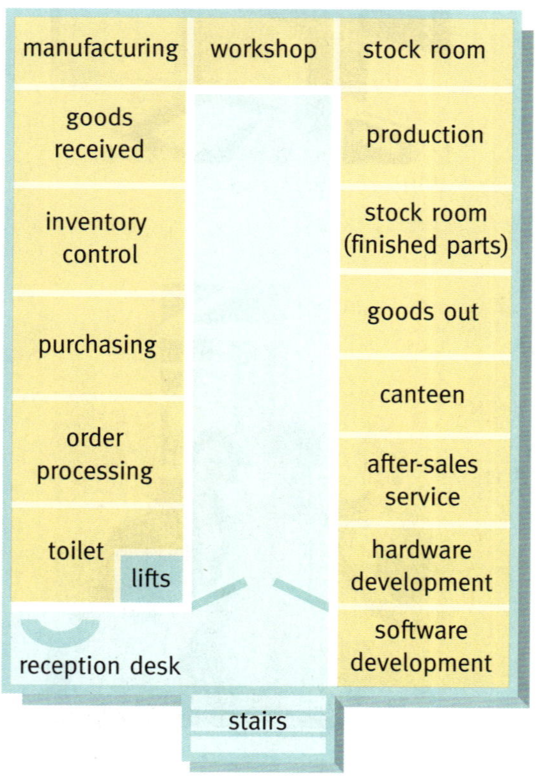

First floor

LANGUAGE

GIVING DIRECTIONS

Go straight on/ahead.
Turn left/right (and left/right again).
Go across the corridor.
Take the lift to the ground/first/second floor.
It's on the right-hand/left-hand side.
It's next to ... .
It's opposite ... .
It's in front of/behind the ... .
It's just after/before the ... .
It's between ... and ... .

3 HOW DO I GET TO ... ?

STUDENT A: Ask how to get:

- **from the purchasing department to the marketing department**
- **from software development to the managing director's office**

STUDENT B: Look at the plan and answer your partner's questions.

Now swap roles.
STUDENT B: Ask how to get:

- **from the reception desk to the archives**
- **from the conference room to the canteen**

STUDENT A: Look at the plan and answer your partner's questions.

4 DESCRIBING YOUR OWN COMPANY

STUDENT A: Draw a rough sketch of the building or site where you work. Don't show it to your partner. Describe the plan of the building or site.

STUDENT B: Listen to your partner's description. Draw the plan on your own sheet of paper.

Compare drawings. Are they the same? Now swap roles.

5

5 PLANNING A PRODUCT LAUNCH

Sven Mortensen meets Klaus Seifert and Gerda Richter of MEDSET.

Listen to the dialogue. What are the job titles of Mr Seifert and Ms Richter? Where in the building does the main discussion take place?

SEIFERT Hello, Mr Mortensen. Nice to meet you. I'm Klaus Seifert, the managing director of MEDSET, and this is Gerda Richter, our sales director.

MORTENSEN Nice to meet you, Mr Seifert, Ms Richter.

RICHTER How was your journey from Copenhagen? Did everything run smoothly?

MORTENSEN Yes, it was fine. We landed on time, and the traffic was light on the way here from the airport.

SEIFERT Good. Let's walk over to the conference room. We can help ourselves to some coffee and biscuits.

A little later ...

MORTENSEN Well, Mr Seifert, I'm glad that you like our new product and that you may be interested in taking over distribution in Germany. How do you want to proceed?

SEIFERT Over to you, Ms Richter.

RICHTER Thank you. First of all, our product management department will carry out a market analysis – to evaluate whether there is a demand for Innocor in Germany.

MORTENSEN I'm sure you will find a ready market for our product.

RICHTER Assuming that you are right, our sales department will send letters to our existing customers, informing them about the product. What sales literature can you give us?

MORTENSEN We have brochures, but they're in English and Danish. Will that present a problem?

RICHTER No. Our marketing department will arrange for German translations to be made right away. The next phase will be an advertising campaign. Marketing will place advertisements in specialist journals, send out mailings and promote the product via our website.

MORTENSEN Excellent.

RICHTER At the same time, our sales and product management departments will brief the sales representatives about Innocor, so that they can demonstrate it to potential customers.

MORTENSEN Do you have a large field sales force?

RICHTER Not that large, but our representatives are experienced, highly skilled negotiators.

MORTENSEN Then hopefully they'll return with lots of orders ...

RICHTER ... so that the order processing department will be kept busy. Then Innocor will be dispatched to the customer.

MORTENSEN Who installs the equipment?

RICHTER Our after-sales service department will send out technicians to install it.

SEIFERT Thank you, Ms Richter ... I think we have settled all the major points for the moment. Are you both ready for lunch?

6 GOING INTO DETAIL

Listen to or read the dialogue again. Copy and complete the organization chart of MEDSET.

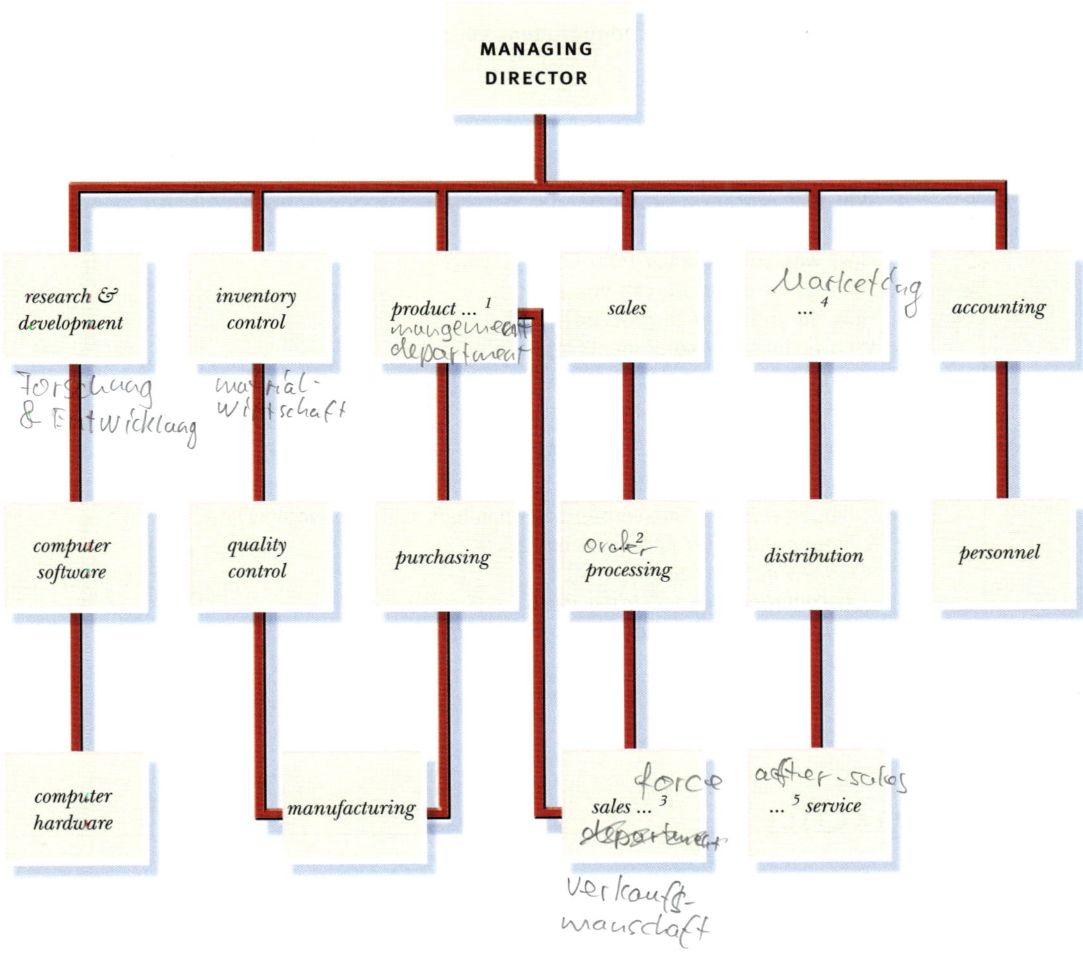

7 FIND THE RIGHT MATCH

1 **Look again at your completed organization chart of MEDSET. First find the English equivalents of these departments:**

a Auftragsabwicklung order processing
b Fertigung manufacturing
c Vertrieb distribution
d Verkauf sales
e Buchhaltung accounting
f Kundendienst after-sales service
g Einkauf purchasing

2 **Now translate the other department names into German.**

8 RESPONSIBILITIES

STUDENT A: Choose a department from the organization chart. (Don't tell your partner which one.) Describe to your partner in English what the people in the department do.

STUDENT B: Decide which department your partner is describing.

Now swap roles.

GRAMMAR

GRAMMAR YOU CAN USE TO ... ASK QUESTIONS

1 **Will** that **present** a problem?
2 **Are** you ready for lunch?
3 How **was** your journey from Copenhagen?
4 What sales literature **can** you **give** us?
5 How **do** you **want** to proceed?
6 Who **installs** the equipment?
7 **Do** you **have** a large field sales force?
8 **Did** everything **run** smoothly?

Das Hilfsverb do *bei der Fragebildung:*

- *ohne* do*:*
  - *Fragen mit den Hilfsverben* have/has/had, will *und* would *(1)*
  - *Fragen mit einer Form von* be *(2, 3)*
  - *Fragen mit Modalverben (4)*
    Ausnahmen: *Modalverben mit* to, *z.B.* want to *(5)*
  - *Fragen mit einem Fragewort, das Subjekt oder Teil des Subjekts ist (6)*
- *mit* do*:*
  - *alle anderen Fragen im* simple present *oder im* simple past *(7, 8)*

9 PRACTICE

Make up appropriate questions for the following answers. There is often more than one solution.

1 Our company was founded in 1987.
2 The managing director is Klaus Seifert.
3 MEDSET has 38 employees.
4 No, we don't. We only have five sales representatives.
5 No. Detlef Bauer is the head of our marketing department.
6 No. Our brochures are only in English.
7 The flight was fine, thanks.
8 Our marketing department will translate the brochure.

LANGUAGE

SMALL TALK

- **Ask about the trip:**
  how he/she got here
  how the journey was
- **Ask about accommodation:**
  where he/she is staying
  whether it's in the centre or far out
  whether the neighbourhood is nice
- **Ask some personal things:**
  where she/he lives
  whether she/he likes it there
  whether this is his/her first trip to Germany
  about his/her first impressions of the country
- **Ask about his/her company:**
  where it is located
  how many people it employs
  whether it operates world-wide

10 WELCOME!

STUDENT A: You welcome a British or American visitor to your company. Introduce yourself and start the conversation with small talk.

STUDENT B: Respond as appropriate.

1 Begrüßen Sie den/die Besucher/in und stellen Sie sich vor.

2 Begrüßen Sie die Person, die Sie abholt.

3 Fragen Sie nach dem Verlauf der Anreise.

4 Geben Sie Auskunft darüber.

5 Fragen Sie, ob Ihr Gegenüber schon früher in Deutschland war.

6 Verneinen Sie dies.

7 Fragen Sie nach der Unterkunft.

8 Sie wohnen in einem kleinen Hotel im Stadtzentrum.

9 Fragen Sie nach dem Heimatland Ihres Besuchers.

10 Erzählen Sie von Ihrer Heimat.

Now swap roles.

CULTURE

WHAT TO AVOID IN SMALL TALK

Topics such as politics, religion, health and salaries are not usually suitable subjects for small talk with visitors from English-speaking countries.

Whilst some British business people are indifferent to the Royal Family, some have definite opinions on the matter, so avoid this topic unless your visitor mentions it first. Try not to contradict anything your visitor has said: many Britons consider it rude to contradict people, even if they are sure that they are wrong!

North Americans may be more open about their opinions, and are less likely to be offended if you are open about yours. Australians usually react positively to a business partner who is open and honest about his or her opinions.

11 MEDSET'S EMPLOYEES

In this company magazine, various employees talk about their responsibilities at MEDSET. Which department is each of them in?

medset
MEDIZINTECHNIK

I'm **Rosa Fernandez**. I work in the sales department. My job involves a lot of written correspondence. I write offers and send out brochures to customers. Apart from that, I am responsible for updating our customer database and the archives. I also arrange appointments for our sales representatives with customers.

My name's **Sven Olsen**. As the head of inventory control, it's my responsibility to ensure the high quality standard of our products. I coordinate all product inspections, organize the checking of incoming goods and make sure that materials and parts are labelled with item numbers. I also approve new suppliers and evaluate the ones that we already have.

I'm the person to talk to about order processing – **Maria Cabana**. Once a product is ready to be dispatched abroad, I prepare all the necessary documents, such as delivery notes, invoices, shipping documents, address labels and so on. I check that the documents exactly correspond with the requirements of the forwarding agent.

I'm **Kashmir Singh**, MEDSET's senior 'trouble shooter'. If there is a problem with one of our products, it's up to me to deal with it. Most technical difficulties can be solved on the phone, but if there is a genuine malfunction, I send out a technician immediately, to either repair the equipment on site or replace it. In our business, after-sales service has to be taken very seriously.

Hello, I'm **Andrew Wright**, and my area of responsiblity is product management. Our department conducts a market analysis for each potential new product. If the result is positive, I coordinate the different departments involved in the production of the product. I also decide how many tests are necessary to ensure that the product works properly. Finally, I write the user manual.

I'm **Olga Smolski**. I'm in charge of the purchasing department. My assistant and I check that we have sufficient stocks of components and materials to meet expected orders. We register all incoming goods in a purchase book, check all suppliers' invoices and liaise with inventory control if there are problems with suppliers.

Find in the text six different ways of saying 'I am responsible for ...'.

12 FINDING THE RIGHT PERSON

Who do the following people need to talk to, and why? Choose the appropriate person from the company magazine.

EXAMPLE:
'I need a list of MEDSET's ten best customers.'
'You need to talk to Rosa Fernandez. She's responsible for updating the customer database.'

1 'We've just bought some equipment from MEDSET. We can't make it work properly.'
2 'There seems to be a mistake in these shipping documents.'
3 'We've just received an order for fifty monitoring systems. Do we need to order more components?'
4 'I've got a great idea for a new product.'

6 13 A NEW APPRENTICE

Klaus Seifert has returned from his business lunch and talks to his next visitor, Cathy Hermanns. She's an American woman who will be doing her apprenticeship at MEDSET. Mr Seifert explains the different phases of the training in English.

Listen to the recording. Put the following departments into the order in which Mr Seifert mentions them:

marketing ▪ order processing ▪ personnel and accounts ▪ production
sales ▪ stock room

Copy the table into your exercise book. Listen to the recording again and complete the table.

Department	Duties
sales	checking invoices

14 A FULL PROGRAMME

In the evening, Cathy explains the different phases of her training to her husband, who is German. Help her to summarize the main points in German.

Advanced materials

KAIZEN

A new management strategy for a new generation of companies

The Japanese term *kaizen* (*kai* 'to change'; *zen* 'good') describes the concept of continuous improvement. It has become the label for a management philosophy adopted by more and more companies around the world. EADS/Airbus is one example.

The context is a world in which the pace of change seems to increase each year. Production processes are constantly evolving; existing technologies are replaced by new ones; work is becoming more varied and complex. The more diversified the processes become, the greater the need for specialists who can work independently. Conventional hierarchical structures are outdated in this context.

Implementing *kaizen* requires completely new management strategies. Here are the five main points:

1. Major decisions are made by strong leadership from the top; bottom-up decision-making processes belong to the past, when decisions were reached in seven or eight steps.
2. Instead of the conventional pyramidal hierarchy, a horizontal network is built up. Specialized work groups organize their own operations as a team. Individual input and merit are the key to higher salaries and promotion, not seniority.
3. The organizational structure is decentralized and flexible, and may be spread across several small bases.
4. Not just maximum profit, but maximum quality and customer satisfaction are the criteria for the success of a company.
5. Consequently, research and development and innovation have more importance than the traditional focus on output. Not 'mass' but 'class' is the first priority.

1 TRADITIONAL VERSUS *KAIZEN*

Put the statements from the text above into two lists: traditional and *kaizen* management methods. Then discuss the pros and cons of each method.

2 *KAIZEN* IN YOUR COMPANY

Develop a questionnaire which incorporates the five main principles of *kaizen*. Then interview people in your organization: do they work according to these principles?

3 A TELEPHONE CALL TO HOLZLAND WULF

1 WARM UP

Answer these questions together with a partner.

Telephone quiz

1 Explain to a British person what these telephone numbers stand for in Germany.
a 030 **b** 040 **c** 089

2 When would you dial these numbers?
a 0044 **b** 0049 **c** 001 **d** 0061

3 Can you identify these German numbers?
a 0170 **b** 0800 **c** 0190

4 When would you call these numbers?
a 999 (UK) **b** 911 (USA) **c** 110 (Germany)

5 A business partner from America asks you for your number. Tell her your country code, area code and number.

1 a area code for Berlin, **b** area code for Hamburg, **c** area code for Munich
2 These are 'country codes'. They are used as follows: **a** when dialling a number in the UK, **b** when dialling a German number from abroad, **c** when dialling a number in the USA, **d** when dialling a number in Australia
3 a mobile phone number, **b** information number, **c** expensive number (chat line, etc.)
4 a, b, c when you need an emergency service

7 2 MAKING CONTACT

HolzLand is a co-operative of 130 timber products stores throughout Germany. One of them, HolzLand Wulf in Ahrensburg, has been a family business for five generations. It has 30 employees and a 1.25-hectare site. Its products include everything from nails to summer houses.

Today the company receives an interesting enquiry ...

Listen to the dialogue. Why does Jessica Wend suggest that Mr Wulf is the person to speak to, do you think?

WEND HolzLand Wulf, Jessica Wend. Guten Tag.

SIMMONS Hello, this is Dan Simmons of Woodworks in Brighton. Do you speak English?

WEND Yes, of course. What can I do for you?

SIMMONS I'd like to speak to someone from your sales department, please.

WEND Yes, certainly. Could you tell me what it's about, please?

SIMMONS I need a price for a bulk order of a certain fence you sell.

WEND In that case you should talk to our managing director, Uwe Wulf. Just one moment, please. I'll put you through ... I'm sorry, his line is engaged. Do you want to hold the line or shall I get him to call you back?

SIMMONS I'd prefer it if he called me back. My number is ...

WEND Just a second, please. I need my pen. OK, go ahead.

SIMMONS Our number is 01273 35281, but you don't dial the zero from abroad, of course.

WEND I'm sorry, I didn't quite catch that. Could you say that again, please?

SIMMONS Certainly. After the country code you dial 1273 for Brighton and then 35281. My extension is 52. Did you get that?

WEND Yes. 1273 35281, extension 52.

SIMMONS That's right.

WEND Thank you, Mr Simmons. I'll get him to call you back as soon as he is free.

SIMMONS Thanks for your help. Who am I speaking to?

WEND My name's Wend, Jessica Wend.

SIMMONS Goodbye, Ms Wend.

WEND Goodbye, Mr Simmons.

Half an hour later, Uwe Wulf calls England:

SECRETARY Woodworks Brighton. Can I help you?

WULF Good afternoon, it's Uwe Wulf calling from Germany. Mr Simmons is expecting my call.

SECRETARY I'm sorry, but Mr Simmons has just gone out. He's going to be out until 4 pm. Can anybody else help you?

WULF I don't think so. I need to speak to him personally. And it's rather urgent.

SECRETARY Then I'll give you his mobile number. It's 079 229 85 46.

WULF 079 229 85 46. Thanks, I really appreciate your help. Goodbye.

SECRETARY You're welcome, Mr Wulf. Goodbye.

At last, Uwe Wulf manages to reach Dan Simmons:

WULF Hello, Mr Simmons. It's Uwe Wulf here, from HolzLand in Germany. You tried to contact me. It was about an order.

SIMMONS Ah, Herr Wulf. Thanks for calling me back … I'm sorry, it's really hard to hear you because the traffic's so loud. I'll get back to you in ten minutes, if that's convenient for you.

WULF Of course. I'll ask my secretary to interrupt me if I'm on the phone again when you call.

SIMMONS Fine, I'll speak to you shortly. Bye.

WULF Goodbye.

Listen to or read the phone conversations again and find the English equivalents for the following.

1. Ich verbinde Sie. I'll put you through
2. Seine Nummer/Leitung ist besetzt. His line is engaged
3. Wollen Sie dranbleiben? Do you want to hold the line?
4. Ich kümmere mich darum, dass er Sie zurückruft. I'll get him to call you back
5. Es ist ziemlich dringend. It's rather urgent
6. Ich gebe Ihnen seine Handy-Nummer. I'll give you his mobile number.
7. Sie haben versucht, mich zu erreichen. You tried to contact me?
8. … , wenn es Ihnen recht ist. if that's convenient for you.

LANGUAGE

ADDRESSING WOMEN

Ms Jones	a married or unmarried woman [mɪz]
Mrs Jones	a married woman [mɪsɪz]
Miss Jones	an unmarried woman [mɪs]

CULTURE

ANSWERING THE PHONE

In the office, the British usually answer the phone with the company name and a phrase like 'How can I help you?' At home, they simply say their telephone number or 'Hello.'

At work, most North Americans pick up the receiver and say their first and last name and the company name. At home they usually just say 'Hello.'

8 3 MESSAGES FOR JESSICA WEND

Jessica Wend has had a busy day. In the afternoon she notices that she has three answerphone messages in English.

1 Listen to the first message and correct Jessica's mistakes.

Maggie Owen aus New York
Lieferung 3566 - beschädigte Türrahmen
dringend zurückrufen: 001-212-870 957

2 Listen to the two remaining messages and note down the important details.

4 PLEASE LEAVE A MESSAGE ...

Read the instructions below and then record your own answerphone message.

Your boss doesn't speak English very well, so he asks you to call Henry Goldman, the import manager of Goodrich Ltd in Southampton. He gives you a memo with the information you are to communicate. Because of the time difference, Mr Goldman is not yet in his office, so you need to leave a message in English.

Henry Goldman benötigt dringend zehn Carports „Variant". Wir haben aber nicht so viele auf Lager und können die Carports FOB Hamburg innerhalb von fünf Tagen liefern. Finden Sie heraus, ob das früh genug ist oder ob er ein anderes Modell möchte, den „Royal" Carport, der sofort lieferbar wäre und innerhalb eines Tages in Southampton sein könnte. Der „Royal" ist allerdings 90 Euro teurer.

VARIANT Doppelcarport

ROYAL Doppelcarport

LANGUAGE

EXPRESSIONS FOR TELEPHONING

- **Making a call:**
  Good morning. Jane Moore here from Universal Ltd.
  Can I speak to Sam Burgess, please?
  Could you put me through to the marketing department, please?
  I'd like to speak to the person in charge of sales, please.

- **Answering a call:**
  Wayland Plastics. How can I help you?
  Good morning, Wayland Plastics.
  Jim Ferguson speaking.

- **Transferring the call/taking a message:**
  One second/moment, please.
  Hold the line, please.
  I'll put you through. / I'll connect you.
  His line is engaged/busy. Would you like to hold?
  Would you like to leave a message?
  Can I take your number / mobile number / email address?

- **Saying what the call is about:**
  I'm calling about ...
  I'd like to know/find out about ...
  I'm interested in ...
  The reason I'm calling is ...

- **Ending the call:**
  Is there anything else?
  We'll be in touch.
  (I'll) speak to you again soon. Bye.
  Thanks for calling. Goodbye.

5 TELEPHONE QUERIES

Role play: use File 2 on page 119 (student A), File 7 on page 121 (student B).

Gartenpavillons

Bezeichnung	PAVILLON ROHBAU	PAVILLON ROHBAU
Artikelnr.	4824	1 × 2246 / 4 × 2201
Abmessungen L × B × H	387 × 387 × 294 cm	194 × 194 × 294 cm
Preis	495	145

AUSVERKAUFT

Gartenmöbel AMELIA

Bezeichnung	SESSEL	TISCH
Artikelnr.	19006	19012
Abmessungen L × B × H	60 × 67 × 80 cm	140 × 80 × 68 cm
Preis	125	195

AUSVERKAUFT

AUSVERKAUFT

Gartenmöbel MIRANDA

Bezeichnung	SESSEL	TISCH
Artikelnr.	19107	19113
Abmessungen L × B × H	64 × 66 × 102 cm	165/225 × 100 × 72 cm
Preis	145	335

Gartenhäuser

Bezeichnung	GARTENHAUS	GARTENHAUS
Artikelnr.	0112	0120
Außenmaß	380 x 296 cm	446 x 380 cm
Nutzfläche	9,56 m^2	14,87 m^2
Wandhöhe	205 cm	205 cm
umbauter Raum	22,65 m^3	34,97 m^3
Preis	1995	2455

AUSVERKAUFT

9

6 TALKING BUSINESS

1 Listen to the conversation between Uwe Wulf and Dan Simmons. Which of these 'telephone expressions' are used?

- **a** Can I take a message?
- **b** Could you repeat that, please?
- **c** Could you speak a little louder, please? ✓
- **d** Sorry, wrong number.
- **e** The line is bad. ✓
- **f** We were cut off/disconnected. ✓
- **g** Could you repeat that more slowly, please? ✓
- **h** Could you spell that, please? ✓
- **i** I think you have the wrong number.

2 Listen to the dialogue again and write Uwe Wulf's email, summarizing what he agreed with Dan Simmons.

LANGUAGE

HOW TO SAY INTERNET AND EMAIL ADDRESSES

www.holzland-wulf.de = www-dot-holzland-dash-wulf-dot-d-e

http://www.contact_home.com = http-colon-slash-slash-www-dot-contact-underscore-home-dot-com

ernest@hemingway.co.uk = ernest-at-hemingway-dot-co-dot-u-k

CULTURE

POLITENESS

English speakers, and particularly Britons, use a lot of 'extra' words to give a polite and helpful impression. This is particularly important on the telephone. If you give short answers, your conversation partner may think that you are angry or rude.

- When making a request, always use 'please', and start your request with 'Could ...' or 'Would you mind ...'. For example:
  Could you call me back, please?
  Would you mind calling me back, please?
- Try to avoid answering with just 'yes' or 'no'. For example:
  'Did you get that?' – 'Yes, I did.'
  'Will the goods arrive by Wednesday?' – 'No, they won't.'

7 CREATING THE RIGHT IMPRESSION

Rephrase these sentences so that they are more polite.

1. Please call me back.
2. Why are you calling?
3. Please email me.
4. Did you call me? – No.
5. Hold the line.
6. Have you got that? – Yes.
7. What's your email address?
8. Thanks. Bye.

8 GETTING IN TOUCH

Act out this telephone conversation with a partner.

HolzLand employee	**British customer**
1 Melden Sie sich am Telefon.	
	2 Stellen Sie sich vor und bitten Sie darum, mit einem Verkäufer verbunden zu werden, der für Gartenhäuser zuständig ist.
3 Herr Leipold betreut gerade einen Kunden. Fragen Sie, ob der Anrufer eine Nachricht hinterlassen möchte.	
	4 Bitten Sie darum, so bald wie möglich unter Ihrer Nummer zurückgerufen zu werden. Es geht um die Bestellung eines Gartenhauses, das heute Vormittag um 9 Uhr geliefert werden sollte und noch nicht da ist.
5 Die Verbindung ist schlecht. Bitten Sie den Anrufer darum, die Telefonnummer zu wiederholen.	
	6 Wiederholen Sie die Nummer und fügen Sie hinzu, dass Sie nur bis 14 Uhr erreichbar sind. Danach sind Sie nicht mehr im Hause.
7 Versichern Sie dem Anrufer, dass Herr Leipold so schnell wie möglich zurückrufen wird.	
	8 Bedanken Sie sich und verabschieden Sie sich.
9 Verabschieden Sie sich.	

LANGUAGE

WHEN THE PERSON ISN'T AVAILABLE

I'm sorry, but ...
... she's gone out for lunch / just taking her lunch break.
... she's with a customer.
... she's in a conference at the moment.
... she's gone for the day.
... she's on holiday (GB) / vacation (US) until July 27.
... she's away on business.
... she's at the Munich trade fair all week.
... she's no longer with this company.

GRAMMAR

GRAMMAR YOU CAN USE TO ... TALK ABOUT THE FUTURE (1)

1 **I'll get** him to call you back.
2 I think you**'ll have** the consignment within two weeks.
3 **Will** the goods **arrive** by Wednesday?
4 You **will have** the consignment by June 24.
5 He's **going to be** out until 4 pm.

will-future = will + *Grundform*

- *In der gesprochenen Sprache kommt die betonte Form* will *selten vor. Meistens (vor allem mit Pronomen) wird die Kurzform* 'll *benutzt. (1, 2)*
- *In Fragen ohne Fragewort ist nur die betonte Form möglich. (3)*
- *In der Schriftsprache ist die betonte Form üblich: Die unbetonte Form wirkt dort informell. (4)*

going to-future = to be going to + *Grundform*

- *Diese Zeitform wird benutzt, um über Pläne oder Absichten zu sprechen. In der gesprochenen Sprache drückt man damit auch aus, dass etwas mit Sicherheit eintreffen wird. (5)*
- *In der Schriftsprache kommt* going to *etwas seltener vor. Dort wird eher das betonte* will-*Futur benutzt. (4)*

Es gibt Situationen, in denen beide Zeitformen ohne erkennbaren Bedeutungsunterschied möglich sind.

9 DELIVERY DETAILS

Uwe Wulf has spoken to his shipping agent about the delivery to Woodworks. He writes another email to Dan Simmons to inform him of what is happening.

Put the verbs in brackets into an appropriate form of the future tense. Use the going to-future at least twice.

Dear Mr Simmons,
We ... (pack) [1] the fencing on pallets for convenient handling. Our shipping agent Kuhn & Co ... [2] (collect) the pallet from our warehouse on Monday, 5 August. They ... [3] (load) the goods into open-top containers. They ... [4] (use) a combination of road and rail transport: they ... [5] (transfer) the containers to railway waggons at the local rail terminal.

The shipment ... [6] (clear) customs at Dover by Thursday, 15 August. Then lorries ... [7] (deliver) the goods to your premises by 9 am on Friday, 16 August. Can you inform me where the exact drop-off point ... [8] (be)? You ... [9] (not pay) a haulage charge since delivery is included in the price.

I ... [10] (send) you the relevant documents as soon as I have them, which should be in the next couple of days.

Kind regards
Uwe Wulf

Advanced materials

How dangerous are mobile phones?

Mobile or cell(ular) phones have become an essential part of modern living. Whether on busy streets or on public transport, in restaurants or schools or at the airport – there's just no getting away from them. Today 50 million Germans have a mobile phone; worldwide there are more than 500 million subscribers to such services. However, there is now concern that mobile phones might present a health risk to their users, due to the electromagnetic radiation they emit, powerful enough to reach aerials many kilometres away. Sleep disorders, depression, allergies, Alzheimer's disease, heart problems and even cancer and brain tumours have been attributed to the hand-held devices. The list is becoming longer and longer.

Children, in particular, may be more vulnerable to health risks from mobile phones: their thinner skulls and developing nervous systems are likely to absorb more of the potentially harmful radiation. There is not yet sufficient scientific evidence to support this theory, but parents would be wise to take certain precautions. Children under the age of 16 should avoid prolonged and frequent use of a mobile phone and just make brief calls. They should not carry the phone in their breast or trouser pocket as this may increase their risk of developing a heart complaint or testicular cancer.

In Germany, mobile networks have existed for over ten years; in Scandinavia, 85 per cent of the population already use mobile phones. Advocates of mobile phones argue that any detrimental effects on the health of users should have been detected by now, but have not. Therefore, they claim, the phones pose no immediate danger to people.

At present, no definite conclusions can be drawn from the discussion of potential health risks. On balance, there seems to be no reason for alarm. Nevertheless, taking obvious precautions and moderating mobile phone use cannot do any harm.

1 A HEALTH RISK?

Read over the text again and list the arguments for and against treating mobile phones as a health risk. Decide where you stand on this issue, then justify your opinion in a class discussion.

2 CASE STUDY

Find out how many students in your class or colleagues in your company have a mobile phone and how much time they spend talking on it. Then look up information on 'specific energy absorption rate' (SAR) on the Internet and see how much radiation these people are being exposed to.

4 TRAVEL ARRANGEMENTS AT BP

1 WARM UP

BP is a global concern with its headquarters in London. Which of these areas of business do you think BP is involved in?

- computer manufacturing
- oil and gas exploration and drilling
- petrochemical manufacturing
- ship building
- solar power generation
- vehicle manufacturing

What might be the job of the BP employee with these stamps in his/her passport?

2 A MEMO FROM MR BRÜGGER

Hans Brügger, head of personnel, has to go to London for a meeting. He passes the following memo to his personal assistant, Hanna Bertram. Ms Bertram will need to phone BP's central travel booking department for Europe, which is located in London.

How would you convey this information in English? What other information might you need to give? Prepare a list of useful expressions.

Deutsche BP **MEMO**

Von: Brügger **An:** Frau Bertram **Datum:** 15. Juni 2002

Liebe Frau Bertram,
bitte buchen Sie für mich:

- Flug Hamburg–London am Donnerstag, 12. Juli (Sitzung beginnt um 11.30 Uhr), zurück am 20. Juli gegen Abend
- Hotel vom 12. bis 13. Juli – Thistle Tower?
- PKW, Mittelklasse, vom 13. Juli bis 20. Juli

Bitte bestätigen Sie mir alle Buchungen.

MfG
Brügger

10

3 A TRIP TO LONDON

Hanna Bertram phones her colleague, Reeta Patel, in the travel booking department.

Listen to the recording. Do they use the language you prepared in exercise 2, or is the information expressed differently?

PATEL Good morning, Patel speaking.

BERTRAM Hi, Reeta, this is Hanna speaking, from Hamburg.

PATEL Hello, Hanna, what a nice surprise! I haven't heard from you for at least two months.

BERTRAM No, I suppose not. None of our executives wanted to fly during the peak holiday season. Besides, I've changed jobs. I'm now PA to Herr Brügger, in personnel.

PATEL Really? How exciting!

BERTRAM Yes, I'm really enjoying it ... Anyway, there's a big meeting next month in London, involving all the senior personnel people. Herr Brügger is our head of personnel, so he needs to go, and I need to book his flights.

PATEL Fine. Could you spell his name for me, please?

BERTRAM Sure, it's B-R-U-Umlaut-G-G-E-R. Initial J, for Johann.

PATEL Sorry – U-Umlaut?

BERTRAM You know, the two dots. But you can spell it U-E, if you want.

PATEL OK, I've got that ... Can you give me the dates, please?

BERTRAM Yes. He needs to fly out on the morning of Thursday the 12th of July. To arrive in London no later than 9 am. The meeting starts at 11.30 am. It ends on Friday afternoon, but Mr Brügger wants to stay on for another week, touring along the South Coast. So he's flying back on Friday the 20th, in the evening.

PATEL Well, ... we have two alternatives. The first is a Lufthansa flight taking off from Hamburg at 08.15, landing at London Heathrow at 08.35 ... and the second is a British Airways flight taking off at 07.45 and landing at 08.05. And for the return flight on Friday the 20th of July there is a Lufthansa flight from Heathrow at 21.00 or a British Airways flight at 21.15.

BERTRAM How long does it take to get from Heathrow to the centre of London?

PATEL It takes about 45 minutes.

BERTRAM OK. He wants to check in at the hotel first, so we'll take the earlier outbound flight, the British Airways one. And he can fly British Airways on the way back, too. Both flights Business Class, please.

PATEL I'll check the flights and ring back in a minute.

BERTRAM Thanks. Speak to you soon.

How much do you remember? Complete the following sentences, then refer back to the dialogue to check your answers.

1 Hanna calls Reeta because ...
2 Reeta works in the ...
3 There are ... for the outbound flight.
4 Hans Brügger is the ...
5 From the airport it takes ...
6 Reeta will ... and ring back.

4 WORKING WITH WORDS

Find English equivalents in the dialogue for the following expressions.

1 Wir nehmen die frühere Maschine für den Hinflug.
2 Er wird Freitag, den 20. zurückfliegen.
3 Mit Ankunft in London bis spätestens 9.00 Uhr.
4 Er will eine weitere Woche bleiben.
5 Abflug um 7.45 Uhr, Ankunft um 8.05 Uhr.
6 Wie lange dauert es von Heathrow bis ins Zentrum?

11 5 CONFIRMING THE BOOKINGS

Ten minutes later, Reeta Patel phones back. Listen to the dialogue and note down the final travel arrangements. Then write an email from Reeta Patel to Hanna Bertram confirming the details.

LANGUAGE

THE 24-HOUR CLOCK

The 24-hour clock is used less frequently in English than in German, particularly in the spoken language. However, it is often used in Britain when making travel bookings. (It is almost never used in North America.)

Written	**Spoken**
07.00	(Oh) seven hundred (hours)*
	Seven am
	Seven (o'clock) in the morning
07.45	(Oh) seven forty-five*
	Seven forty-five am
	(A) quarter to eight in the morning
21.00	Twenty-one hundred (hours)*
	Nine pm
	Nine (o'clock) in the evening
21.15	Twenty-one fifteen*
	Nine fifteen pm
	(A) quarter past nine in the evening

**travel schedules (GB only)*

6 MAKING TRAVEL RESERVATIONS

Role play: use File 3 on page 120 (student A) and File 8 on page 122 (student B).

7 BOOKING A HOTEL

Write a fax for Hanna Bertram to enquire about a room for Hans Brügger at the Thistle Tower Hotel, using the prompts in the boxes. Refer to the dialogues above and your notes for the information you need.

State:
- your company
- name of the person
- date and approximate time of arrival
- date of departure
- kind of room wanted

Ask:
- price?
- what is included?
- company discount?
- other discounts?
- which credit cards accepted?

8 BROWSING FOR HOTEL INFORMATION

While she's waiting for a response to her fax, Hanna Bertram visits the Thistle Hotels website. Read the web page on page 38: what features at the Thistle Tower might these symbols refer to?

1 

2 

3 

4 

5 

Thistle Tower

THISTLE HOTEL
Tower

Hotel Details

Check prices

Situated on the banks of the River Thames, next to the Tower of London and Tower Bridge and very close to the financial district, this modern four-star hotel offers 801 well-equipped bedrooms, apartments and suites, all with superb views.

Other facilities include City Club floor with gym facilities and early check-in guaranteed by 10.00 latest, 19 airconditioned meeting rooms and a wide range of restaurants including a lounge. Car parking and a water taxi to nearby Canary Wharf for easy access to the financial area are available, both at an additional charge.

Check-in Notice
From 14.00. If rooms are available earlier we will be happy to check you in. For City Club Rooms we can offer 10.00 check-in guaranteed and 18.00 check-out.

Check-out Notice
12 Noon, but late check-out may be possible by prior arrangement.

Leisure Facilities

Check prices

* Coffee Shop
* Fitness Centre
* Gift Shop
* In Room Movies
* Lounge Bar or Suite
* Pub Style Bar
* Satellite Television

Dining Facilities

Check prices

CARVERY RESTAURANT
opening hours:
06.30–10.00, 12.30–15.00, 17.30–22.00 daily
A traditional English carvery serving roasts and specialities of the day.

WWWATER CAFE
Informal cuisine from around the world
opening hours:
07.00–11.00, 12.00–23.00 daily
A vibrant café, nautically themed, with affordable food.

GALLERY LOUNGE
opening hours:
10.00–23.00 daily
A comfortable lounge offering afternoon teas, sandwiches and snacks.

THAMES BAR
opening hours:
17.00–01.00 daily
Informal bar with splendid views of Tower Bridge.

COMOTION COFFEE BAR
opening hours:
06.30–22.30 Mon–Fri; 06.30–late Sat–Sun
All-day coffee bar serving deli-style foods, freshly made sandwiches and salads. Specialising in variety coffees, it also offers a full bar service.

HAAGEN-DAZS CAFE
Premier ice cream, plus snacks and beverages.
opening hours:
10.30–19.00 daily

Roomexpress

Roomexpress is our room service brand, which aims to provide flexibility and choice to our guests throughout the day and night. We always aim to give our guests what you want and need. Roomexpress is designed to give you both of these – in the comfort of your room.

9 RELEVANT INFORMATION

Read the web page again. Make a German summary of useful information for Hans Brügger.

Hans Brügger likes to keep fit, but he also likes British beer. He hates airline food, so he's looking forward to a good breakfast at the hotel before he goes to his meeting on Thursday. He wants to check in no later than 10.15 am. He will be going out to dinner with his colleagues on Thursday evening, but he is looking forward to a quiet evening on Friday before he sets off for the South Coast early on Saturday.

12 10 THE RIGHT CHOICE?

Jamina Robertson, manageress of the Grand Hotel, describes the attractions of her hotel to a potential guest.

Listen to Ms Robertson and compare the facilities mentioned with those at the Thistle Tower. Does the Grand Hotel have anything extra to offer?

CULTURE

HOTELS IN BRITAIN

Britain has plenty of hotel accommodation of all kinds. Large **hotel chains** are comfortable, and offer good business services, but tend to be bland and internationalized: you could equally be in Frankfurt, New York or Hong Kong. If you need something special, look for **country-house** or **'heritage'** hotels, which range from modest country hotels to grand old houses and ancient castles.

If cheaper accommodation is required, look for bed and breakfast establishments or **B&Bs** (also called **guesthouses**). They are small to medium-sized, inexpensive hotels with an informal atmosphere. They offer accommodation and breakfast, but not generally lunch or an evening meal. They are usually unlicensed (alcohol may not be bought or drunk on the premises). The best B&Bs offer excellent value for money; the worst are very bad indeed. Rely on personal recommendations or good guide books.

There is no single system for **rating** hotel accommodation, but the national tourist boards and organizations such as the AA (Automobile Association) and RAC (Royal Automobile Club) show the quality of accommodation by awarding hotels one to five rosettes, crowns, stars or other symbols. A rating of five indicates the most luxury (and the highest price).

The King's Head Hotel
Lymnor
Tel: 0197 4304

English Tourism Council ★★★ HOTEL | AA ★★★ Hotel | RAC ★★★ Hotel

13 11 HIRING A CAR

After the meeting, Hans Brügger intends to tour the South Coast. As he plans to stay in B&Bs, he only needs Ms Bertram to hire a car for him.

Listen to the dialogue and note down the following information.

1 Period of hire
2 Type of car
3 Hire fee per day/week
4 Additional fee per mile
5 Other costs incurred
6 Number of service points in Britain
7 Where to return the car to
8 What Carol asks for

12 FILL THE GAPS

Below you see the website of Car Rental London. Fill in the blanks using the words in the box:

deliver or collect ▪ easy reach ▪ escorted ▪ online quotation system proximity ▪ quality and selection ▪ regular updates ▪ well equipped

Car Rental London

Home
Quotation Request
View Vehicles
Prestige Collection
Meet & Greet
FAQ
E-mail

Car Rental London

We are based in Wimbledon, London SW19 and are within … [1] of Wimbledon Park Tube Station, which is on the District Line.

We are also in close … [2] to the following South and West London locations: Croydon, Purley, Kingston, Brixton, Chelsea, Clapham, Earl's Court, Fulham, Raynes Park, Heathrow, South Kensington, Stockwell, Battersea, Balham, Barnes, Putney, Streatham, Tooting, Wandsworth and Colliers Wood.

We pride ourselves on the … [3] of our rental cars. We have chosen vehicles that are … [4] – most with power-assisted steering, electric windows and central locking. All vehicles are covered by a breakdown and emergency service cover. This can be extended to cover the continent.

We provide vehicles to London residents and visitors using a simple … [5] with a quick response time.

We offer a meet-and-greet-service at London Airport, Heathrow and Gatwick. You will be met in arrivals and … [6] to your rental car in the short stay car park near the terminal.

We will … [7] a vehicle anywhere, any time in the Greater London area.

Join our opt-in mailing list and receive … [8] on our promotions and special offers by email.

Car Rental London

13 MATCH IT

Match each answer to the appropriate question.

1 What is the minimum age requirement for vehicle rental?
2 What is the maximum age requirement?
3 I have just passed my test. Can I drive?
4 What are the requirements for renting?
5 What means of payment are required?
6 What else is necessary for renting?
7 Can I take the vehicle abroad?

a An acceptable valid driver's licence, issued in your country of residence.
b Yes, but we need to know where you intend to travel so that we can extend the insurance cover abroad.
c No, you need to have held your licence for a minimum of two years.
d A deposit/payment for hire is taken on most major credit cards.
e 23
f Identification. In addition to the licence, two forms of identification are needed.
g 74

GRAMMAR

GRAMMAR YOU CAN USE TO ... TALK ABOUT THE FUTURE (2)

1 He's **staying** at the Thistle Tower Hotel.
2 There'**s** a big meeting next month.
3 It **takes off** at 21.00.
4 The meeting **starts** at 11.30 am.

- *Das* present continuous *und das* simple present *können beide für zukünftige Ereignisse verwendet werden, für die ein Plan, eine Verabredung oder ein Programm vorliegt. (1–4) Dies gilt insbesondere, wenn eine Zeitangabe Missverständnisse mit der Gegenwart ausschließt. (2–4)*
- *Beim Vollverb* be *ist in diesem Zusammenhang nur das* simple present *möglich. (2)*
- *Bei anderen Verben wird das* simple present *verwendet, wenn die zukünftigen Ereignisse als feststehend betrachtet werden, z.B. wenn es sich um Fahrpläne oder Stundenpläne handelt. (3, 4)*

14 PRACTICE

Translate these sentences into English, using either the simple present or the present continuous. Where both tenses are possible, write two versions.

1 Er nimmt die Maschine um 07.00 Uhr am Freitag.
2 Die Tagung endet um 17.00 Uhr.
3 Sie wird morgen in Frankfurt sein.
4 Es nehmen noch zehn weitere Personen teil.
5 Wir unterschreiben die Verträge am Mittwoch.
6 Das Taxi kommt um 19.00 Uhr.
7 Die Sitzung findet in Birmingham statt.
8 Ich sehe ihn heute Abend.

Advanced materials

HSBC

gives you more control

Why have a credit card?

A credit card gives you convenience. Financial flexibility. So you can make better use of your money. The way you want to.

- Instant purchasing power at millions of outlets around the world
- No need to write cheques or carry cash
- An agreed credit limit
- Take advantage of sale bargains
- Shop over the phone
- Spread the cost of larger purchases
- Separate business and personal spending
- Cash withdrawals from cash machines and over the counter at banks worldwide
- Itemized monthly statements

Why have our cards?

Our credit cards offer many advantages. More than you might think.

- No annual fee for the first year for MasterCard, Visa card or Gold Visa card
- No annual fee for MasterCard and Visa card if you spend £1200 or more each year (excluding cash advances, refunds, interest and any other charges)
- Special introductory interest rate
- Up to 8 weeks' interest free credit
- No additional charges for occasional late payment or for going over your credit limit
- Option to make minimum payment by Direct Debit
- Plus earn exclusive Choice points to redeem for goods and services

1 WHAT DOES IT MEAN?

Read the text and look up any words you don't know in a dictionary. Explain in English what each of these phrases means, using your own words.

1 instant purchasing power
2 an agreed credit limit
3 cash withdrawals
4 itemized monthly statements
5 special introductory interest rate
6 interest free credit
7 occasional late payment
8 going over your credit limit

2 PROS AND CONS

Some companies issue credit cards to their executives. What are the advantages and disadvantages? Make two lists in English.

5 A MEETING AT KUBALD GMBH

1 WARM UP

1 You are responsible for organizing an important business meeting. What do you need to do (a) before the meeting; (b) during the meeting; (c) after the meeting? List at least six ideas, then compare with the rest of the class.

2 Think about a meeting you have attended (not necessarily a business meeting). Did you feel that the meeting was a success or a failure? Give reasons.

14 2 ARRANGEMENTS FOR A MEETING

Kubald GmbH ranks among Europe's leading signware suppliers. The company is currently negotiating a large contract with Texaco Europe, part of the ChevronTexaco group, to supply signware for Texaco service stations throughout the Benelux countries. Peter Kubald has invited Jodi Tinner of Texaco UK and Jean Moreau of Texaco Benelux to a meeting to finalize the contract.

Peter Kubald receives a phone call from Jodi Tinner. Listen to the dialogue and answer these questions.

1 What does Mr Kubald do to be helpful and hospitable?
2 How and at what point does Ms Tinner signal that she wants to 'get down to business'?

KUBALD Kubald.

TINNER Hello, Peter. It's Jodi Tinner here.

KUBALD Hello, Jodi. How are you?

TINNER Couldn't be better, thanks. And yourself?

KUBALD Yes, I'm fine. What can I do for you?

TINNER I'm calling about the hotel. The last one left a lot to be desired. This time I thought I should ask your advice before booking.

KUBALD Well, there is a small but very good and comfortable hotel with an excellent restaurant about 10 km from here. It's the Waldhotel in Garbsen. Shall I make a reservation for you?

TINNER Thanks. It would be a great help if you did that for me.

KUBALD What are your travel plans?

TINNER I'm planning to take flight BA445 on Thursday, which is due to arrive at Hanover-Langenhagen at 5.20 pm. I need to fly back the next day, straight after the meeting. There's a plane at 7.45 pm.

KUBALD If you don't mind, I'll come and meet you at the airport and take you to the hotel. In the evening I'd like to invite you and Jean to be my guests for dinner.

TINNER Thank you very much. It'll be a pleasure ... Now, about the meeting: I have the agenda and the minutes of the last meeting, which you very kindly sent me, but I want to agree a timetable. If we hadn't run out of time in the last meeting, the contract would have been finalized by now. What do you propose?

KUBALD Well, if it's OK with you, I suggest we start at nine o'clock with the terms and conditions. We can break for lunch from twelve to one. After lunch, I'd like to show you the production plant. That should take us until two. Then we can discuss the delivery schedule. We should be through by five, don't you think?

TINNER That sounds fine to me. I suggest that you check with Jean, though.

KUBALD Of course. Once I've spoken to him, I'll send you a short confirmation. I hope you have a good trip. Bye now.

TINNER See you soon. Bye.

3 WORKING WITH WORDS

Read the dialogue and find the English equivalents of the following words.

1 Rat
2 einladen
3 Tagesordnung
4 Protokoll
5 zum Abschluss gebracht
6 vorschlagen
7 Bedingungen
8 Fertigungsanlage
9 Liefertermine
10 Bestätigung

4 CONFIRMING THE ARRANGEMENTS

Peter Kubald phones Jean Moreau to discuss the arrangements for the meeting on Friday 10 August. As Mr Moreau needs to fly to Brussels at 6.30 pm, they agree to start the meeting at 8.30 am and continue over lunch if necessary, so that they can finish an hour earlier.

Write an email to Jean Moreau and Jodi Tinner confirming the new arrangements.

15

5 THE MEETING

It is 8.30 am on Friday 10 August. Mr Kubald welcomes his business partners. After a few words of friendly small talk, they get down to business.

Listen to the dialogue, then look at the agenda. Which point does the meeting reach by the end of this recording?

KUBALD Well, why don't we begin? First of all, welcome to Kubald GmbH. I'm sorry that we had to bring forward the start of the meeting, but it's better than *postponing* the whole meeting until a later date.
As we agreed beforehand, I shall *chair* today's meeting. Ms Baumann will be taking the minutes.
What we hope to accomplish during the course of the meeting is the final draft of the delivery and maintenance contract between Kubald GmbH and ChevronTexaco Global Lubricants. I have *circulated* the agenda together with the minutes of our last meeting. Are there any matters *arising from* the minutes?

TINNER Yes, Peter. Just one point: the minutes don't mention that the meeting was interrupted because we had to consult our solicitors.

KUBALD Let me see ... No, you're quite right. Ms Baumann, please note that correction to the minutes of the last meeting. Jean, do you have anything to add?

MOREAU No, everything else seems fine.

KUBALD Excellent. The next *item on the agenda* is the specific terms and conditions of the contract. You have before you our estimate, which has been *revised* in the light of our discussions at the last meeting. Can I have your views, please?

MOREAU I do have one *objection* to the proposed terms, Peter. This is a substantial contract – it has a volume of €711,000. Under these circumstances, we would expect the supplier to bear all delivery costs. I therefore *propose* that the terms should be Free Domicile, rather than Ex Works.

TINNER Yes, I would definitely *support* that proposal.

KUBALD Hmm ... Maybe we can *reach a compromise position* on this issue ...

Kubald GmbH

Meeting with Texaco Europe representatives
Friday 10 August 2002, 8.30 am

AGENDA

1 Acknowledgement of the agenda
2 Minutes of the meeting on 23.04.02.
3 Specific terms and conditions of the contract
4 Scheduling the delivery
5 Any other business

Neustadt, Wednesday 29 July 2002
P. Kubald

6 WORKING WITH WORDS

Study the dialogue text. Find the words or expressions in italics which have the following meanings.

1. changed
2. to be responsible for keeping order
3. to agree with a suggestion
4. to result from
5. to make a formal suggestion
6. to find a solution which is acceptable to both sides
7. to distribute
8. matter to be discussed
9. argument against something
10. to put something off until a later time

16

7 THE DISCUSSION CONTINUES

Listen to the recording. What is the main issue here? What is Peter Kubald's standpoint? What is Jodi Tinner's standpoint?

8 FORMAL LANGUAGE

Formal language helps business people to stop a disagreement turning into an argument. Match the formal phrases (1–11) with what they really mean (a–k).

What you say

1. Furthermore, I'd like to point out that ...
2. We are not far from each other's position.
3. I'm sure that you're right, but ...
4. I have to support ... in this.
5. Correct me if I'm wrong, but ...
6. That alone won't help us, I'm afraid.
7. To be quite frank, ...
8. That isn't the main issue here.
9. Could I come in at that point?
10. Have you taken into account ... ?
11. Let's consider the matter further.

What you mean

a I don't agree with you.
b I'm about to say something harsh.
c I'm fairly sure I'm right.
d Be quiet and let me speak.
e I haven't made up my mind yet.
f I agree with ...
g I want to continue speaking.
h I'm prepared to compromise if you are.
i That isn't important to me.
j You've forgotten ...
k That's not relevant.

17

9 TAKING THE MINUTES

It has been a long, hard day at Kubald GmbH, but finally the meeting comes to an end. Listen to the rest of the dialogue and complete the minutes.

The parties agreed that Kubald GmbH should be responsible for the … [1] of the Texaco service station signware for the Benelux countries. The contract should include all necessary … [2] and maintenance work, and should … [3] with the Belgian service stations in June 2003.

The following specific … [4] were agreed: 660 units in total as per prototype (see attached specification) at a cost of … [5], Free Domicile. Payment to be settled after the … [6] of every 50 units.

Ms Tinner emphasized that talks with the Global Purchase Division regarding signware for Texaco UK service stations would follow soon after the announcement of the new bidding period.

The following … [7] was agreed: 200 units on demand from 1 June 2003 to 15 December 2003; … [8] further units from 10th January 2004 to 15th December 2004.

Ms Tinner promised that Texaco Europe would draw up the contract on the basis of the agreed … [9].

Mr Kubald undertook to confirm the agreement within 14 days of receipt.

There was no other … [10].

Mr Kubald concluded the meeting by … [11] the participants for the pleasant and … [12] atmosphere.

Neustadt, Friday 10 August 2002

Baumann

10 SAY IT IN ENGLISH

Was würden Sie auf Englisch sagen, wenn Sie …

1 … eine bestimmte Person bitten möchten, das Protokoll der Sitzung zu führen?
2 … die Anwesenden um ihre Meinung bitten möchten?
3 … einen Vorschlag unterstützen möchten?
4 … höflich, aber bestimmt widersprechen wollen?
5 … fragen möchten, ob es weitere Wortmeldungen gibt?
6 … einen Vorschlag unterbreiten wollen?
7 … den Teilnehmerinnen und Teilnehmern für ihre Beiträge danken möchten?
8 … die Sitzung schließen wollen?

CULTURE

CULTURAL KNOWLEDGE – A VITAL TOOL OF BUSINESS

Knowledge about the business culture of the people you want to do business with is essential. Not knowing can spoil all the hard work you have invested.

Here are some examples from different parts of the world (Asia, Africa and South America) that will show how meetings can become a nightmare or a success.

China

- The Chinese are keen on exchanging business cards, so be sure to bring a plentiful supply. Ensure that one side is in English and the other side is in Chinese.
- When receiving a business card, make a show of examining it carefully for a few moments; then carefully place it into your card case or on the table.

Egypt

- In accordance with tradition, an Egyptian will welcome you several times at your first meeting.
- Be aware that Arabic is a language of hyperbole. For example, when an Egyptian says 'yes', he may actually mean 'possibly'.

Argentina

- When you enter the meeting room, wait to be told where to sit. Customarily, the highest-ranking participants are seated across from each other.
- Making 'small talk' and smiling frequently are vital to establishing rapport with your colleagues. But it would be wrong to assume that you can joke with Argentines from the start. To imply that someone or something is not to be taken seriously is a grave insult in this culture.

11 CULTURAL BRIEFING

You are writing a cultural briefing for North American and British business people visiting Germany. What advice will you give? Discuss ideas with a partner, then write up a paragraph of advice in a similar style to the text in the box.

In the box you will find some hints to get you started.

- In Britain and North America, it is not usual to have university qualifications printed on your business card.
- British and especially North American business people are used to using first names.
- Many British and North American companies have quite flat hierarchies, and their employees may not be very status-conscious.

GRAMMAR

GRAMMAR YOU CAN USE TO ... EXPRESS CONDITIONS: IF-CLAUSES

	if-clause	**main clause**
1	*simple present* If you **don't** mind,	*future* I **will come** and meet you.
1a	*simple present* If I **press** this button,	*simple present* the bell **rings**.
2	*simple past* If you **did** that,	*conditional* it **would be** a great help.
3	*past perfect* If we **hadn't run** out of time,	*past conditional* the contract **would have been finalized**.

- *Sätze vom Typ 1 drücken eine erfüllbare Bedingung aus.*
- *Sätze vom Typ 1a drücken eine zwangsläufige Folge aus.*
- *Sätze vom Typ 2 drücken eine Bedingung aus, die möglicherweise erfüllbar ist.*
- *Sätze vom Typ 3 drücken eine Bedingung aus, die nicht erfüllt wurde.*

12 PRACTICE

Fill the gaps with the correct tense of the verb in brackets.

1 I will pick you up from the airport if you ... me to. (want)
2 If you don't have enough time, we ... to postpone the meeting. (have)
3 You will hear from me if I ... the letter. (receive)
4 If you sent the letter this week, he ... it in time. (get)
5 I would have booked another hotel if I ... of one. (know)
6 Mr Moreau wouldn't complain if he ... no reason to do so. (have)
7 Texaco would have chosen another supplier if they ... better terms. (offer)
8 If I had seen the contract in advance, I ... the terms of payment. (not accept)
9 Students can fail the exam if they ... . (not work)

13 TRANSLATION

Translate the following sentences.

1 Herr Moreau wird kommen, wenn er sein Flugzeug nicht verpasst.
2 Wäre der Nebel nicht gewesen, hätte ich es rechtzeitig geschafft.
3 Wenn Sie jetzt nichts gesagt hätten, wäre ich sehr enttäuscht gewesen.
4 Falls ich Sie abhole, werde ich gleich die Rechnung zahlen.
5 Er sagte, dass er seine Maschine nicht verpasst hätte, wenn der Taxifahrer schneller gefahren wäre.
6 Wenn ich frei habe, hole ich ihn ab.
7 Der Taxifahrer meinte jedoch, dass Sie die Maschine leicht erreicht hätten, wenn der Fahrgast eher angerufen hätte.

14 A FORMAL MEETING

Read and follow the instructions below.

You are a senior manager at RM plc, the leading supplier of IT software, services and systems to the UK education market. Your classmates are your colleagues. You have to hold a meeting to decide the location of your next annual sales conference.

RM headquarters, Milton Park, near Oxford

Alveston Manor, Warwickshire

1. Elect a chairperson to lead the meeting.
2. Refer to File 4 on page 120 (student A), File 9 on page 122 (student B) and File 11 on page 123 (chairperson).
3. Agree an agenda for the meeting.
4. Consider your point of view and make some notes in preparation for the meeting.
5. Conduct the meeting and make a decision.

Advanced materials

Companies switch on to virtues of global vision

Videoconferencing is increasingly popular with businesses, reports

Violet Johnstone

IMAGINE a meeting of senior BP executives, one group sitting round a table in Anchorage, another in Houston, a third in London, a fourth in Stavanger, a fifth in Aberdeen and a sixth in Azerbaijan – all discussing the assessment of the next four quarters' capital requirements of related businesses.

It is the sort of scene that is on the increase as more and more organisations take up videoconferencing to enable groups of people to see and speak to each other while thousands of miles apart.

BP has used the big studio systems for almost 15 years. It was one of the earliest companies in the world to do so. The immediate advantage is obvious – less need to travel, cutting costs, saving time and reducing stress. The National Economic Research Association estimates that by 2007 videoconferencing could replace 20% of business travel. Users extol other benefits, too. A banking executive claims his new-found ability to observe and make eye contact is valuable: 'I know whether my message is getting through.'

It brings people into meetings who do not normally travel, says a multinational manufacturer of electronic materials. Some technical people realise they are working on the same projects and can exchange ideas and information.

Additional people can be pulled into meetings at short notice if specialist contributions are required, says a motor manufacturer. 'The opportunity to see someone's body language is an advantage,' says one consultant. 'It's a carrier of meaning.'

Videoconferencing at BP

Most relevant of all, it speeds decision-making, says Mike Haynes, of Unilever, which began with two studios in London and Rotterdam seven years ago and now operates videoconferencing in 120 locations in 20 countries. About half the locations have studio-based systems. 'A system which cost us £250,000 ten years ago when we began videoconferencing has come down to £20,000 – and the equipment is far more reliable,' says Tony Vincent, project leader for Voice and Video Services at SmithKline Beecham.

'The opportunity to see body language is an advantage'

The company has 31 studios globally and is adding Brazil and Australia to the list. Fifteen to 20 meetings take place daily around the world, generally lasting two hours.

To Mr Vincent one of the biggest advantages of videoconferencing is that it enhances the feeling of team working. 'We operate in 104 countries, yet work as a virtual community,' he says. Half an hour's training is sufficient to familiarise people, says Mr Vincent. Even if they feel intimidated at first, as soon as they start talking they forget the technology and get involved in the meeting.

The explosion will come with PC videophones, says Kevan Hall of Global Integrations, a feeling shared by Jim Hood, information technology leader at BP, where expanding videoconferencing from studios to desktops and small meeting rooms has been the significant change in the past two or three years. 'It is not just about cutting down on travel, but about improving the frequency and quality of meetings and having the contact that otherwise would not take place,' he says.

For small companies such as that of David Attinger, who found that his advertising agency in Dorset 150 miles from London created a geographical image problem for clients, PC videophones have proved their worth. He will pay £4,000 to £5,000 for a client to have the system installed if the client's contract is big enough to justify it.

As well as being able to look someone in the eye in a video meeting, the document conferencing facility enables the agency to show digital layouts, artwork, 3D models, copy and advertising schedules and both parties can read, alter and edit the documents at the same time.

PC-based videoconferencing is a practical tool, says Mr Attinger. 'It's just like using the phone – except you have to remember to keep your clothes on,' he quips.

1 UNDERSTANDING THE TEXT

Read the article and answer the questions.

1 What predictions are made for the effect of videoconferencing on business travel?
2 What benefits does videoconferencing have for technical people who might not normally travel?
3 What is the typical length of a videoconference at SmithKline Beecham?
4 How has the organization of videoconferences changed recently at BP?
5 Are meetings now held more often or less often at BP?
6 What problem did David Attinger's advertising agency have, and how did he solve it?
7 What does he use videoconferencing for, other than face-to-face contact with clients?

2 THE ADVANTAGE IS ...

List and describe in your own words the advantages of videoconferencing mentioned in the article.

3 ON THE OTHER HAND ...

If videoconferencing is as practical as the article claims, why do people continue to travel to meetings? Note down your own thoughts first, then compare ideas with a partner.

4 WHAT IF ... ?

If the meeting between Kubald GmbH and Texaco Europe had been conducted via a videoconferencing facility, would this have made a difference to the negotiations? Conduct a class discussion. Consider the following aspects, and any others you can think of.

- efficiency
- personal relationships
- atmosphere
- bargaining position
- likely outcome

6 A PRESENTATION AT CHEVRONTEXACO CORP

1 WARM UP

What do you think are the ingredients of a good presentation? Think of ideas to complete the diagram.

enough preparation

clear objective

interesting material

18 2 FEEDBACK ON A PRESENTATION

Management trainees at Devtec Engineering take a course in presentation skills. One trainee, Anthony Thane, has just finished giving his first presentation, and now the trainer, Dr Anne Rider, invites the other trainees to give feedback.

Listen to the dialogue. Note down any important tips for giving presentations.

ANNE ... Thank you, Anthony. Well done. Now, everyone: what did you think of the presentation? Meera?

MEERA I thought it went very well. But he could have provided handouts at the end.

ANNE Good point. Seventy-five per cent of what an audience hears will be forgotten within 24 hours. Probably more with this lot, Anthony ... Unless you put the most important points on a handout. What material could he have presented as a handout?

MEERA Some of the visual aids that he used in his presentation. For example, those sales figures that he presented as pie charts. He could have used those as handouts.

ANNE Hmm ... Yes. But he would have needed to add some explanatory text. Handouts have to make sense *after* the presentation as well as *during* it. Otherwise, you won't remember how they were relevant to the presentation. But that brings me to another point: Anthony's visual aids were excellent. Remember: visual aids are very effective in keeping an audience's attention and helping them to remember what you have said. Any other observations? Gavin?

GAVIN Yes. Anthony's tone of voice was a bit, well ... monotonous. Sorry, Anthony!

ANNE Yes, that is something you need to work on, Anthony. You need to vary your speech more, use stress and intonation effectively. Studies show that voice quality accounts for more than one third of the impact of a presentation. Now, let's pick up on some more good points. Anyone?

MEERA The structure of Anthony's talk was very clear. And he kept to the time limit.

ANNE Absolutely! Never steal your listeners' time by rambling on. Anthony's presentation was an excellent example of KISS: 'Keep It Short and Simple'. It was very thoroughly prepared, too. Some experts say that one *hour* of *preparation* is needed for every *minute* of *presentation*. What do you think, Anthony?

ANTHONY Er, yes. I'd say that's about right.

ANNE One final thought. When preparing a presentation, always think about your audience. In particular, take into account any cultural differences ... OK, that's it for today, folks. Take a copy of my handout as you leave the room, please.

How good was Anthony's presentation, do you think? Award him points for each of the following aspects. 0 points = very poor, 3 points = very good.

- handouts
- visual aids
- voice
- organization
- preparation

3 WORKING WITH WORDS

Read the handout and fill the gaps with appropriate words from the dialogue.

Golden rules for presentations

1. Prepare handouts. Seventy-five per cent of what an … [1] hears will be forgotten within 24 hours.
2. Use visual aids. Visual aids have been found to be very … [2] in keeping your audience's attention and helping them to remember what you have said. An audience is 43% more likely to be persuaded by your arguments if you use good visual aids.
3. Use your voice effectively. Put strong stress on important words, and use … [3] (the rise and fall of your voice) to make your presentation sound lively and interesting. Studies show that voice quality accounts for more than one third of the impact of a presentation and that listeners often get bored by … [4] speeches.
4. Keep it short and simple. The most effective presentations have a clear … [5] and are kept as short as possible. In fact one of the worst mistakes of a poor speaker is 'stealing' the listeners' time. You can best reach your objective by the principle of KISS: 'Keep It Short And Simple.'
5. Prepare thoroughly. Some experts say that one hour of … [6] is needed for every minute of … [7].
6. Take account of … [8] differences. Many presentations 'across borders' (i.e. to people from other countries or cultures) fail because the presenter does not take such differences into account when preparing or giving his or her talk.

4 PRESENTATION TOOLS

Below you see various tools which can be used in a presentation, and situations in which they can be used.

Match each tool to the most appropriate situation.

a laptop, projector

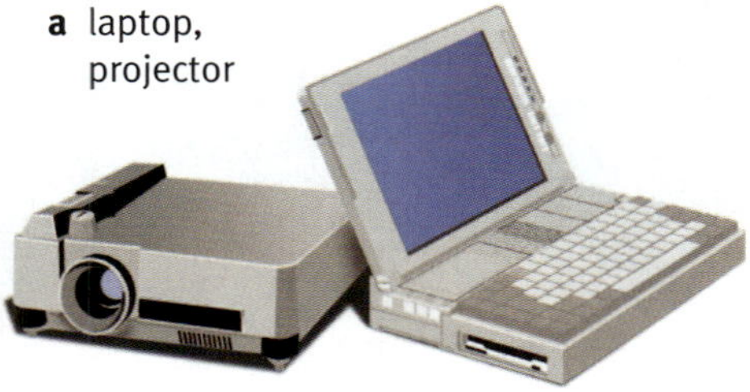

b flipchart

c whiteboard

d TV

e cassette recorder

f OHP, OHTs

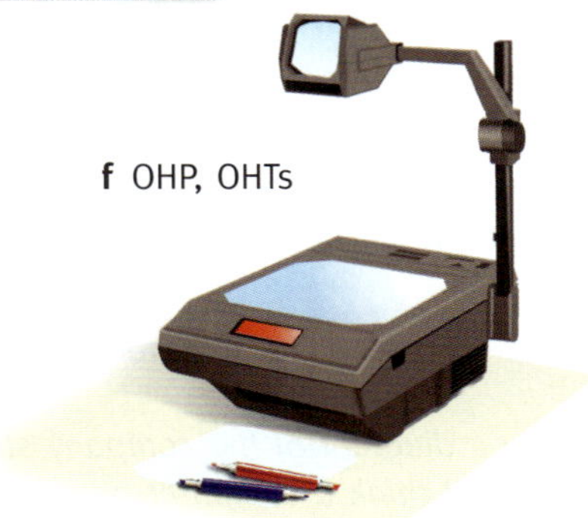

g postcards

1. You want to conduct a workshop session: participants will discuss ideas in pairs and then report back to the group.
2. You want to present static graphics and text. You also want to be able to write notes on your visuals during the presentation.
3. You want to present animated graphics and text. You also want to show various websites.
4. You want to present short written statements and simple hand-drawn diagrams, which you will prepare before the presentation. You also want to brainstorm ideas. You don't want to turn the lights off.
5. You want to write key ideas during the presentation. You also want to gather ideas from the participants.
6. You want to show your company's promotional video.
7. You want your audience to listen to a jingle for an advertising campaign.

5 CHOOSING THE RIGHT TOOLS FOR THE JOB

Peter Kubald, managing director of Kubald AG, has been invited to the headquarters of ChevronTexaco Corp in the USA. He is going to give a presentation about his company and its new coating technique for signs. Below you see his overview of the talk he intends to give.

1 Begrüßung, kurze Einleitung
2 Kubald AG – Entwicklung, Allgemeines
3 Lackiertechnik erläutern (Bilder)
4 Fragen beantworten
5 Handout verteilen

What tools do you think that he should use to give this presentation? Why? Make notes in English.

6 PAIRWORK

Choose one of the roles and work with a partner.

STUDENT A: You are Kubald AG's American marketing director. Suggest what tools Mr Kubald should use for each stage of his presentation.

STUDENT B: You are Peter Kubald. Find out why your marketing director thinks these tools are appropriate. If you disagree, say why.

EXAMPLE:
A: *You could use an OHT to present the company history.*
B: *Why is that?*
A: *So that you can show a diagram of the company structure.*
B: *I'm not sure about that. I think a computer presentation would look more professional ...*

LANGUAGE

- **Making suggestions:**
  How about an OHT?
  You could use a flipchart.
  I would use a whiteboard.
- **Asking for reasons:**
  Why is that?
  Why do you say/think that?
  Do you think so? Why's that?
- **Giving reasons:**
  So that you can ...
  Because that allows you to ...
  That way, you can ...
- **Expressing doubts:**
  I'm not sure about that.
  I'm not so sure.
  I don't think that's such a good idea.
- **Making counter-suggestions:**
  I think it would be better to use a whiteboard.
  It might be better to use a flipchart.

7 GRAPHICS

Peter Kubald wants to give his audience some background information about his company. Amongst other things, he wants to illustrate the growth in his company's turnover over several years. He experiments with several ways of presenting the statistics.

1 Look at the different graphs. Which one would you choose to present these statistics and why?

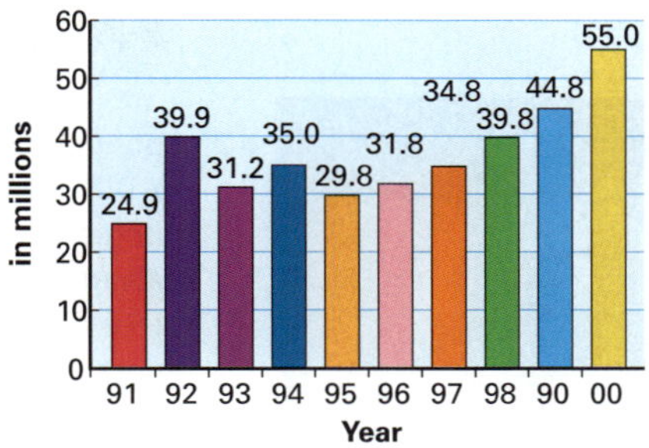

bar chart

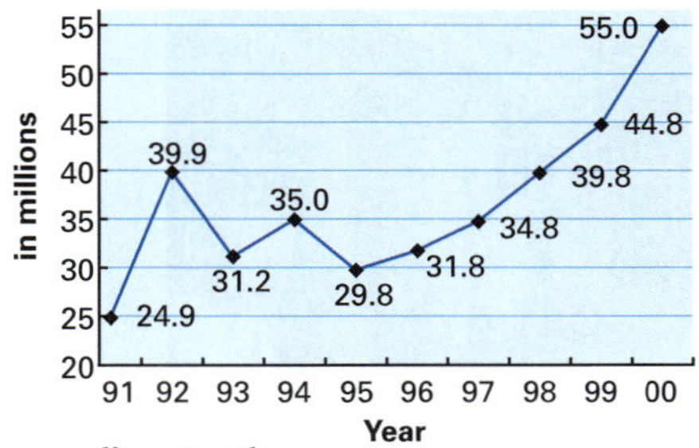

line graph

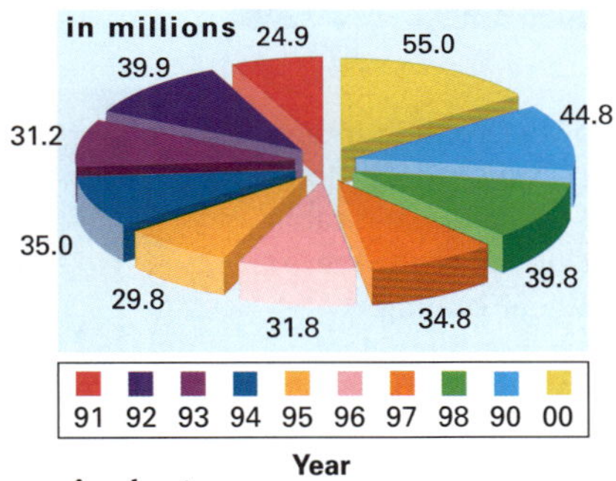

pie chart

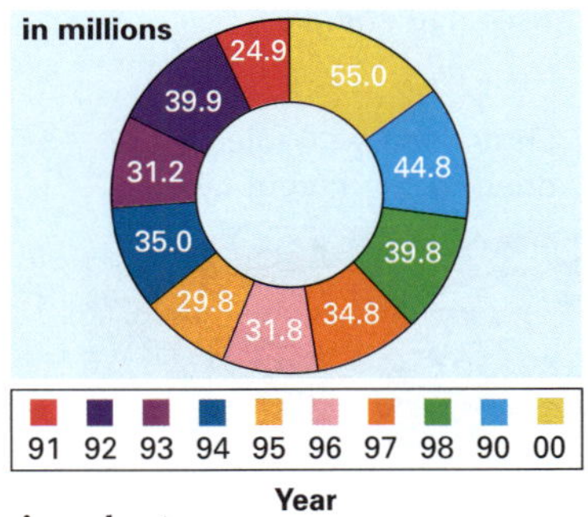

ring chart

2 Which type of chart would you use to illustrate the following statistics?

a Currency exchange: euro–dollar rates over three years
b Per capita income in the UK and Germany over three years
c The contribution of five different products to a company's annual turnover
d Two companies' advertising spending on TV, radio, newspaper and internet advertising for one year

---

CHOOSING THE RIGHT CHART

Choosing the best type of chart for a set of statistics means considering several different factors. Here are some 'rules of thumb' to help you:

Simplicity more important than precision:	pie chart, ring chart, bar chart
Precision more important than simplicity:	line graph
Comparing one item over time:	line graph, bar chart
Several items to compare:	pie chart, ring chart, bar chart

N.B. These are only general suggestions: every case is different!

---

8 VISUALS

Peter Kubald also wants to illustrate the new coating technique. The process is highly technical, but the members of his audience are not from technical backgrounds. Below are the major stages in the coating process.

How would you present this material? Suggest presentation tools to use, and write down exactly what you would say about each stage in the process.

1 Work-piece feed and discharge station

2 Spray chromating according to DIN 50939. Here, the unfinished aluminium or galvanized steel work-pieces are pre-treated to guarantee the best adhesion of the coating.

3 Chromated work-pieces are dried in the drying oven.

4 Powder coating in any desired shade is done in the automatic cabin or optionally in the manual coating chamber if required.

5 The stoving process at temperatures of 160–200°C is the final stage.

19 9 THE PRESENTATION BEGINS

It is now 10.15. Peter Kubald expected to start his presentation at 10.00. John Page, head of station maintenance at ChevronTexaco, greets the audience.

Listen to the recording, then note down your impressions of how the presentation started.

10 NOT QUITE WHAT I EXPECTED …

After his visit to ChevronTexaco, Peter Kubald writes an email to an American friend.

Read the email and compare Mr Kubald's impressions with your own notes from exercise 9. Are they similar?

I had prepared everything thoroughly and was looking forward to the presentation. I had all the relevant material at hand, including slides and transparencies, and I had some brochures ready to hand out.

The presentation was due to start at ten o'clock. Well, I was there in plenty of time, but the audience chatted amongst themselves and didn't want to sit down! It must have been at least a quarter past ten before I could start. I guess that German punctuality and American punctuality aren't quite the same thing.

Then, Mr Page introduced me. I was a bit surprised that I was expected to use first names. I keep forgetting how informal you Americans are. And then Mr Page started joking again with his colleagues.

Anyway, I was just about to get started with my first point, but then there was another interruption. Instead of asking about the product, Mr Page seemed very interested in asking about Hanover and telling me about his wife's holiday adventures.

When I was allowed to start, everyone listened very politely, and I think the talk went very well. All things considered, this was a very interesting experience, and I learned a lot about the American way of conducting meetings.

CULTURE

BODY LANGUAGE

People 'communicate' with their bodies as well as their words. Here are some examples.

Description	**Meaning**
Mouth tightly closed, cheeks puffed out	Aggressive rejection: 'Forget it!'
Stroking your nose	Scepticism: 'I'm not sure that I agree.'
Body turned away from partner	Arrogance, rejection: 'I'm not interested in you.'
Eyes wide open, eyebrows raised	Surprise: 'I wasn't expecting that.'
Hand around chin and jaw	Thinking hard: 'I need to find a good argument.'
Looking down, tense posture	Lacking self confidence: 'I don't believe in myself.'

11 CULTURAL DIFFERENCES

What can you conclude from Peter Kubald's experiences about the differences between presentations in Germany and in the United States? Draw up a table:

Germany	USA
Surnames used	First names used

GRAMMAR

GRAMMAR YOU CAN USE TO ... TALK ABOUT THE PAST

1 Anthony's visual aids **were** excellent.
2 He **kept** to the time limit.
3 Peter Kubald **has been invited** to the headquarters of ChevronTexaco Corp.
4 You address your neighbour by his surname, even if he **has lived** next door for years.
5 I **had prepared** everything thoroughly and was looking forward to the presentation.

- *Das* simple past *bezieht sich auf abgeschlossene Handlungen und Ereignisse in der Vergangenheit. (1, 2)*
- *Das* present perfect *wird verwendet, wenn ein Ereignis oder eine Handlung in der Vergangenheit begonnen hat und bis zur Gegenwart andauert bzw. noch in der Gegenwart sichtbar oder fühlbar ist. (3, 4)*
- *Man darf das* simple past *und das* present perfect ***nie verwechseln,*** *wenn eine Zeitangabe vorliegt:* five minutes ago *oder* in 1989 *sind Beispiele für Zeitadverbien, die das* simple past *fordern; mit* since 1989 *und* for the last five minutes *muss das* present perfect *benutzt werden.*
- *Das* past perfect *wird benutzt, wenn man innerhalb einer Beschreibung in der Vergangenheit eine frühere Zeit erwähnt. (5)*

12 PRACTICE

Complete the following sentences with the correct tense of the verb in brackets.

1 Peter Kubald's father ... the company in 1935. (found)
2 Mrs Baumann ... there for 20 years. (work)
3 Their turnover ... since 1990. (increase)
4 Peter Kubald was confident about his presentation: he ... everything. (prepare)
5 John Page's wife and her friends ... to Hanover in 2000. (go)
6 He ... there yet. (not be)
7 The new production method ... in use for two years now. (be)
8 It ... the first one installed in Germany. (be)

13 OVER TO YOU

Prepare a short presentation about your company (or another company you know well). Give the presentation, with the rest of the class acting as your audience. Use any presentation tools which are available and appropriate.

Advanced materials

ExecutivePlanet.com

Let's Make a Deal! What you should know before negotiating in Germany

* Bring plenty of business cards, as Germans tend to be keen about receiving and exchanging them. Include your full title or position, and any university degrees you have earned or professional organizations with which you are affiliated.
* Your business cards can be printed in English, since most German businesspeople are familiar with this language. It is unnecessary to have the reverse side translated into German.
* The initial meeting is usually conducted in the office, where your German counterparts will make an assessment of you, your proposal and company.
* The German side will arrive at the meeting well-informed, and will expect the same from you.
* Germans tend to be intensely analytical thinkers. Objective facts are the basis for truth in German business culture; feelings are irrelevant, especially in negotiations.
* There can also be a tendency among German businesspeople to be unreceptive to new ideas and concepts. Moreover, they do not freely share information among levels of the same organization. The younger generation, however, is becoming more open.
* Flexibility and spontaneity are not prominent traits in German business culture. Concepts such as "brainstorming", "risk-taking", or challenging rules and authority are not necessarily considered desirable.
* Generally, German businesspeople are reluctant to do something differently unless the reason is not only extremely convincing, but also proven.
* It's important that you bring a carefully planned, logically organized proposal to the meeting.
* Ensure you have plenty of data and other empirical evidence to support your proposals and arguments. Exaggerations of any kind will not be tolerated.
* When you are preparing promotional or presentation material, be aware that German businesspeople are usually unimpressed by glitzy advertising, illustrations, and memorable slogans.
* Germans will sometimes look for deficiencies in your products or services and will criticize you openly if you fail to live up to all of your claims.
* German businesspeople will not make concessions easily. Be warned that any attempts to be aggressive and confrontational with a sizeable German company are usually counterproductive.
* Germans can be very sensitive to criticism themselves, so you should do everything you can to avoid embarrassing them, even unintentionally.
* Germans, generally, are very private people; never discuss personal matters during business negotiations.
* Business meetings are treated as serious occasions, so trying to convince your German counterparts to "lighten up" is inappropriate. Moreover, humour and jokes are reserved for socializing.
* Refrain from interrupting others; allow each speaker to make his or her point before responding.
* Expect a lot of long-range planning to take place during meetings rather than spontaneous, direct action.
* Decision-making in German business culture is slow, protracted, and every detail relating to your proposal will be painstakingly examined.
* Contracts are taken very seriously in German business culture; anything agreed to in writing is virtually guaranteed. Likewise, your German counterparts will expect you to follow through with anything you have agreed to in a contract.
* Refrain from complimenting your colleagues until you have established a close personal relationship. Unsolicited praise is not necessarily expected or welcome.
* At the end of a meeting, Germans sometimes signal their approval or thanks by gently rapping their knuckles on the tabletop instead of applauding.
* Once a decision is finally made, it's unchangeable.

1 COMPREHENSION

Read the text, then find words which mean the following.

1 calling into question
2 something which is given to an opponent
3 claims which are beyond what is true
4 not suitable
5 not willing to accept
6 people at the same level or in the same situation
7 seeking an argument
8 impressive-looking
9 things which are not good enough
10 trying to reach an agreement
11 suggestion
12 to stop oneself (from doing something)
13 unwilling
14 the ability/readiness to do something without preparation
15 taking a long time
16 to indicate
17 not asked for

2 DISCUSSION

Do you think that the points made in the text are true? Which ones do you find least valid? Which do you find most valid?

3 VICE VERSA

The text was written for North American business people. What does it tell you about their business culture? Write a similar article about business culture in the USA, using the text, your own knowledge and further research.

7 A MARKETING CAMPAIGN AT BEIERSDORF

1 WARM UP

1. What do you associate with the term 'marketing'? Make a list of key words, then compare your ideas with a partner's.

2. Think of some brands you know: describe any advertisements that relate to the products.

3. Have you ever bought a product because you liked its advertising? Which one(s)?

4. Have you ever been put off buying a product because of its advertising?

(20) 2 PLANNING MARKET RESEARCH

Anke Seidel is a marketing executive at Beiersdorf. She is talking to the company's American marketing adviser, Neil Brown, about how to launch a new product on the American market.

Listen to the recording. What is the new product, and who are likely to be the main customers?

SEIDEL Hi, Neil. I'm glad you could make it. We need your advice about the launch campaign for Nivea Beauté in the States.

BROWN No problem. What would you like to know?

SEIDEL First of all, how do you see Nivea's position in the US market?

BROWN Well, Nivea is a well-established brand name in the US and has a reputation for high-quality products.

SEIDEL Excellent. So the question is, how to differentiate the new product from the rest of the Nivea product range – in other words, how to develop an individual brand personality.

BROWN Yes, I'd say that's correct.

SEIDEL We're planning to engage a market research firm to get a better picture of the competitive situation in the market. Which market research methods would you recommend?

BROWN Let me think ... How do you define your target group?

SEIDEL Young women in their late teens and their twenties, who are fashion-conscious and trendy.

BROWN OK, I'd advise you to conduct face-to-face surveys on the street, in drugstores and in trendy bars.

SEIDEL That's pretty much what I was thinking. And how extensive should the research be, do you think?

BROWN I'd say that approximately 1,000 women should be interviewed.

SEIDEL OK ... How long do you think I should give the market researchers to undertake the study and submit their report? I need some feedback pretty quickly.

BROWN Once the survey questionnaire has been finalized, the survey can be completed within a month, I'm sure. So give them two months in total.

SEIDEL Fine. Do you think that an image analysis should be conducted as well?

BROWN No, I don't think that will be necessary. We already know that Nivea has an excellent reputation amongst the target group. On the other hand, have you considered using focus groups of say, six to eight women, so that we can get their opinions in more depth?

SEIDEL Yes, but we'll leave that until a later stage, when we're planning the advertising campaign in detail ... So, I think that's all the questions I have for now. The next step is to devise the questionnaire. I'll need your help with that, too.

BROWN We can get started on it right away, if you like.

SEIDEL Great! Now I was thinking ...

3 SUMMARY IN GERMAN

Ms Seidel sends an email to a colleague, summarizing the main points of the conversation in German. Write the email.

4 WORKING WITH WORDS

Find synonyms in the dialogue for the following expressions:

1 to hire
2 to suggest
3 to carry out
4 about
5 to question
6 needed
7 to think about
8 to draw up

5 MARKETING TERMINOLOGY

Find these marketing terms in the text. Then define in your own words what they mean.

1 launch campaign
2 brand name
3 individual brand personality
4 market research
5 competitive situation
6 target group
7 image analysis
8 focus group

6 QUESTIONNAIRE

1 **Study the questionnaire which Anke and Neil have written. Add two questions of your own.**

2 **Would you also ask interviewees for their name and address/email address? Why (not)?**

1 How old are you?

- ☐ Under 15
- ☐ Between 15 and 20
- ☐ Between 20 and 25
- ☐ Over 25

2 How often do you use cosmetics?

- ☐ Every day
- ☐ Sometimes
- ☐ Never

3 Do you use one or all of the following?

- ☐ Lipstick
- ☐ Eye shadow
- ☐ Nail polish
- ☐ None of the above

4 Have you heard of Nivea?

- ☐ Yes
- ☐ No

If yes, what do you associate with this brand?

____

5 Would you try a new cosmetic series with seasonal trend colours?

- ☐ Yes
- ☐ Possibly
- ☐ No, I never change my brand

6 How much do you pay for lipstick, eye shadow and nail polish per month?

- ☐ Up to 10 dollars total
- ☐ Up to 20 dollars total
- ☐ Up to 30 dollars total

7 Which kind of advertising do you take most notice of?

- ☐ Ads in papers and magazines
- ☐ TV/radio ads
- ☐ Billboards
- ☐ Internet
- ☐ Other media

7 RESULTS OF THE MARKET RESEARCH

A market research company, Perception Marketing, is commissioned to carry out the survey. Below is the summary page of the report.

Read the summary page. Then compare it with the questionnaire. Which questions relate to which findings in the report?

P perception marketing

10.1 *Summary*

In order to test consumer reaction to the new product, a representative survey of 1,000 women in the target group between 15 and 25 years of age was carried out in New York, Los Angeles, Houston and Seattle.

Statistical analysis:

- 80% of interviewees know the brand Nivea. It is associated with good quality and reasonable prices.
- 74% of interviewees use cosmetics on a daily basis:
  Lipstick is used by 67%, eye shadow by 54% and nail polish by 63%.
- When asked what they were willing to pay per month for these cosmetics, the most common response (49% of all interviewees) was "up to 20 dollars".
- 68% of interviewees consider the name "Nivea Beauté" appealing, although many interviewees found it difficult to pronounce and mainly said "Beauty".
- 70% of interviewees said that they were willing to try out new cosmetics.
- TV advertisements have the best resonance (59%), followed by billboards (43%). Magazine advertisements are overlooked by many interviewees (73%).

10.2 *Conclusions*

On the basis of these findings, there is certainly a demand for such a product as Nivea Beauté, despite the fact that there is a vast range of lipstick, eye shadow and nail polish brands on the US market. The advantage of Nivea is its reputation, which indicates excellent market potential.

10.3 *Recommendations*

10.3.1 In order to achieve the greatest success, Nivea Beauté should be launched shortly before spring, with countrywide TV advertisements between programs favored by young women. A list with suggestions for programs is attached to this report (Appendix C).

10.3.2 A billboard campaign could target public places such as Times Square in New York and similar locations in other major cities. Placement costs would be considerable, however.

10.3.3 Press advertising should be very selective, concentrating on the three or four magazines which are most often read by younger women (Appendix D). A press advertising campaign should last for no more than three months.

8 *Market Research Report for Nivea Beauté, Beiersdorf, Germany*

8 WORKING WITH WORDS

Find the English equivalents in the report:

1 Befragte	**5** Ruf
2 ansprechend	**6** auf den Markt gebracht
3 Ergebnisse	**7** bevorzugt
4 riesig	**8** sich konzentrieren auf

9 CONVEYING THE MESSAGE

After reading Perception's report, Anke Seidel goes to see the head of the marketing department, Beate Neumeier. Since Ms Neumeier's English is not good, Anke summarizes the content of the report in German.

Prepare a summary in German for Anke.

GRAMMAR

GRAMMAR YOU CAN USE TO ... MAKE IT SOUND OFFICIAL:
THE PASSIVE VOICE (1)

1 Lipstick **is used** by 67%.
2 Magazine advertisements **are overlooked** by many interviewees.
3 Approximately 1,000 women **should be interviewed**.
4 The survey **can be completed** within a month.
5 A representative survey of 1,000 women **was carried** out.

- *Das Passiv wird oft verwendet, wenn man auf eher unpersönliche Art und Weise über Fakten, Vorgänge und Zahlen berichtet.*
- *Das* present simple passive *wird mit* am/is/are + *Partizip Perfekt (3. Verbform) gebildet. (1, 2)*
- *Das Passiv mit Modalverben* (must, should, can, could, have to *usw.) wird mit dem Modalverb* + be + *Partizip Perfekt gebildet. (3, 4)*
- *Das* simple past passive *wird mit* was/were + *Partizip Perfekt gebildet. (5)*

10 PRACTICE

Make sentences in the passive by using the following words. Select an appropriate tense for each sentence.

1 advertisement / magazine / last week / place / full-page
2 company's / special offers / advertise / latest catalogue
3 promote / in TV adverts / brand products / like Nivea
4 Internet / digital shop window / to display products / companies / use
5 this advertisment / on billboards / display / last year
6 advertising / sell / merchandise / a lot of / because of
7 products / direct mail / promote / new / could
8 research methods / utilize / the marketing agencies / different

11 NIVEA – MORE THAN JUST A PRODUCT?

1 **Look at the four advertisements which accompany the brochure text on the next page. What impression do you think each picture is trying to give? Write down any relevant English words you can think of. Then compare notes with a partner.**

2 **The four advertisements are taken from Nivea advertising in four different decades of the 20th century. Decide which decade each advertisement dates from.**

3 **Read the text. Can you find clues to confirm your dating of the advertisements?**

a

b

c

d

The advertising history of a classical brand name

Nivea Creme, the first ever moisturizer, was developed in 1911. To transform a mere product into an established 'brand personality', Beiersdorf, the German manufacturer of Nivea, used marketing techniques which captured the spirit of the times. The first jars were designed in an Art Nouveau/Art Deco style, which remained unchanged until the mid-1920s.

Then Juan Gregorio Clausen, head of the Beiersdorf marketing department, came up with the combination of white text set on a blue background. This apparently simple design used 'colour psychology' in a sophisticated way: the blue represented sky and water, the white stood for inner and outer purity.

This was a time when sports, outdoor activities and sunbathing became fashionable. Nivea expressed this in its advertisement campaigns: naturalness, youthfulness and freshness prevailed. The Nivea models of the 1920s and 1930s wore no jewellery or other accessories – in order to stress that the brand was affordable for everybody.

After the drab and depressing post-war period, Nivea advertisements of the 1950s mirrored a new optimism and dynamic spirit which had taken hold of the West. People started to look to the future full of confidence. This was also an age which celebrated glamour, beauty and romance – the age of the beauty queen.

In the 1960s travel became more affordable for ordinary people. This was the start of the travel boom which endures to this day. People bought their first cars and started to spend the weekends at the beach or in the mountains. Nivea reflected this new trend in its advertising.

Characteristic of the 1980s was the 'singles trend'. Self-confident, unmarried professionals made demanding consumers. Nivea captured the *zeitgeist* with advertisements depicting self-confident young women, rather than couples or parents with children. Differentiated product lines for different skin types were produced.

In the 1990s Nivea continued to diversify and expand its product range. 'Globalization' was the buzzword of the decade. All Nivea product groups received new international names (like Nivea Body, Nivea Visage) and new packaging, whilst the logos and advertisements were internationally standardized to enhance the recognition of the brand all over the world. TV ads, for example, all started and ended with the 'Blue and White' melody, which functioned as an 'acoustic logo'. Visual recognition continued to be secured through the blue colour and the Nivea typeface.

12 MARKETING STRATEGY

Copy the timeline into your exercise book. Now read the brochure text again and make notes about Beiersdorf's marketing/advertising strategy for Nivea next to each of the decades in the timeline.

Consider the following factors:

- social trends
- Nivea advertising themes
- impression Beiersdorf wanted to give

1920s

1950s

1960s

1980s

1990s

13 IT'S YOUR TURN

1. **What should be the characteristics of an advertisement for Nivea Beauté, to capture the spirit of *our* times? Brainstorm key words with a partner or in a group.**
2. **You need to commission a series of advertisements for Nivea Beauté in the United States. Write a brief for an American advertising agency. Use these notes to help you. Take into consideration everything you have learned about the Nivea Beauté brand.**

- Context: where will the advertisements appear, and who are they aimed at?
- What impression should the advertisements give?
- What 'traditional' elements of the Nivea brand image should be kept?
- Find suitable pictures in magazines or on the Internet, to show what type of 'look' we want.
- Produce a first draft of an ad, including text, pictures and layout.

Advanced materials

CI

two letters for a whole business philosophy

Over the last century, company structures have undergone a process of radical change. Once, men like Werner von Siemens or Gottlieb Daimler determined the identity of their company – a company which concentrated on one product range. Those days are over: nowadays, huge corporations diversify more and more, with new product ranges and with the acquisition of other companies. The result is conglomerates such as General Electric, which sells everything from aircraft engines to refrigerators.

Furthermore, the market is saturated with a wide variety of similar products: the consumer attempting to buy a simple bottle of shampoo is confronted by literally hundreds of 'haircare products' on the supermarket shelves. Globalization is flooding domestic markets with international products and making competition fiercer.

With ever more products entering the market ever more quickly, it is becoming increasingly difficult to maintain a distinctive product image.

Moreover, customers are growing more critical and selective. They are less prepared to buy a product simply for its function: instead, they pay attention to its design, prestige, quality, eco-friendliness and how economical it is to use.

In these times of interchangeable products, increasing competition and hypercritical customers, companies consider it vital to stand out from the crowd and to project a corporate identity which gives their employees, customers and suppliers an orientation to hold on to.

How do companies achieve this corporate identity – CI for short? The three main elements are corporate design, corporate communications and corporate behaviour.

Corporate design focuses on the visual presence of a company. It aims to create a sense of identity through the unified design of products; through uniform logos, colours and typefaces and through the uniform style of correspondence. It may even go so far as to dress employees in uniforms and apply a uniform style to the architecture and interior design of buildings.

Corporate communications aims to ensure that advertisements, brochures, employee newsletters and customer instruction manuals convey a coherent, consistent message. Memorable slogans are employed to reinforce public 'brand recognition'.

Corporate behaviour focuses on people's treatment of each other: how leadership is handled, what manners prevail, how conferences are conducted and how criticism is expressed and received. The goal is to create a team spirit and a sense of belonging – in recognition of the fact that employees who identify with their company and products are more motivated, more effective and more productive.

1 WORD SPIDER

Use expressions from the text to create a word spider. Start like this:

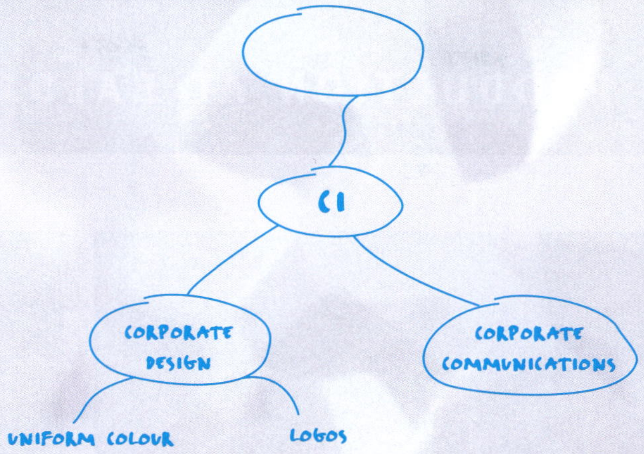

2 FROM McDONALD'S TO ...

Think of companies you know which have a strong CI. How is this expressed? Consider each of the elements of CI described in the text.

3 DISCUSSION

Do you think that CI has the desired effect? What are the advantages and disadvantages of this business strategy? Make a list, then compare ideas with the rest of the class.

4 CI WITHIN ARM'S REACH

1 Write a questionnaire and conduct a survey in your company to find out whether the employees experience the 'sense of belonging' and 'team spirit' mentioned in the text.

2 Write a report on your findings and present it to your class. Make recommendations about how your company could use CI more effectively.

8 PRODUCTION AT BALDA AG

1 WARM UP

What is the core task of a company's production department? Work with a partner to draw up a description in one sentence. Then compare descriptions with the rest of the class. In the box are some ideas to get you started.

to organize ▪ co-operation ▪ to produce ▪ quantity ▪ quality ▪ cost

(21) 2 ONLY PLASTICS?

Balda AG:
Kathrin Breitensträter

Balda AG is a leading manufacturer of mobile communications equipment. Kathrin Breitensträter of Balda AG is taking Brian Page on a tour of the Balda site. Mr Page is an analyst and fund manager at Dorman Brothers, London. Ms Breitensträter wants to give him an overview of her company's products and production processes.

Listen to the dialogue and make a note of the production processes you hear mentioned.

BREITENSTRÄTER ... And so, to meet increasing demand, the manufacturing process has been split into two parts, which we call Business Units 1 and 2. Business Unit 1 includes activities such as product design, industrial engineering, software development, mould making and tool making. Business Unit 2 includes assembly, system components and surface treatments.

PAGE I see. Sorry, but what exactly is your core business?

BREITENSTRÄTER Essentially, we develop and manufacture plastic components for the mobile telephone, medical engineering and satellite communications industries. But we also assemble components such as microphones, loudspeakers and aerials which are provided by our suppliers.

PAGE You mentioned 'early supplier involvement' just now. How does that work?

BREITENSTRÄTER We are very much involved in our customers' new product development. We go to them to discuss the feasibility of their ideas. In this way, we nurture our relationships with our customers. At the same time, we reduce production costs, because we avoid costly mistakes.

PAGE Excellent ... How long does it take for a new product to be developed?

BREITENSTRÄTER Obviously, that depends on the product, but take a mobile phone cover as an example. From the first meeting to the final product, the process takes about 15 months. That's also how long it takes for one mobile phone model to reach the point of market saturation ... but let's continue with the tour. We'll take a look at the moulding process next and how we use modern technologies such as CIM.

PAGE CIM?

BREITENSTRÄTER Computer-integrated manufacture. This way, please ...

The pictures show production processes at Balda AG. Match the appropriate caption to each picture. Then assign each picture to Business Unit 1 or Business Unit 2. Refer back to the dialogue as necessary.

1

2
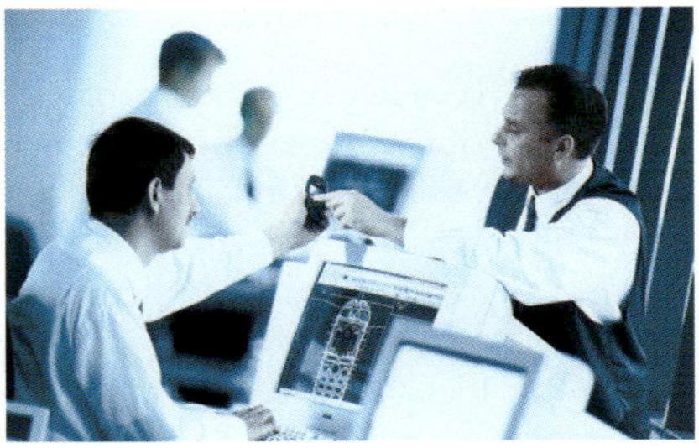

3

4
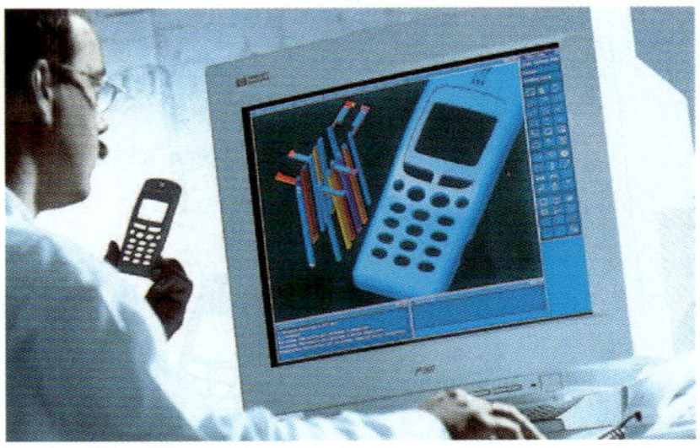

a **Product design team**
b **Tool making**
c **Assembly of electronic components**
d **Surface treatment**

3 WORKING WITH WORDS

Match the expressions from the dialogue with the appropriate definitions.

1 design
2 software development
3 mould making
4 suppliers
5 saturation
6 process
7 to assemble
8 feasibility
9 costly

a the stage at which no more can be absorbed
b to fit parts together to form a whole
c manufacturing a hollow container into which a liquid will be poured
d whether something is possible
e expensive
f writing and improving programs for computers
g a series of actions or operations performed in order to do, make or achieve something
h developing a plan or drawing from which something may be made
i people or organizations that provide goods or services

4 GOING FROM STRENGTH TO STRENGTH

Read the press release. What kind of publication do you think that this text is aimed at? What can you say about the choice of language?

Balda Group on the right track

At a press conference Mr Gerhard Holdijk, Chairman of the board of management of Balda Group, gave his views on Balda's production activities.

In order to go ahead as planned with the expansion of Balda Group, he said, it was first of all essential *to increase* the available capacity. The company succeeded in meeting all of its *targets* in this respect in the year under review.

Pursuing a growth-oriented manufacturing strategy, efforts were made to increase the production *volume* of tools and machines. *Systematic* progress was made in the field of innovative production technologies. New methods of computer-integrated manufacture will be *implemented* soon.

In the year under review, the group made investments totalling 46.8 million euro in *plant*. During the course of the year, production capacity doubled, while at the same time production cycles were significantly shortened by Balda's production engineers. Production management structures were reorganized, and the level of automation was increased yet again.

The company tested new production technologies successfully and introduced them into mainstream *operations*. The group greatly expanded its *product portfolio*. Balda's ultimate aim is to become a manufacturer of all plastic *components* related to the mobile communications market.

Balda is still the only company in the industry worldwide to offer the complete range of manufacturing technologies for plastic hardware used in mobile communication products. Mr Holdijk concluded his statement by pointing out that in setting up facilities for assembly work and for the processing of electronic components such as microphones, loudspeakers and aerials, the group has *fulfilled* its strategic goal of transforming itself from a components supplier into a *fully fledged* systems supplier.

5 WORKING WITH WORDS

Read the text again. Replace each expression in italics with one of the expressions below.

1 following
2 range of products
3 parts
4 to expand
5 buildings and equipment
6 quantity
7 methodical
8 put into practice
9 business activities
10 completely developed
11 achieved
12 goals

6 DEFINITIONS

Write English definitions for the following words.

1 chairman
2 tool
3 progress
4 reorganization
5 innovative
6 production capacity
7 production cycle
8 automation
9 mainstream

7 TV INTERVIEW

You are to give a short interview on American television about the successes of Balda AG. Prepare a brief outline of Balda's business activities, and its successes in the past year. You will find all the necessary information in the dialogue and the press release above. Make sure that your presentation is short and simple enough to be understood by a non-technical audience.

22

8 PRODUCTION PROCESSES

Kathrin Breitensträter and Brian Page make their way to the production unit of Balda AG. Mr Page is very impressed with the production facilities ...

Listen to the dialogue. Put the photos in the order in which the processes are mentioned.

a Typical flow-shop system: component assembly

b Mould cutting

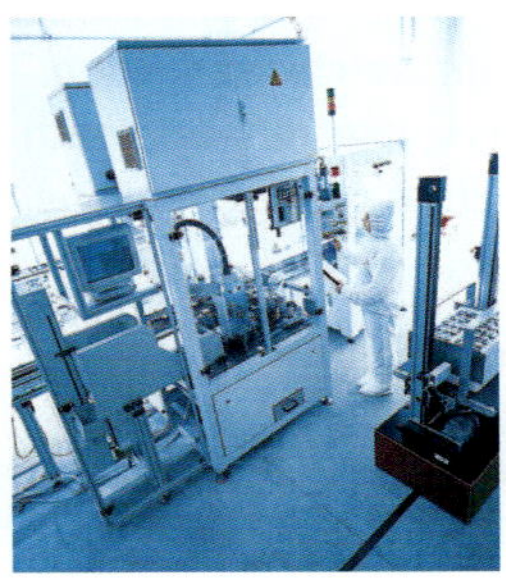

c CIM supports the manufacturing process

d Surface treatment

9 GOING INTO DETAIL

Listen to the dialogue again. Answer the following questions.

1 What is manufactured using the job-shop system at Balda?
2 Why do Balda AG produce the moulds in their own workshop?
3 What is the main difference between a job-shop and a flow-shop system?
4 Why is the flow-shop system used for the integration of all components into the manufacturing process?

Collect material on the production process in your company (or a company you are familiar with) and prepare a short presentation. Include visual materials if possible.

INFORMATION

METHODS OF PRODUCTION

There are different ways to produce different types of goods.

Job production
Job production is also known as 'unit' production. A single unit is produced from start to finish. It is based on the individual specification of the customer. It is a very labour-intensive – and therefore cost-intensive – production method.

Mass production
Mass production is also known as 'flow-shop' production. Each product is passed on from one stage to the next in a production line. It is a typical production method for the production of large numbers of identical products as cheaply as possible. It is a capital-intensive method but it is not labour-intensive. It requires skilled employees to operate the machines.

Batch production
If a customer requires a small number of similar products, they are often made in batches. This production method is a combination of job and mass production.

10 YOU DECIDE

Working with a partner, decide whether each item below is most suitable for job production, mass production or batch production. Then discuss your answers with the whole class, giving reasons.

1 a house
2 a luxury car
3 a CD player
4 a textbook

GRAMMAR

GRAMMAR YOU CAN USE TO ... DESCRIBE PROCESSES: THE PASSIVE VOICE (2)

1 The manufacturing process **has been split** into two parts.
2 Systematic progress **was made**.
3 But we also assemble components ... which **are provided** by our suppliers.
4 New methods of computer-integrated manufacture **will be implemented**.
5 It **is being controlled** by the computer over there.
6 How long does it take for a new product **to be developed**?
7 You'll also hear it **referred** to as the job-shop system.

- *Durch den Gebrauch des Passivs wird das Prädikat hervorgehoben. Das Passiv wird daher oft verwendet, wenn die beschriebene Handlung wichtiger ist als der Handelnde.*
- *Der Gebrauch des Passivs gibt die Möglichkeit, den Handelnden wegzulassen, wenn die Angabe nicht wirklich wichtig ist. (1, 2, 4, 6, 7)*
- *Das Passiv wird mit der entsprechenden Form von* be *+ Partizip Perfekt gebildet. Wie im Aktiv können alle Zeiten gebildet werden. Die Kriterien für deren Gebrauch sind dieselben wie im Aktiv. (1–4)*
- *Die Verlaufsform (*be + -ing*) kann im Passiv sinnvoll nur im* present *oder im* past *gebildet werden. (5)*
- *Infinitivkonstruktionen mit dem Passiv sind ebenfalls möglich. (6)*
- *‚Von' und ‚durch' werden undifferenziert durch* by *ausgedrückt. (3, 5)*
- *In Passivkonstruktionen mit Verben der Wahrnehmung wie* see, hear *usw. wird* be *manchmal unterdrückt. (7)*

11 PRACTICE

Your boss asks you to help prepare a presentation. Rewrite the text in English.

Die Produktivität im 1. Quartal wurde gesteigert. Ein Grund dafür war, dass mehr Formen als erwartet von den Werkzeugmechanikern gebaut wurden. Hinzu kommt, dass die Maschinen mit höherer Geschwindigkeit gefahren werden können. Durch Qualitätskontrolle und die Integration von Computerprogrammen konnte der Ausschuss reduziert werden. Alles in allem wurde Balda auf den richtigen Weg gebracht. Die Wettbewerbsfähigkeit ist erheblich gesteigert worden.

12 DESCRIBING A MANUFACTURING PROCESS

Describe the process using the passive voice of the given sentences. (Decide whether the subject of each active verb should be mentioned.)

EXAMPLE:

The raw parts are carried to the supply and monitoring desk ...

AUTOMATED MANUFACTURING UNIT

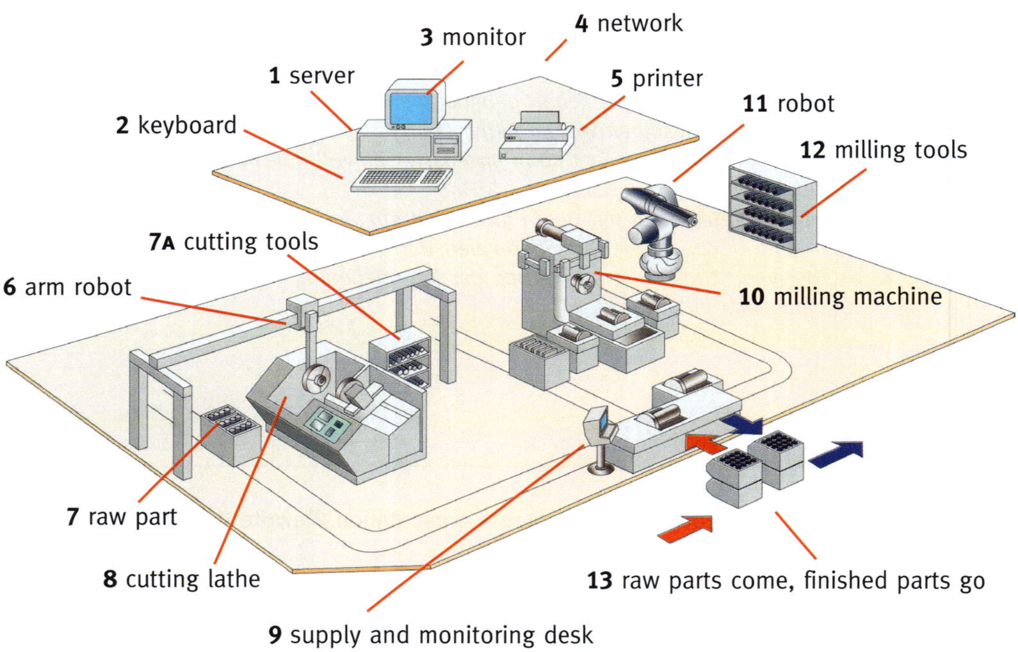

The Driverless Transportation System (13) carries the raw parts to the supply and monitoring desk (9). There the operator puts the parts into a computer steered box (7). The arm robot (6) picks up one raw part and delivers it to the cutting lathe (8). If the unit requires another tool, the arm robot takes it from the cutting tool box (7a). The server (1) controls the whole process. Our programmers wrote and installed the software. We will start production after technicians have tested the whole process thoroughly.

13 TIME FOR A CHANGE

Below you see three different Balda mobile phone covers. What do you think made Balda AG change the design? From what you have read in this unit, how often do you think the designs change?

Now read the article to check your answers.

IT WON'T LAST FOREVER

Products have a limited lifespan, from both the consumer's and the manufacturer's viewpoint. For example, a particular mobile phone cover might last 15 to 20 months. New inventions and technology (eg smaller phones, or a different keypad layout) can make this part of a mobile phone obsolete. But fashion also plays its part.

'For our products, fashion is a major influence,' says Kathrin Breitensträter of Balda AG in Bad Oeynhausen, Germany. 'The kids are really crazy about the fancy covers. The product itself is close to being unbreakable, but it's "in" to have the latest covers on their phones.'

This tendency can be recognized in the economy at large. A product has to be both usable and fashionable. Some products survive because they have found a new niche within their original market, as Richard Traube of Pelikan AG knows: 'Fountain pens have become less popular in everyday life due to the success of biros. But in the "quality pen" sector they are now very profitable.'

Products have a life cycle. A mobile phone might have a life cycle of 15 months, a car one of 5 to 20 years and certain fountain pens even longer. What they all have in common are the different stages of their life cycles. There is usually a stage of development, followed by a stage of introduction. After a period of growth (hopefully), the peak is reached with a stage of maturity, followed by a period of decline.

A product's lifespan can often be extended in some way. Companies often seek to 'improve' their product by modifying its style or content. This is usually linked to marketing strategies such as changes in packaging or advertising – or even taking the product off the market for a period of time. 'Taking our product off the market turned out to very successful in the longer term,' comments Robert Hütli of Ferrero Swiss.

14 THE PRODUCT LIFE CYCLE

The diagram shows a product life cycle. Decide which of the stages (1–5) each description (a–e) applies to.

- **a** low sales, negligible profits, few competitors
- **b** fast growth, peak-level profits, mass market
- **c** decreasing sales, low profits, few customers
- **d** no sales, no profits, high costs
- **e** slow growth, declining profits, mass market

15 OVER TO YOU

List some products made by your company, or a company you are familiar with. What stage do you think each product is at in its life cycle? How could its life cycle be extended? Choose one of the products: prepare and give a short presentation about how its life cycle could be extended. Use visual aids as appropriate.

Computer companies step forward to increase industrial output

At an 18th century villa in the Veneto region of Italy, some of the country's most talented young footwear artisans gather to learn the century-old craft of shoemaking – with a difference. Here, at Villa Loredan, the headquarters of the Shoe Designer's School of the Riveria del Brenta, conventional classes in theory and leather working are supplemented by instruction in the use of computerized shoe design.

Even the most tradition-bound crafts and professions have found ways to use information technology (IT), and for the most basic of business reasons: to save money, to improve quality, to gain competitive advantage. In Italy, where employee costs are the highest in Europe (when taxes, pensions and social security obligations are included), computer-assisted design (CAD) and computer-assisted manufacturing (CAM) have become indispensable adjuncts to the flexibility for which the country's workers are famous.

Thanks to advances in microelectronics, automation products are becoming more powerful and almost as flexible as the workers they assist – and sometimes replace. Performance is rising, while costs are decreasing, and, as in the overall IT market, software and engineering – rather than hardware – represent more than half the expenditure.

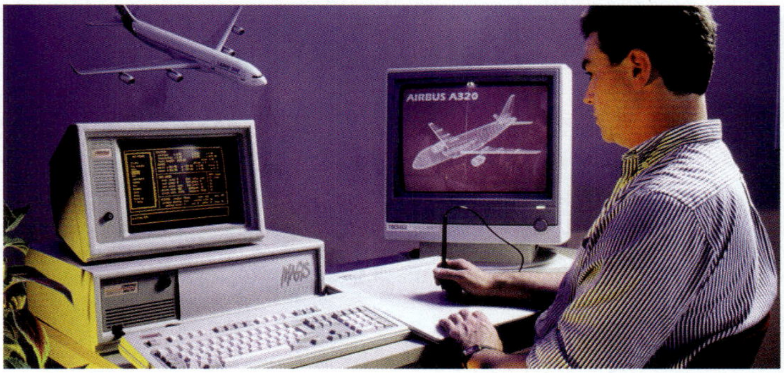

What you see is what you get: *an aeronautical development engineer uses specialized computing power to modify, on screen, the design of a jet aircraft engine.*

Paralleling general IT trends, the automation sector is moving toward open system architecture, with integration of diverse elements in the manufacturing process and built-in scalability – in other words, room to grow in the future. Equally important is the move to more user-friendly systems, so that engineers can concentrate on their technical objectives without having to become computer experts.

Klaus Wucherer, head of the Industrial Automation Systems Division of Siemens Automation Group, said at the INTERKAMA Trade Fair: 'Customers not only buy software or hardware products, they buy solutions to their problems.' Because more functionality is being integrated into software, Siemens have been able to develop 'engineering tools that translate the description of a technological task into the language of the target system, requiring hardly any programming knowledge on the part of the user,' he explained. This means that a chemical engineer can think in chemical process terms, and the mechanical engineer can focus on his machine design.

1 CIM, CAM OR CAD?

Decide whether each description best matches CIM, CAM or CAD.

1. These programs allow the companies to alter, improve or change the design of their product, eg to carry out a customer's order.
2. A design can be incorporated into the production process by using this computer system. It is an all-inclusive network of computer technology.
3. These programs carry out production on the basis of processing data, production plans, material lists, etc.

2 THE IMPORTANCE OF IT

Read the text again. Make notes about the importance of IT in the following industries:

1. industrial automation
2. chemical engineering
3. the shoemaking industry

3 MAXIMIZING PERFORMANCE

Identify an industry where increased use of IT could improve performance and profitability. Discuss and compare ideas with a partner.

9 CONTRACTS AND PAYMENT AT HABERMANN & FALKE

1 WARM UP

1 **Your company wishes to purchase goods from a trading partner outside the Euro Zone. What matters need to be agreed between the supplier and the customer before the goods can be dispatched? Make a list.**

2 **Who issues each of these documents: the supplier or the customer?**

a delivery note
b order acknowledgement
c quotation
d sales enquiry
e invoice
f purchase order
g remittance advice

3 **Can you put the documents in chronological order?**

2 A LETTER FROM TAYLOR & PENTON

Peter Weiche, purchasing manager at Habermann & Falke AG, receives a letter from a British company.

Read the letter on the next page. Why has it been sent, and what is its purpose?

Taylor & Penton

Habermann & Falke AG
Pastorenweg 12–14
30168 Hanover
Germany

10 Avro Way
Brooklands
Weybridge
Surrey KT13 QYR

Telephone (01932) 336181
Facsimile (01932) 336182

Our ref MS/ft G17
Your ref HAN

12 November 2002

For the attention of Mr Weiche

Dear Mr Weiche

Office Suite 2000/205

Many thanks for your email enquiry concerning our Office Suite 2000/205. Based on the office plan you made available, we submit our quotation as follows:

Item No	Quantity	Description	Order No	Price
1	1	work station	63140	£ 650.00
2	1	deep drawer chest	63124	£ 125.00
3	1	pull-out keyboard shelf	63045	£ 29.00
4	1	open shelf unit	63058	£ 139.00
5	1	shelf unit with two doors	65057	£259.00
Total	1	complete unit		£1,202.00

To give you detailed information we have pleasure in enclosing our latest catalogue.

Terms of payment: Total less 2.5% cash discount for settlement within 30 days. Our prices are FOB Harwich.

We would be pleased to receive an order from you. Please do not hesitate to contact us if we can be of any further assistance.

I look forward to hearing from you.

Yours sincerely

M Sampson

Margaret Sampson
SALES MANAGER

Enclosure

Answer the following questions about the letter.

1 What did Peter Weiche send to Taylor & Penton?
2 What is Taylor & Penton's business?
3 What item does the word 'Enclosure' refer to?
4 Has Peter Weiche agreed to buy the goods? How can you tell?

23 3 QUERIES

Jonas Hanke is a trainee at Habermann & Falke. Peter Weiche asks him to phone Taylor & Penton to discuss some points about the letter which seem to be unclear.

Listen to the dialogue. What information was missing from the letter?

SWITCHBOARD Taylor & Penton, good morning. Can I help you?

HANKE Good morning. Could you put me through to Ms Sampson, please?

SWITCHBOARD Who's calling, please?

HANKE This is Jonas Hanke from Habermann & Falke. I'm calling from Germany.

SWITCHBOARD Just a moment, please. I'll see if she's in the office ... Ms Sampson can speak to you now, Mr Hanke. I'm putting you through.

SAMPSON Hello, Mr Hanke, sorry to keep you waiting. What can I do for you?

HANKE Hello, Ms Sampson. I'm ringing about your quotation, which we received this morning. Mr Weiche asked me to check some details with you about your Office Suite 2000/205 for our main office in Hanover.

SAMPSON Of course, Mr Hanke. Could you please tell me the number behind the initials on the reference line?

HANKE It's G70.

SAMPSON G70 isn't possible, I'm afraid. Could it be G17?

HANKE You're right, Ms Sampson, it's G17.

SAMPSON ... Here we are. Our offer includes a complete office unit ...

HANKE Yes, that's right. But we couldn't check the dimensions, because there was no catalogue enclosed.

SAMPSON Oh, I'm sorry about that. It should have been sent with the letter. You will have it tomorrow morning by express courier.

HANKE Thank you. There was also nothing in the letter about the delivery date.

SAMPSON Right. You should give us 28 days from receipt of your order.

HANKE Twenty-eight days ... That might be acceptable. As we are interested in purchasing 15 complete units, I would like to ask for a quantity discount, an introductory offer and a change in the trade terms. We prefer CIF Hamburg.

SAMPSON Perhaps we could discuss the discount first. We grant a quantity discount of ten per cent on orders exceeding ten units. We can't grant introductory offers; that's company policy, I'm afraid. Now, the trade terms ... FOB Harwich seems a fair deal to me. In effect, the costs are shared fifty-fifty.

HANKE Very well, Ms Sampson. We'll have to compare your quotation with offers from German suppliers. But we'll let you have our decision soon. Thank you very much.

SAMPSON You're welcome. Thank you for calling. Goodbye, Mr Hanke.

HANKE Goodbye.

4 TAKING NOTES

Write a short memo in German to Peter Weiche, informing him about Jonas Hanke's conversation with Margaret Sampson.

5 WORKING WITH WORDS

Find the English equivalents of these expressions, in the letter or in the dialogue.

1 zu Händen von
2 Zeichen
3 Anfrage
4 bezüglich
5 zur Verfügung stellen
6 vorlegen
7 Preisangebot
8 Mengenrabatt
9 Lieferant

6 DEFINITIONS

Explain in English the following expressions from the letter or the dialogue.

1 settlement within 30 days
2 be of any further assistance
3 terms of delivery
4 introductory offer
5 that's company policy

7 ADOPTING THE RIGHT TONE

In business dealings, inappropriately informal language will be taken as a sign of an unprofessional attitude.

Find in the letter or the dialogue more formal ways of expressing the following.

1 There's a copy of our catalogue with this letter.
2 Give us a call if you need more help.
3 Thanks for asking about our ...
4 Here's what it will cost: ...
5 That might be alright.
6 I want some money off, because we're buying a lot of things.
7 We'll tell you when we've made up our minds.
8 Those are our rules.

8 ASKING THE RIGHT QUESTIONS

Write appropriate questions for the answers below.

1 They need it for their main office in Hanover.
2 Yes, we can give you ten per cent.
3 We can let you have it when we've compared your quotation with other offers.
4 They will send it by express courier.
5 Twenty-eight days from receipt of order.

9 DISCREPANCIES IN THE ORDER FORM

1 **Compare the order form with the terms which Margaret Sampson and Jonas Hanke agreed upon. What is wrong?**

2 **Write a short email to Ms Sampson to apologize for the mistakes and to rectify the order.**

Habermann & Falke AG

Pastorenweg 12–14
D-30168 Hannover

Tel: 0511 / 85 99 99
Fax: 0511 / 85 99 91

Margaret Sampson
Taylor & Penton
Avro Way
Brooklands, Weybridge
Surrey KT13 QYR
Great Britain

Our ref: PW/HAN
Your ref: MS/ft G17

24 November 2002

Dear Ms Sampson

Office Equipment Series 2000/205

With reference to your offer dated 12 November 2002 and your phone call with Mr Hanke, we are pleased to place the attached order in line with the negotiated terms.
We look forward to receiving the units within the agreed delivery period.

Yours sincerely

P Weiche

Peter Weiche
Purchasing Manager

Enclosure

Habermann & Falke AG

Pastorenweg 12–14
D-30168 Hannover

Auftragsnummer/Order No: 2002/195
Datum/Date: 24 November 2002

Bitte liefern Sie/Please supply:

Lfd. Nr. Item No	Menge Quantity	Beschreibung Description	Katalognr. Catalogue no.	Preis Price	Gesamtbetrag Total
1	15	Office Suite 2000/205		£ 1,202.00	£ 18,030.00

Quantity discount: 15%

Terms of delivery: CIF Hamburg
Terms of payment: 5.2% cash discount
Delivery period: 21 days

10 WRITING AN ENQUIRY

Read the following instructions and write the letter in English.

Für die Jahresbestellung an Büromaterial werden drei Angebote eingeholt. Im vergangenen Jahr hat die Firma Sanford UK, Oldmeadow Road, King's Lynn, Norfolk, PE30 4JR, im Rahmen einer europaweiten Ausschreibung das günstigste Angebot vorgelegt. Schreiben Sie eine Anfrage an den Verkaufsleiter, Jonathan McGuire, und bitten Sie ihn um ein Angebot auf der Grundlage der Vorjahresbestellung, mit der Sie sehr zufrieden waren. Fragen Sie nach Preisnachlässen, Liefer- und Zahlungsbedingungen.

LANGUAGE

OPENING AND CLOSING A BUSINESS LETTER

You open a letter with	when	and you close with
Dear Sir or Madam	you don't know the name	Yours faithfully
Dear Mr Rush	you are writing to a man	Yours sincerely
Dear Ms Rush	you are writing to a woman	Yours sincerely
Dear Mrs Rush	you know that Mrs is correct	Yours sincerely
Dear Miss Rush	you know that Miss is correct	Yours sincerely
Dear Dr Rush	the person has PhD/MD after his/her name	Yours sincerely

For more information about writing business letters, see the appendix on page 108.

11 ACKNOWLEDGING AN ORDER

Where are the following points addressed in the acknowledgement below?

a Methods of transport
b Payment methods and timing
c Currency exchange risk
d Unambiguous description of goods
e Terms of trade
f Documentation

Dear Mr Dobbs

Acknowledgement of Order No. 2001

We are pleased to confirm your order as follows:

Article:	1,500 circular saws, model Electronics 225
Delivery:	To be effected within 30 days from the date of the acknowledgement, FOB Hamburg
Packing:	Consignment comes boxed for sale in 5 crates, sea-packed
Origin:	Certificate of Origin that the circular saws are of German origin will be supplied together with the shipping documents.
Payment:	To be made by bank transfer within 10 days after receipt of invoice
Price:	€ 25 per unit
Total price:	€ 37,500
Guarantee:	We guarantee the quality of the circular saws for a period of 12 months commencing on the date of retail sale.

Please rest assured that we will execute your order to your entire satisfaction.

Yours sincerely

12 THE INCOTERMS

The International Chamber of Commerce has produced a set of internationally accepted definitions for the most commonly used terms in international trade, known as 'Incoterms' (INternational COmmercial TERMS). These terms allow exporters and importers to agree precisely on their respective responsibilities and duties.

(For the full set of Incoterms and detailed explanations, see page 111.)

Match the appropriate English term (a–g) and explanation (i–vii) to each abbreviation (1–7).

1	FOB	**a**	Carriage paid
2	FAS	**b**	Cost, insurance and freight
3	CIF	**c**	Ex works
4	DDP	**d**	Delivered duty paid
5	CPT	**e**	Free alongside ship
6	EXW	**f**	Free carrier
7	FCA	**g**	Free on board

i The buyer pays for the goods to be delivered and insured.
ii The seller pays for the goods to be delivered to the carrier at an agreed place.
iii The seller pays for the goods to be delivered on board the ship.
iv The seller pays for the goods to be delivered to a named place in the destination country, and also pays minimum insurance cover.
v The seller pays for the goods to be delivered to an agreed place in the destination country, and to be cleared for import.
vi The seller pays for the goods to be delivered to the ship, but not loaded onto it.
vii The seller pays for the goods to be delivered to a named place in the destination country, but does not provide insurance cover.

13 TERMS OF PAYMENT

Here you will find some of the most commonly used terms of payment. Match each German term to its English equivalent.

1 cash in advance
2 payment on invoice
3 cash on delivery (COD)
4 payment within ...
5 ... % for cash
6 cash against document (CAD)
7 documents against acceptance (D/A)
8 payment by irrevocable and confirmed letter of credit

a ... % bei Barzahlung
b Kasse gegen Dokumente
c Vorauszahlung
d Zahlung bei Rechnungserhalt
e Zahlung durch unwiderrufliches und bestätigtes Dokumentenakkreditiv
f Zahlung gegen Dokumente
g Zahlung gegen Nachnahme
h Zahlung innerhalb ...

GRAMMAR YOU CAN USE TO ... EXPRESS POSSIBILITIES AND REQUIREMENTS: MODAL VERBS

1 Ms Sampson **can** speak to you now.
2 We **can't** grant introductory offers.
3 **Could** you put me through to Ms Sampson, please?
4 We **couldn't** check the dimensions.
5 That **might** be acceptable.
6 You **should** give us 28 days from receipt of your order.
7 It **should** have been sent with the letter.
8 We'll **have to** compare your quotation with offers from German suppliers.
9 You **must not** send an invoice yet.
10 We **don't have to** pay until the goods are received.

Modale Hilfsverben haben folgende Eigenheiten:

- *Sie haben in allen Personen dieselbe Form. (1–7, 9)*
- *Bei der Verneinung gibt es zusammengezogene Formen. (2, 4)*
- *Sie werden mit dem Infinitiv ohne* to *verwendet. (1–7, 9)*
- *Wenn andere Zeitformen nötig sind, benutzt man die Ersatzverben* to be able to (can), to be allowed to (may), to have to (must). *(8)*
- *Achtung:* must not *bedeutet ‚darf nicht';* do(es) not have to *bedeutet ‚muss nicht'. (9, 10)*

Positive	**Negative**		**German**
	Full	**Contracted**	
can could	cannot could not	can't couldn't	*können* *konnte/könnte*
may might	may not might not	– mightn't	*dürfen* *dürfte*
shall should	shall not should not	shan't shouldn't	*sollen* *sollte*
must	must not	mustn't	*müssen; nicht dürfen*

14 PRACTICE

1 Read the dialogue on page 85 again, list the modal verbs and note the German translation in that context.

2 Translate the following sentences into English.

a Sie sollten das berücksichtigen.
b Ich musste das erst mit meinem Abteilungsleiter besprechen.
c Die Unterlagen müssen Sie nicht per Express schicken.
d Wir wären bereit, Ihnen einen Preisnachlass zu gewähren.
e Wir wären dann in der Lage, die Ware zu liefern.
f Sie brauchen das nicht zu bestätigen.
g Können Sie mir bitte helfen?
h Hier dürfen Sie nicht rauchen.

15 WRITING AN ENQUIRY

As you have more than 200 packages each day to send to other countries, you are considering changing from Deutsche Post to another provider. The packages vary between 200 g and 5 kg and need to arrive at their destinations within five working days.

Write an enquiry (letter, fax or email) to UPS®.

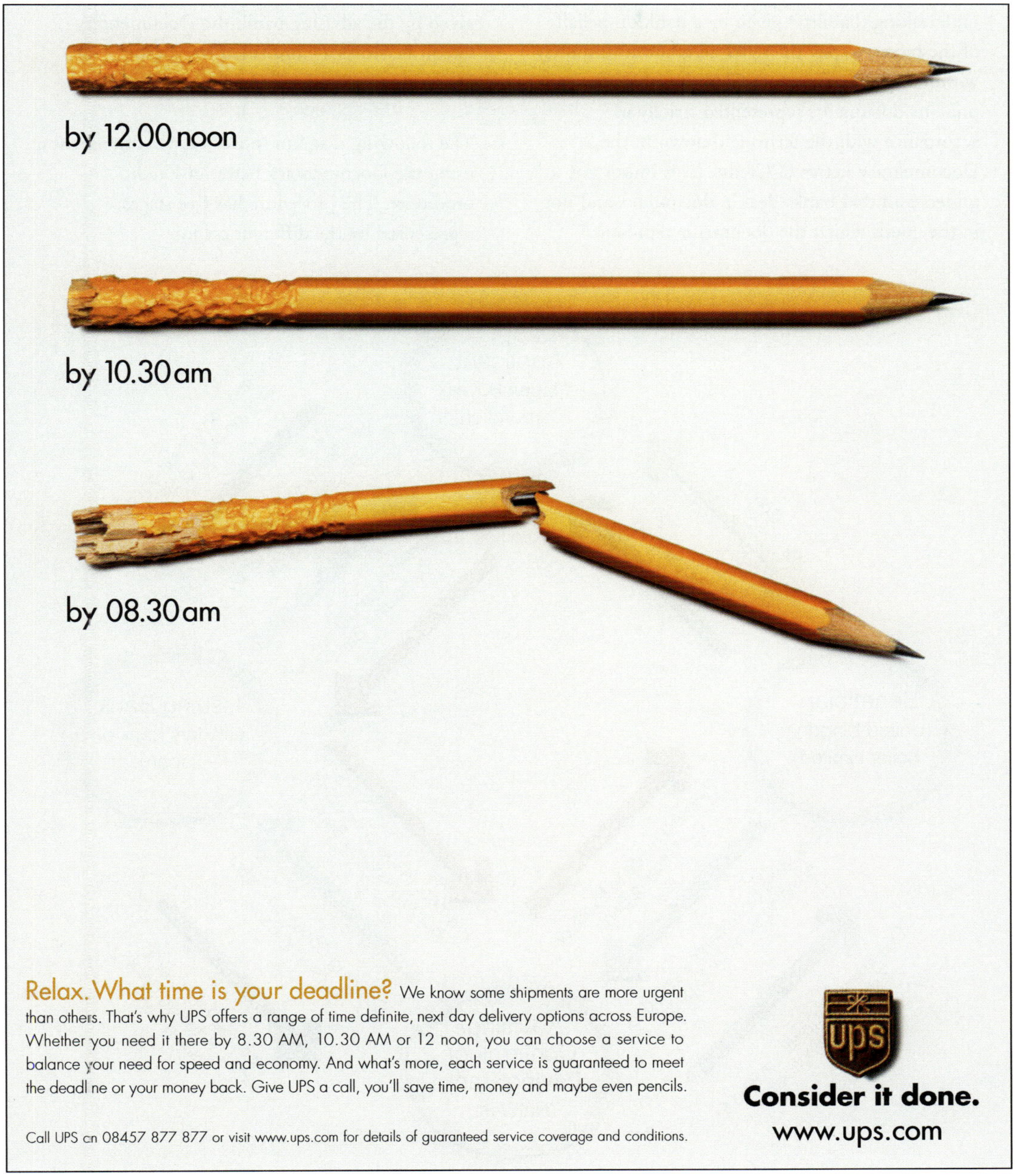

Advanced materials

A Documentary Credit transaction

A Documentary Letter of Credit is a written undertaking (liability) given by a bank on behalf of the buyer, to pay the seller an amount of money within a specific time, provided that the seller presents documents represented strictly in accordance with the terms laid down in the Documentary Letter of Credit. (It is important to understand that banks deal in documents and not in the goods which the documents represent.)

When trading with a country experiencing political or economic difficulties, a seller may insist on the additional security of the legal and binding undertaking of the advising bank in his own country. If this additional undertaking is given by the advising bank, the Documentary Credit becomes a Confirmed Irrevocable Documentary Letter of Credit.

The following diagram shows a typical transaction using the Documentary Letter of Credit procedure. The procedure has five stages, represented by the different colours.

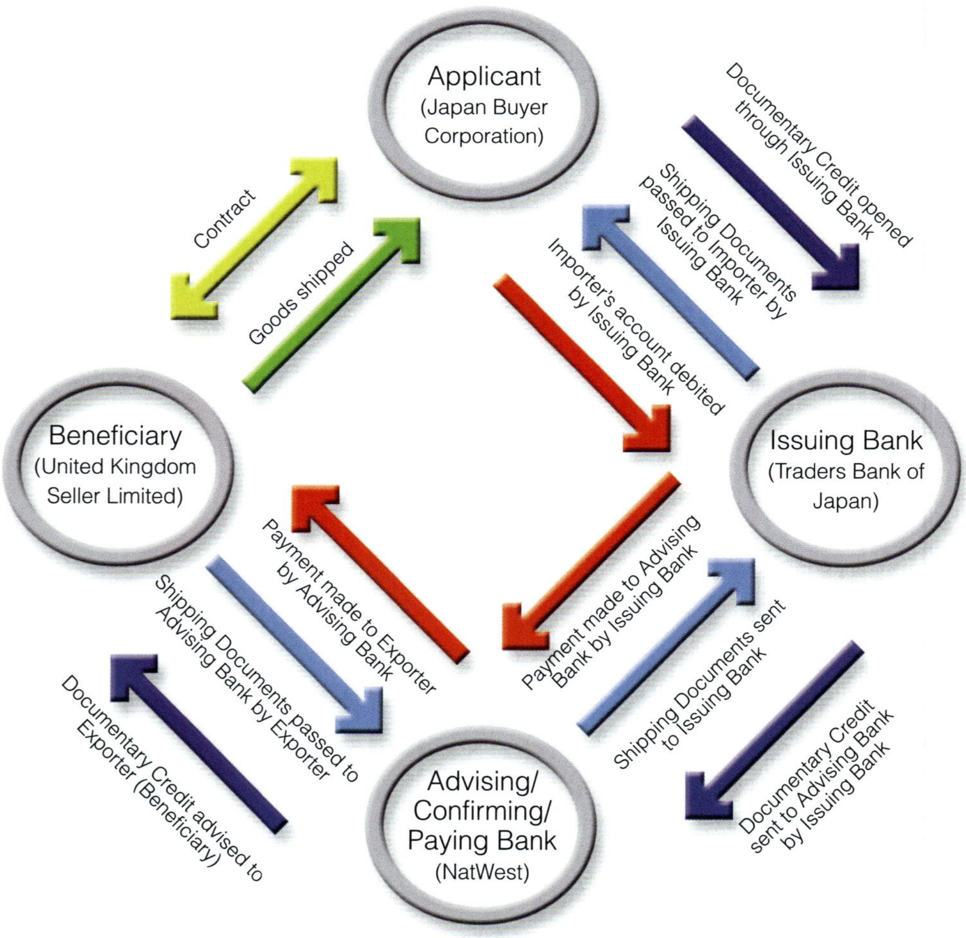

1 COMPREHENSION

Find expressions in the text or the diagram which have the following meanings.

1 a promise to do something
2 in agreement with
3 an exchange of money for goods
4 not able to be cancelled
5 a set series of actions
6 safety
7 to charge money to
8 to transport (goods)

2 FIND THE SEQUENCE

Put the colour-coded arrows in the correct chronological order.

1 → 2 → 3 → 4 → 5 →

3 SUMMARY

Summarize the procedure in German.

10 ETH UMWELTTECHNIK: DEALING WITH PROBLEMS

1 WARM UP

a

b

c

d

Answer questions 1–4 for each cartoon.

1 What is the problem? Select one problem from the box.

damaged in transit ▪ delayed consignment ▪ error in invoice ▪ faulty goods ▪ incomplete consignment ▪ wrong consignment

2 What could have happened?
3 What might be the reasons for it?
4 Suggest a solution.

24 2 PROBLEMS WITH A CONSIGNMENT

ETH Umwelttechnik is an environmental technology company which processes waste products in order to reintegrate them into the economic cycle. Organic materials and industrial waste are processed to be reused at sewage works or on construction sites. One of ETH's customers is the Danish construction company DanCon A/S in Kolding. There is a problem with a consignment of gravel and sand which has arrived at ETH from DanCon. Grit Beyer at ETH phones Søren Jensen at DanCon.

Listen to the conversation. How would you describe the tone of the conversation?

BEYER Hi Søren, how are you?

JENSEN Hello Grit, fine thanks. What can I do for you?

BEYER We received a consignment of gravel and sand from you this morning.

JENSEN Yes? Is there a problem with it?

BEYER I'm afraid there is. It's of inferior quality, compared with what we usually get from you. It appears to be contaminated with oil.

JENSEN Oh dear! Do you have the consignment number?

BEYER Yes, it's 3672.

JENSEN Thanks ... Can you use the delivery at all?

BEYER Unfortunately we can't. The material can't be recycled cost-effectively.

JENSEN I'm very sorry about that. This is the first time anything like this has happened. As you know, we're normally very reliable. What do you suggest we do?

BEYER We don't want to cancel the contract, so I'd prefer a replacement instead.

JENSEN That sounds fair. I'll make sure that you receive the replacement as soon as possible. As far as this consignment is concerned, you can send it back at our expense.

BEYER Alright. I'll see to it personally that the consignment is returned immediately.

JENSEN And I'll clear up the error and let you know when you can expect the new delivery. I'm really sorry about the inconvenience we have caused you.

BEYER Never mind. Things like this happen. As long as it doesn't happen again ...

JENSEN I certainly hope it won't! I'll see to it that the quality is checked more carefully in future. I'll look into the matter right away.

BEYER Thanks for your help. Bye for now.

What ways of saying sorry are used in the dialogue?

3 WORKING WITH WORDS

Match the words below with expressions in the dialogue that have the same meaning.

1 delivery	**3** dependable	**5** cost	**7** examined
2 not as good	**4** substitute	**6** trouble	**8** investigate

4 MEMO

Write a memo in German to Grit Beyer's superior, Frauke Ehrich, explaining the problem and the solution which has been agreed upon.

5 ALTERNATIVE SOLUTIONS

What would have been another solution to the problem? Gather ideas with a partner and present your suggested solution in class.

6 DEALING WITH COMPLAINTS

Respond to these emails, following your boss' instructions. Use any appropriate phrases from the language box on the next page.

Dear Mr Müller,

Due to faulty packing some pieces of the shipment you sent were damaged in transit and are unsaleable now. On unpacking we found that the wood was splintered on ten chairs and seven cupboards. We wish to return them at your expense. Please let us know whether you agree to this.

With kind regards,

Tony Harrison

Schreiben Sie Tony Harrison, dass er die Stühle zurückschicken kann. Wir werden den Fall mit unserer Versicherung klären.

Dear Sir or Madam,

I am writing to inform you of an incorrectly addressed consignment (No. 2003) which we received today. Due to a mistake in your shipping department we received a delivery of 100 sweaters destined for a company in Ireland. Please get in touch with me to discuss the matter.

Regards,

Ian Banks

Danken Sie Ian Banks für die Information. Er soll die Sendung per Kurier nach Irland schicken. Wir übernehmen natürlich die Kurierkosten.

Dear Ms Nordmann,

We regret to inform you that the five cases of pineapples we received are not the first-grade quality products we ordered but are of inferior quality. We are willing to keep the consignment, but demand a price reduction of 20 per cent.

Best wishes,

Linda Evans

Sagen Sie Linda Evans, dass wir ihr keinen Preisnachlass gewähren. Die Ware hat in einwandfreiem Zustand und in der gewünschten Qualität unser Lager verlassen.

LANGUAGE

RESPONDING TO COMPLAINTS IN WRITING

- **Apologizing:**
  We are extremely sorry that ...
  We were extremely concerned to learn that ...
  We are afraid that ...
  We apologize for ...
  Please accept our sincere apologies for ...
  ... the error.
  ... the delay.
  ... the inconvenience caused.
- **Giving reasons:**
  The delay was due to ...
  The late delivery was caused by ...
  The error was the result of ...
  The damage resulted from ...
  ... circumstances beyond our control.
- **Offering solutions:**
  We have made arrangements to ...
  We are trying to ...
  We are doing our best to ...
  ... make up the delay.
  ... rectify the matter.
- **Giving reassurance:**
  We will do everything in our power to ensure that this does not happen again.

7 PROBLEMS WITH PAYMENT

DanCon's new consignment of gravel and sand is received and processed; ETH sends an invoice for the processing. Three weeks pass, but ETH receives neither the amount due nor an explanation. Sabine Heller, accounts clerk at ETH, writes a first reminder.

Read the reminder on the next page. Write Mr Jensen's reply.

2 September 2002

Dear Mr Jensen,

Our invoice no. 10025 of 12 August

We refer to the above invoice, which has not been settled yet. As you usually clear your accounts promptly, we assume that you have overlooked this invoice. Please settle your account in the next few days.

If you have already remitted the amount due, please ignore this letter.

Yours sincerely,

S Heller

Sabine Heller
Accounts

LANGUAGE

WRITING REMINDERS

- **First reminder (still friendly):**
  We refer to our invoice no. 123 dated 23 August which has not been settled yet.
  We wish to draw your attention to invoice no. 123 ...
  We are writing concerning your outstanding August account.
  As you usually clear your accounts promptly, we assume that you have overlooked invoice no. ...
  If you have already remitted the amount due, please ignore this letter.
  Would you please settle your invoice by 1 September?
  Could you please clear your account/send us a remittance?
  May we ask you to transfer the amount to our account?
- **Second reminder:**
  In reply to our letter of 1 June you promised clearance of the account by (+ date)
  We must now insist on your clearing our invoice within eight days.
  We must press you to remit the amount by 2 May.
- **Final reminder:**
  Since we wrote we have received neither a reply nor a remittance from you.
  If we have not received the sum by 28 June, we will be forced to take legal action.
  Unless we receive your remittance within the next ten days, our solicitors will be instructed to start legal proceedings.
- **Replying to a reminder:**
  We intended to clear our account as promised, but due to unforeseen circumstances ...
  We regret that we were unable to settle our account for the last quarter, but ...
  We would appreciate it if you could grant us an extension of credit for four weeks.

8 FIRST, SECOND OR FINAL REMINDER?

Study the extracts from reminders. Are they suitable for first, second or final reminders, or is there more than one possibility? Give reasons for your answers.

1. We will give you a further seven days to remit the amount due, after which the matter will be dealt with by our solicitors.
2. Please send us a cheque to settle your invoice.
3. We must now insist on your clearing your account within the next ten days.
4. We would be grateful if you could send your remittance by the end of September.
5. Although we have written twice, we still have not received any remittance.
6. We must press you to transfer the sum by 18 February.

9 THE SECOND REMINDER

After the first reminder, ETH receives no reply from DanCon A/S. Sabine Heller writes a second reminder. Put the pieces together in the correct order.

a 12 September 2002

b Further to our reminder of 2 September we are surprised that we have still not received payment of the above invoice.

c **Account no. 10025, second reminder**

d S Heller
Sabine Heller
Accounts

e We have been waiting for four weeks for either a remittance or an explanation as to why the balance has not been cleared, but have received neither.

f Your order was carried out promptly in accordance with your wishes.

g Yours sincerely

h We must now insist on your clearing our invoice within seven days.

i Dear Mr Jensen

10 THE FINAL REMINDER

DanCon A/S does not respond to the second reminder. On 22 September Sabine Heller receives instructions to send a final reminder. Write the reminder for her in English.

Schreiben Sie bitte einen Brief an DanCon A/S und beziehen Sie sich auf die Rechnung vom 12. August und die erste und zweite Mahnung. Bestehen Sie darauf, dass der Betrag innerhalb von sieben Tagen beglichen wird. Ansonsten behalten wir uns rechtliche Schritte vor.

11 THE REPLY

ETH eventually receives the following reply. Read the letter and explain in your own words DanCon's reasons for non-payment.

Sabine Heller
ETH Umwelttechnik
Buchhaltung
Einsiedeldeich 15
20539 Hamburg

DanCon A/S

Jensenvej 25
DK4579 Kolding
Tel: +45 969 30440
Fax: +45 969 30441

23 September 2002

Dear Ms Heller

Invoice no. 10025, 12 August

Thank you for your letter of 22 September.

Firstly let me apologize on behalf of DanCon S/A for not having cleared your August statement. However, we are surprised that you did not receive our letter of 17 August, in which we stated that due to unforeseen circumstances we are not able to settle your invoice at present.

Some of our heavy digging machinery failed without warning and had to be replaced at short notice. Furthermore, some of our regular customers are in arrears with their payments, but have assured us that we can expect payment within the next week.

Once we receive these payments your overdue account will be settled in full. We know you will understand the situation and hope you can bear with us for a few days more.

Yours sincerely

Knut Cederholm

Knut Cederholm
Finance Director

12 A CREDIBLE EXPLANATION?

Evaluate the situation. Do you believe DanCon's excuses? How should ETH react to the letter? Discuss the next steps and the possible consequences in class.

13 CREDIT CONTROL PROBLEMS

Inquire in your company about the system for the collection of outstanding debts. Find answers to the following questions.

1 How many days' credit does your company give its clients? Does this vary from client to client?
2 After how many days are the first, second and final reminder sent?
3 What is the relevant German and EU legislation?
4 How many final reminders has your company sent in the last 12 months?
5 How many legal proceedings has your company initiated for non-payment?

GRAMMAR

GRAMMAR YOU CAN USE TO ... DESCRIBE ACTIONS: ADVERBS

1 Your order was carried out **promptly** ...
2 ... compared with what we **usually** get from you.
3 The material can't be recycled **cost-effectively**.
4 The consignment arrived **late**.
5 The goods were packaged **well – better** than the last shipment.
6 I'll see to it that the quality is checked **more carefully** in future.

Adjektive und Adverbien sind im Deutschen meistens identisch in der Form. Das ist im Englischen nicht der Fall.

- *Die meisten Adverbien werden durch Anhängen von* -ly *an das Adjektiv gebildet. (1–3, 6)*
- *Einige wenige Adverbien haben dieselbe Form wie das Adjektiv: z.B.* fast, late, early. *(4)*
- *Zum Adjektiv* good *gehört als Adverb* well. *(5)*
- *Die meisten Adverbien werden durch den Gebrauch von* more *und* most *gesteigert. (6)*
- *Folgende Adverbien haben unregelmäßige Steigerungsformen:* well – better – best; badly – worse – worst. *(5)*

14 PRACTICE

Use these words as adjectives or make adverbs from them to complete the following sentences. More than one answer may be possible.

immediate ▪ urgent ▪ normal ▪ regular ▪ good ▪ late ▪ complete ▪ exact

1 The goods arrived ... because of a truck drivers' strike.
2 The boss said he needs the consignment ... .
3 Please let us know the ... shipment date as soon as you can.
4 This item is ... sold out.
5 I called ... to confirm that the shipment had arrived on time.
6 We have had a ... business relationship with this company for generations.
7 They are some of our most ... and reliable customers.
8 ... they pay their invoices promptly, but not this month.

15 SOLVING PROBLEMS

As you have seen in this unit, a lot of problems can occur when companies interact and there are mostly no standard solutions to rely on. This week ETH Umwelttechnik encounters new problems.

1 Conduct the two role plays.

STUDENT A: Refer to File 5 on page 121.

STUDENT B: Refer to File 10 on page 123.

2 Present your solutions to the class.

16 LEARNING FROM EXPERIENCE

Conduct a class discussion as follows.

1. Tell your class about some typical problems which your company has encountered.
2. Let your classmates try to find a solution.
3. Finally, tell them how the problem was actually solved.

Advanced materials

Just In Time

Make, assemble, sub-assemble, press, paint, weld or machine the right part in the right quantity and at the right quality. Then get it to the right place at the right time. This is the goal of Just In Time.

The Just In Time concept can help your organization by eliminating waste, which is inherent within all production environments. Producing more than required, having large amounts of stored product before and within the process and carrying large stocks of finished items – all are manifestations of lost profit and waste within the production system.
Just In Time systems can be broken down into three main categories:

KANBAN

TAKT TIME

SINGLE PIECE FLOW

Kanban: one of the most common terms of Lean Manufacturing. *Kanban* in Japanese means 'ticket'. It has come to describe a system where a downstream process sends messages to an upstream process to produce components and subcomponents just in time for use by the downstream process.

This system reduces:
- the amount of inventory required
- the amount of storage space
- overproduction

Takt Time: *Takt* is a German word meaning 'pace', Takt Time is exactly that – the pace at which items must be produced to satisfy the customers' demands.

Takt = operational time available ÷ customer demand rate

EXAMPLE
The customer requires 900 items per shift, the available time to produce that product is 7.5 hours (450 minutes or 27,000 seconds) = 27,000 ÷ 900. Therefore, if we produce a product every 30 seconds, we are producing the right product at the right time.

Single Piece Flow: this is a system where one item is produced as required by the following process and passed on immediately.

BENEFITS
- reduces manufacturing space
- reduces inter-process inventory to a single piece
- reduces customer lead-time
- improves material flow

1 ADVANTAGES

According to the text, what problems does Just In Time solve?

2 DISADVANTAGES

What problems could the introduction of Just In Time *cause*? Discuss ideas with a partner, then present your ideas to the class.

APPLYING FOR A JOB

1 JOB HUNTING ON THE INTERNET

Kai Schumann is currently working for a telecommunications company in Germany. He is looking for a new job with an international company in order to improve his career prospects. Since he is fluent in spoken and written English, he decides to look for a job with a company based in the United Kingdom. Kai starts to search the Internet and finds the following:

JobHunt

We have the right job for you! You'll find more than 15,000 vacancies in our online database. If one of the jobs suits you, simply click on 'apply'.

keyword search: [ ] go

search by category: **select a profession** ▼

home | **about us** | **contact**

Export specialist, €28,000–32,000

We are a British manufacturer and supplier of electronic equipment. We require an **export specialist** to join our subsidiary in Hanover.

You will deal with enquiries and orders from German customers and send information in English to our headquarters in London. In addition, you will enter data into our SAP system and coordinate logistics.

The successful applicant will be a native speaker of German with excellent spoken and written English. He/She will have had two or more years' experience in commercial sales for industry.

apply

2 THE LETTER OF APPLICATION

Kai receives an application form, which he fills out. He encloses the following letter of application:

Ringstraße 21
28211 Bremen
Germany
Telephone: +49-421-35 68 262
kschumann@usernet.de

21 November 2003

Paul Smith
Personnel Manager
Easycall UK PLC
Easycall House
Tunbridge Street
London W6 5HJ

Dear Mr Smith

Your advertisement for an export specialist, reference 3H45

I am responding to your Internet advertisement for an export specialist to join your Hanover branch.

I have been working for two years as a sales assistant for AB&T, one of the largest German telecommunications companies. In this position I deal with new customers over the telephone, prepare quotations and handle complaints. Previously, I received in-company training at Nordmann AG, a German manufacturer of electronic equipment. With this professional background I should be well equipped to meet the requirements of the advertised position.

I've visited the United Kingdom several times to take language training courses and have always enjoyed my stays, especially in London, my favourite European city. This would be a great opportunity for me to work for an international company.

I hope I will have the opportunity to support you in your Hanover subsidiary. If you require any further information, I would be delighted to supply it.

I would have to give one month's notice in my present position.

I enclose a completed application form, my CV, a diploma from the chamber of commerce and a diploma showing my language qualifications.

I look forward to receiving your response to my application.

Yours sincerely

K Schumann

Kai Schumann

Encs: application form, CV, diplomas

Main points of a letter of application:

- Salutation
- Reference to the advertisement
- Information about your current job
- Relevant qualifications and experience
- Reasons for the application
- Period of notice
- Complimentary close
- Enclosures

3 THE CURRICULUM VITAE

Look at the CV (curriculum vitae) which Kai Schumann has written. How does it differ from German CVs?

Curriculum Vitae

Name	Kai Schumann
Address	Ringstraße 21, 28211 Bremen, Germany
Telephone	+49-421-35 68 262
Email	kschumann@usernet.de
Date of birth	2 May 1975
Place of birth	Bremen
Marital status	single
Nationality	German

Education and qualifications

1998–2000	Berufsschule 3 Bremen (part-time vocational school)
1989–1998	Ernst-Barlach-Gymnasium, Bremen (grammar school)
1985–1989	Grundschule (primary school)

Professional training and qualifications

April 2000	Examination by the Chamber of Commerce, Bremen, and certification as Industriekaufmann (Commercial Clerk for Industry). Final assessment: Grade 2
1998–2000	In-company training with Nordmann AG, Bremen, Germany (manufacturer of electronic equipment)

Work experience

2000–present	AB&T, Hanover, Germany (telecommunications company). Sales assistant, responsible for new customer accounts including preparation of quotations and dealing with complaints

Additional information

Languages	German: native speaker English: excellent oral and writing skills French: good writing skills
PC skills	Windows NT, Office 2000
Interests	Travel, volleyball, theatre
References	supplied on request

4 PRACTICE

Read the following advertisement and apply for the job. Write your own letter of application and an English CV as above.

Wir sind ein expandierendes, weltweit tätiges Fashion-Unternehmen und suchen zum nächstmöglichen Termin für unsere Münchener Hauptniederlassung eine

Kundenbetreuung für unsere ausländischen Kunden

Sie verfügen über ausgezeichnete Englischkenntnisse und gute Umgangsformen, sind wortgewandt und haben eine hohe Einsatzbereitschaft. Eine abgeschlossene Ausbildung als Industriekauffrau/mann und einige Jahre Berufspraxis setzen wir voraus.

Wir bieten Ihnen einen interessanten, abwechslungsreichen Job, ein gutes Gehalt und eine Mitarbeiterbeteiligung am Unternehmen.

Bitte senden Sie Ihre aussagefähigen Unterlagen in Englisch mit Angabe zur Gehaltsvorstellung und frühestmöglichem Eintrittstermin an Mike Higgins, Human Resources, International Style PLC, PO Box 212, Oxford, OX9 7HG.

1 A BUSINESS LETTER

1 Office Furnishing plc

2 Habermann & Falke AG
Pastorenweg 12–14
30168 Hanover
Germany

Shires House
10 Midland Grove
Cheltenham
GL54 1XX
United Kingdom

Telephone +44 (0)1242 939000
Facsimile +44 (0)1242 911166

Email joel@office_furnishing.co.uk
URL www.office_furnishing.co.uk

3 Our ref JS/mp Your ref WEI

4 14 November 2002

5 For the attention of Mr Weiche

6 Dear Mr Weiche

7 **Office System Futura**

8 Many thanks for your email enquiry concerning our Office System Futura. Based on the office plan you made available, we submit our quotation as follows:

Item No	Quantity	Description	Order No	Price
1	1	large work station	12-118	£ 550.00
2	1	deep drawer chest	12-115	£ 135.00
3	1	open shelf unit	12-235O	£ 119.00
4	1	shelf unit with doors	12-235D	£ 249.00
5	1	pull-out keyboard shelf	12-216	£ 35.00
Total (excl. VAT)				£ 1,088.00

To give you further information we enclose our full catalogue and price list.

We would be delighted to receive an order from you. Please do not hesitate to contact me if I can be of any further assistance.

I look forward to hearing from you.

9 Yours sincerely

10 *M Patterson*

pp Joel Shaw
Sales Manager

11 Encs: catalogue, price list

There is no standard layout for business letters in English, but you should use a clear, consistent layout and always include the following information:

1 Letterhead

In the English-speaking world, there are no rules about the design and content of company letterheads. However, the letterhead always shows the company's registered name and address, and its telephone and fax numbers. These days it often gives an email address and a website address as well.

2 Inside address

This is the recipient's address. Note that the house number comes before the street name and that no commas are used.

3 Reference line

When you are answering a letter from another company, give the reference of the original letter under 'Your ref:' and your own reference under 'Our ref:'.

The reference shows who wrote the letter (in capitals), who typed it (in small letters) and possibly other information such as a date or order number.

4 Date

The most common formats are '6 May 2003' (GB) and 'May 6, 2003' (US), but other formats are possible, eg '6th May 2003'. Don't change formats within a letter.

Never use 'number-only' dates like '6.5.2003'. In Britain, this means '6 May 2003' but in the USA and Asia it means 'June 5, 2003'.

5 Attention line

This shows who the letter is for. Alternatively, you could include this information in the inside address:

Mr Weiche
Habermann & Falke AG
...

6 Salutation

If you know the name of the person you are writing to, then use it, eg 'Dear Mr Weiche'. If you normally use the other person's first name, then use it in routine business letters too, eg 'Dear Peter'.

For more information on the salutation, see page 88: *Opening and closing a business letter.*

7 Subject line

This states what the letter is about, in a few words. It is usually written in bold letters or underlined. It comes immediately after the salutation, not before it.

8 Body

This is the main part of the letter. Keep it brief and use short paragraphs. Leave a space between the paragraphs.

9 Complimentary close

Finish your letter with 'Yours sincerely' if you used a name with the salutation (eg 'Dear Mr Weiche'). If you used the salutation 'Dear Sir or Madam', then finish with 'Yours faithfully'.

Americans also use 'Yours truly' or 'Truly yours' instead of 'Yours faithfully'.

For more information on the complimentary close, see page 88: *Opening and closing a business letter*.

10 Signature block

If the letter is signed by somebody other than the writer (eg an assistant or secretary), then pp or per pro (*per procrationem = im Auftrag von*) must be put before the writer's name below the signature.

This is not the same as the German ppa (*per procura*).

If you are writing a letter for your company, not as a private individual, always state your position below your name.

11 Enclosure(s)

If you have enclosed something with the letter, then say so using 'Enc' or 'Enclosure' (for one item) or 'Enclosures:' or 'Encs:' (for two or more items). If enclosing two or more items, list them.

INCOTERMS

When goods are bought from a supplier in another country, who has to pay for transportation (*Fracht*) and insurance (*Versicherung*)? Who pays any customs duty (*Zoll*)? When does the buyer actually own the goods? These matters have to be agreed between the buyer and seller using the Incoterms – a set of commercial terms which apply (*gelten*) all over the world.

= water transportation only

EXW
Ex works
Ab Werk

The buyer is responsible for the goods as soon as they leave the seller's door.
The buyer owns the goods from this point.

FCA
Free carrier
Frei Frachtführer

The seller is responsible for clearing the goods for export and delivering them to the carrier (*Frachtführer*) and for insurance up to this point.
The buyer owns the goods when they are delivered to the carrier.

FAS
Free alongside ship
Frei Längsseite Schiff

The seller is responsible for clearing the goods for export and delivering them alongside ship and for insurance up to this point.
The buyer owns the goods when they are alongside ship.

FOB
Free on board
Frei an Bord

The seller is responsible for clearing the goods for export and delivering them on board ship and for insurance up to this point.
The buyer owns the goods when they are on board ship.

CFR
Cost and freight
Kosten und Fracht

The seller is responsible for delivering the goods on board ship and for insurance up to this point. The seller additionally pays for transportation to the destination port (*Bestimmungshafen*).
The buyer owns the goods when they are on board ship.

CIF
Cost, insurance and freight
Kosten, Versicherung und Fracht

The seller is responsible for delivering the goods on board ship. The seller additionally pays for transportation and insurance to the destination port.
The buyer owns the goods when they are on board ship.

CPT
Carriage paid to
Frachtfrei

The seller is responsible for delivering the goods to the carrier. The seller additionally pays for transportation to the destination (*Bestimmungsort*). The buyer owns the goods when they are delivered to the carrier.

CIP
Carriage and insurance paid to
Frachtfrei versichert

The seller pays all transportation and insurance costs.
The buyer owns the goods when they are delivered to the carrier.

DAF
Delivered at frontier
Geliefert Grenze

The seller is responsible for delivering the goods to a named point on the border of the next country. The buyer pays any customs duty.
The buyer owns the goods when they are delivered to the border.

DES
Delivered ex ship
Geliefert ab Schiff

The seller is responsible for delivering the goods to the destination port.
The buyer owns the goods when the ship is at the destination port.

DEQ
Delivered ex quay (duty paid)
Geliefert ab Kai (verzollt)

The seller is responsible for bringing the goods to the destination port and paying any customs duty.
The buyer owns the goods when they are cleared for import and on the dock (*Kai*).

DDU
Delivered duty unpaid
Geliefert unverzollt

The seller is responsible for transporting the goods to the destination. The buyer pays any customs duty.
The buyer owns the goods when they arrive at the destination.

DDP
Delivered duty paid
Geliefert verzollt

The seller is responsible for transporting the goods to the destination and pays any customs duty.
The buyer owns the goods when they arrive at the destination.

1 BILL OF LADING

BILL OF LADING FOR COMBINED TRANSPORT SHIPMENT OR PORT TO PORT SHIPMENT

Shipper
The Black Horse Co Ltd
Ache Road
Moorgate,
LONDON

B/L No.123456

Reference: .BH-1

Atlas CONTAINER LINE

390 High Road, Ilford, Essex IG1 1UH England

Consignee
ORDER

Notify Party/Address It is agreed that no responsibility shall attach to the Carrier or his Agents for failure to notify (see clause 16 on reverse).
THE IMPORTING CO LTD
QUEENSWAY
NEW YORK
USA

Place of Receipt (Applicable only when this document is used as a Combined Transport Bill of Lading)

Place of Delivery (Applicable only when this document is used as a Combined Transport Bill of Lading)

Vessel
FILLY NOIR

Port of Loading
SOUTHAMPTON

Port of Discharge
NEW YORK

Marks and Nos: Container Nos:	Number and kind of Packages; description of Goods	Gross Weight (kg)	Measurement (cbm)
HORSE NEW YORK 1-10	10 CASES STC 2 X 15 HP POWER UNITS	310	1.35m³

Specimen

ABOVE PARTICULARS AS DECLARED BY SHIPPER **ORIGINAL**

Total No. of Containers/Packages
10

Type of Service

Freight and Charges (indicate whether prepaid or collect)

Origin Inland Haulage Charge	Paid
Origin Terminal Handling/LCL Service Charge	Paid
Ocean Feight	Paid
Destination Terminal Handling/LCL Service Charge	Collect
Destination Inland Haulage Charge	Collect

SHIPPED in apparent good order and condition, except as noted, marked and numbered as above. Number of packages, marks numbers and contents (contents and description measurements weights quantity and condition quality and value as declared by shipper) as above are considered as unknown. In using this Bill of Lading the shipper, consignee, owner or holder expressly accepts and agrees to all its stipulations exceptions and conditions whether written, printed stamped or otherwise incorporated on both pages as fully as if they were all signed by the shipper, consignee, owner or holder. In witness whereof the company has signed original Bills of Lading as mentioned above, all of this tenor and date, one of which Bills of Lading being accomplished the other(s) to stand void.

Number of Original Bills of Lading	Place and Date of Issue
3	LONDON 20 May 1998

Validfleet Limited Registered in England No: 2630747 Registerd Office: 2 Bloomsbury Street, London WC1B 3ST

For Atlas Container Line –
The Carrier

2 CERTIFICATE OF ORIGIN

1 Consignor
The Black Horse Co Ltd
Ache Road
Moorgate, LONDON

No. PQ 74459 ORIGINAL

2 Consignee
The Importing Co Ltd
Queensway
New York, United States of America

3 Country of Origin
European Communities - United Kingdom

EUROPEAN COMMUNITY

4 Transport details (Optional)
Ship - Filly Noir

5 Remarks

CERTIFICATE OF ORIGIN

Specimen

6 Item number, marks, numbers, number and kind of packages; description of goods			7 Quantity
10 Cases	Horse New York 1 - 10	Power Units	310 kilos

8 THE UNDERSIGNED AUTHORITY CERTIFIES THAT THE GOODS DESCRIBED ABOVE ORIGINATE IN THE COUNTRY SHOWN IN BOX 3

THE HERTFORDSHIRE CHAMBER OF COMMERCE AND INDUSTRY

Place and date of issue; name, signature and stamp of competent authority

Hatfield

....

....

The Hertfordshire Chamber of Commerce and Industry

3 IRREVOCABLE LETTER OF CREDIT

Advice for the beneficiary

NAME OF ISSUING BANK ABC Bank Plc, International Division, 1, Broadway, London EC27 Place and date of issue London 15th April 1998	Irrevocable documentary credit — Number 62340 Place and date of expiry at counters of advising bank 31st August 1998
Applicant – Playtime Toys Limited Blisset Street London W36	Beneficiary – The Orient Toy Company Cornwall Road North Hong Kong
Advising Bank – Ref. No. – Bank XYZ Duke Road Hong Kong	Amount – HK$ 9,000 (Hong Kong Dollars nine thousand)
Partial Shipments: ☐ allowed ☒ not allowed Transhipment: ☐ allowed ☒ not allowed	Availability ☐ by sight payment ☒ by acceptance ☐ by negotiation ☐ by deferred payment at against the documents detailed herein
Shipping/despatch/taking in charge from/at Hong Kong for transportation to: Heathrow Airport, London	☒ and beneficiary's draft at 90 days sight on Bank XYZ, Duke Road, Hong Kong

INVOICE IN THREE COPIES ALL ORIGINALLY SIGNED certifying that the goods are in accordance with Playtime Toys Limited Order Number 51 dated 4.2.1998.

AIR CONSIGNMENT NOTE evidencing goods dispatched to Playtime Toys Limited London W36 marked "Freight Paid".

PACKING LIST IN TRIPLICATE

We are informed that insurance is being arranged by our principals.

DESCRIPTION OF GOODS

Plastic toy cars

CFR Heathrow Airport, London.

Documents to be presented within days after the date of issuance of the transport document(s) but within the validity of credit.

We hereby issue the Documentary Credit in your favour. It is subject to the Uniform Customs and Practice for Documentary Credits (1993 Revision International Chamber of Commerce, Paris, France, Publication No. 500) and engages us in accordance with the terms thereof. The number and the date of the credit and the name of our bank must be quoted on all drafts required. If the credit is available by negotiation, each presentation must be noted on the reverse of this advice by the bank where the credit is available.

ABC Bank Plc, International Division
1, Broadway, London EC27

This document consists of signed page(s)

4 BILLS OF EXCHANGE

No. 120

Exchange for £2,560 1st March 1998

AT SIGHT of this FIRST BILL of Exchange

(SECOND of the same tenor and date being unpaid) pay to the

order of OURSELVES the sum of

TWO THOUSAND FIVE HUNDRED AND SIXTY POUNDS ONLY

To ABC BANK PLC

1 BROADWAY, LONDON EC27

FOR AND ON BEHALF OF
J D P CLOTHING LTD

DIRECTOR

Specimen

No. 156

Exchange for £8,240 1st March 1998

90 DAYS after DATE of this FIRST BILL of Exchange

(SECOND of the same tenor and date being unpaid) pay to the

order of OURSELVES the sum of

EIGHT THOUSAND TWO HUNDRED AND FORTY POUNDS

To ABC BANK PLC

1 BROADWAY, LONDON EC27

FOR AND ON BEHALF OF
BAKER DISTRIBUTION LTD

DIRECTOR

Specimen

5 CERTIFICATE OF INSURANCE

Advice for the beneficiary

NAME OF ISSUING BANK
ABC Bank Plc, International Division,
1, Broadway, London EC27

Place and date of issue
London 15th April 1998

Irrevocable documentary credit | Number 62340

Place and date of expiry
at counters of advising bank 31st August 1998

Applicant –
Playtime Toys Limited
Blisset Street
London W36

Beneficiary –
The Orient Toy Company
Cornwall Road North
Hong Kong

Advising Bank – Ref. No. –
Bank XYZ
Duke Road
Hong Kong

Amount –
HK$ 9,000 (Hong Kong Dollars nine thousand)

Availability
☐ by sight payment ☒ by acceptance ☐ by negotiation
☐ by deferred payment at
against the documents detailed herein
☒ and beneficiary's draft at 90 days sight
on Bank XYZ, Duke Road, Hong Kong

Partial Shipments
☐ allowed ☒ not allowed

Transhipment
☐ allowed ☒ not allowed

Shipping/despatch/taking in charge from/at Hong Kong
for transportation to: Heathrow Airport, London

INVOICE IN THREE COPIES ALL ORIGINALLY SIGNED certifying that the goods are in accordance with Playtime Toys Limited Order Number 51 dated 4.2.1998.

AIR CONSIGNMENT NOTE evidencing goods dispatched to Playtime Toys Limited London W36 marked "Freight Paid".

PACKING LIST IN TRIPLICATE
We are informed that insurance is being arranged by our principals.

DESCRIPTION OF GOODS
Plastic toy cars

CFR Heathrow Airport, London.

Documents to be presented within days after the date of issuance of the transport document(s) but within the validity of credit.

We hereby issue the Documentary Credit in your favour. It is subject to the Uniform Customs and Practice for Documentary Credits (1993 Revision International Chamber of Commerce, Paris, France, Publication No. 500) and engages us in accordance with the terms thereof. The number and the date of the credit and the name of our bank must be quoted on all drafts required. If the credit is available by negotiation, each presentation must be noted on the reverse of this advice by the bank where the credit is available.

ABC Bank Plc, International Division
1, Broadway, London EC27

This document consists of signed page(s)

6 COMMERCIAL INVOICE

The Black Horse Co Ltd
Acche Road
Moorgate, London

The Importing Co Ltd
Queensway
New York
United States of America

Invoice No: 6789

2	15 HP "Power Units" @ £345.00 each		
	Total value ex works	£690.00	
	f.o.b. Charges plus Insurance Premium	£127.00	
	Sea Freight Charges	£ 90.00	
Marks & Nos.	Total C.I.F. NEW YORK	STG£907.00	
Horse New York 1 - 10	Goods manufactured in UK by A. Power Co. Ltd. Power Road, Peterborough UK		
	Total No. of pieces: 10 cases Nett Weight: 292 kilos Gross Weight: 310 kilos Cube: 1.35 cubic metres Despatched per vessel - Filly Noir		
	Certified True & Correct for THE BLACK HORSE CO LTD		

File 1 *Unit 1, Exercise 7*

Student A

Boeing 747-400	
overall length	71 m
height	19 m
wingspan	64 m
number of engines	4
passenger load	416–524
flight range	13,750 km
cruising speed	910 km/h
fuel capacity	216,840 l
max. takeoff weight	397 tonnes
first delivery	1988

File 2 *Unit 3, Exercise 5*

Student A

Dialogue 1

You are head of sales at HolzLand. Call your stock room and check whether the pergola, article number 4820, is in stock. A customer wants it right away.

Dialogue 2

You are a salesperson at HolzLand. A customer calls. Check whether the item he/she wants is in stock, using the catalogue information on page 29. If the item is not in stock, offer an alternative. Give a discount. The customer should pick up the item this evening. Your opening hours are from 9.30 a.m. to 8 p.m.

Dialogue 3

You are a HolzLand customer. You ordered summerhouse type 0112 but received type 0120. Call HolzLand and complain.

File 3 *Unit 4, Exercise 6*

Student A

Dialogue 1

You work in the travel department at BP. A colleague calls. Try to find the best flights, using the information below. Take the booking.

1 British Airways

from	to	date	depart	arrive	flight
London Heathrow	Milan Malpensa	03/12	11:50	14:55	BA566
Milan Malpensa	London Heathrow	12/12	08:45	09:45	BA571

Business Class and Economy Class available

2 Alitalia

from	to	date	depart	arrive	flight
London Heathrow	Milan Malpensa	03/12	12:35	15:40	AZ231
Milan Malpensa	London Heathrow	12/12	19:25	20:25	AZ231

Economy Class only available

3 bmi british midland

from	to	date	depart	arrive	flight
London Heathrow	Milan Linate	03/12	10:30	13:30	BD451
Milan Linate	London Heathrow	13/12	08:15	09:25	BD452

Business Class and Economy Class available

Dialogue 2

You work in the finance department at Deutsche BP. You need to book flights for your boss, Ms Siobhan O'Brien [ʃə'vɒn ˌəʊ'braiən] Call the travel department and book the best flights, using the information below.

20 August: Berlin–Belfast; arrive before 2 pm
28 August: Belfast–Berlin; leave after 3 pm
Business Class if possible, otherwise Economy will do.

File 4 *Unit 5, Exercise 14*

Student A

You believe that the sales conference should be held at Alveston Manor. This is a hotel and conference centre near Stratford-upon-Avon in Warwickshire.

Your reasons are:

1. Alveston Manor is an impressive location: a magnificent old house in beautiful gardens.
2. There is plenty of space for the 150 participants. They can also stay at the hotel, which has 114 bedrooms.
3. The conference facilities are excellent.
4. The senior managers of partner companies in Europe and the USA will be attending, so it's important to make a good impression.

You can make up further reasons of your own.

During the meeting, you must use each of the following expressions at least once at an appropriate point:

- If we hold the conference at Alveston Manor, ...
- I have one objection.
- I support that proposal.
- I'd like to point out that ...
- Could I come in at that point?

File 5 *Unit 10, Exercise 15*

Case study 1

Student A

ETH has just received a consignment of compost from ComPo, but the consignment weighs 6 tons instead of the agreed 13 tons. The driver was not aware that the consignment was incomplete.

You work for ETH. Phone ComPo, explain the problem and try to find out what went wrong.

Case study 2

OLB has sent ETH a delivery of clinker bricks to be processed as an ingredient for cement.

You work for OLB. You receive a call from ETH complaining about the quality of the bricks. You are sure that the quality was good. Suggest a solution.

File 6 *Unit 1, Exercise 7*

Student B

Airbus A380	
overall length	73 m
height	24 m
wingspan	79.8 m
number of engines	4
passenger load	555 or 650 (extended version)
flight range	14,800 km
cruising speed	910 km/h
fuel capacity	310,000 l
max. takeoff weight	560 tonnes
first delivery	2006

File 7 *Unit 3, Exercise 5*

Student B

Dialogue 1

You work in the stock room at HolzLand. You receive a call from the sales manager about an item. Check the catalogue information on page 29. If you cannot find the item, ask questions to find out which item the sales manager really wants. If the item is not in stock, suggest an alternative.

Dialogue 2

You are a customer. In a HolzLand advertisement you see that AMELIA pine garden chairs and tables are on sale – 20% off the normal price. You want four chairs and a table. Call the store to find out whether these articles are already sold out and whether they can keep one set for you until tomorrow.

Dialogue 3

You are a salesperson at HolzLand. A customer calls: he/she wants to exchange an item. Check whether the item he/she wants is in stock. If not, try to convince the customer that he/she should keep the item.

File 8 *Unit 4, Exercise 6*

Student B

Dialogue 1

You work in the marketing department at BP. You need to book flights for your boss, Dr Cedric Coveney ['sedrɪk 'kʌvni]. Call the travel department and book the best flights, using the information below.

3 December: London–Milan; leave after 10 am
12 December: Milan–London; leave after 8 pm
Must be Business Class. Could come back early on 13 December if necessary.

Dialogue 2

You work in the travel department at BP. A colleague calls. Try to find the best flights, using the information below. Take the booking.

1 British Airways, bmi british midland

from	to	date	depart	arrive	flight
Berlin Tegel	London Heathrow	20/08	11:00	12:05	BA991
London Heathrow	Belfast City	20/08	13:20	14:40	BD86
Belfast City	London Heathrow	28/08	11:10	12:30	BD85
London Heathrow	Berlin Tegel	28/08	14:30	17:20	BA922

Business Class and Economy Class available

2 Lufthansa, British European

from	to	date	depart	arrive	flight
Berlin Tempelhof	London City	20/08	10:40	11:35	LH2356
London City	Belfast City	20/08	12:00	13:30	BE177
Belfast City	London City	28/08	14:55	16:45	BE180
London City	Berlin Tempelhof	28/08	18:05	20:55	LH2357

Business Class fully booked on BE180; Economy Class available

File 9 *Unit 5, Exercise 14*

Student B

You believe that the sales conference should be held at the RM headquarters in Milton Park.

Your reasons are:

1. It won't cost the company anything.
2. It's an opportunity to show your company's modern building to business partners.
3. There will be less disruption to the company's normal working routine.
4. It's convenient for participants travelling from abroad – Birmingham International and Heathrow airports are only an hour away by train or car, and Oxford has several suitable hotels for your visitors.

You can make up further reasons of your own.

During the meeting, you must use each of the following expressions at least once at an appropriate point:

- If we held the conference at RM headquarters, ...
- I propose that ...
- Have you taken into account ... ?
- To be quite frank, ...
- That isn't the main issue here.

File 10 *Unit 10, Exercise 15*

Student B

Case study 1

ComPo has recently sent a consignment of 13 tons of compost to ETH.

You work for ComPo. You receive a call from ETH complaining that the consignment was incomplete. Give an explanation and suggest a solution.

Case study 2

ETH has received a delivery of clinker bricks to be processed as an ingredient for cement.

You work for ETH. The quality of the bricks was too low to be recycled. Therefore the consignment had to be taken to the waste disposal site. Phone OLB and explain that you are not willing to pay for the disposal of the bricks, which amounted to 130 euros.

File 11 *Unit 5, Exercise 14*

Chairperson

Try not to take sides in the discussion. Your task is to make sure:

1 that the meeting is well organized
2 that all the points on the agenda are discussed
3 that all participants get a fair opportunity to express their views
4 that the meeting does not continue for too long

During the meeting, you must use each of the following expressions at least once at an appropriate point:

- What we hope to accomplish is ...
- Do you have anything to add?
- Can I have your views, please?
- Correct me if I'm wrong, but ...
- To sum up: ...

UNIT WORD LIST

Die neuen Wörter sind in der Reihenfolge ihres Vorkommens im Text verzeichnet. Hier sind jedoch die Wörter, die zum Grundwortschatz gehören, nicht aufgeführt. Die Zahl am linken Rand gibt die Seitenzahl an.

p = das Wort befindet sich im *Pairwork File*.

t = das Wort befindet sich im *Transcript*.

Unit 1

6	**federal state** [ˌfedərəl ˈsteɪt]	Bundesland
	be located [bi ləʊˈkeɪtɪd]	sich befinden
	correlation [ˌkɒrəˈleɪʃn]	Korrelation, Wechselbeziehung
	aviation industry [ˌeɪviˈeɪʃn ɪndəstri]	Luftfahrtindustrie
	be based in [bi ˈbeɪst ɪn]	seinen Sitz haben in
	site [saɪt]	Stelle, Platz
	electronics [ˌɪlekˈtrɒnɪks]	Elektronik
	ship building [ˈʃɪpbɪldɪŋ]	Schiff(s)bau
	textiles [ˈtekstaɪlz]	Textilien
	vehicle manufacturing [ˌviːəkl ˌmænjuˈfæktʃərɪŋ]	Fahrzeugproduktion
7	**electronic** [ˌɪlekˈtrɒnɪk]	elektronisch
	component [kəmˈpəʊnənt]	(Bau-)Element, Bauteil
	delayed [dɪˈleɪd]	verspätet
	meanwhile [ˈmiːnwaɪl]	inzwischen
	personal assistant [ˌpɜːsənl əˈsɪstənt]	(persönliche/r) Assistent/in
	take care of [teɪk ˈkeər əv]	sich kümmern um
	feel at ease [fiːl ət ˈiːz]	sich wohl fühlen
	pleased to meet you [ˌpliːzd tə ˈmiːt ju]	es freut mich, Sie kennen zu lernen
	do business with [du ˈbɪznəs wɪð]	Geschäfte machen mit
	opportunity [ˌɒpəˈtjuːnəti]	Gelegenheit
	operation [ˌɒpəˈreɪʃn]	Betrieb
	actually [ˈæktʃuəli]	eigentlich, tatsächlich
	found [faʊnd]	gründen
	at that time [ət ðæt ˈtaɪm]	zu jener Zeit
	diversify into [daɪˈvɜːsɪfaɪ ɪntə]	die Produktion ausweiten auf
	aircraft [ˈeəkrɑːft]	Flugzeug
	merge with [ˈmɜːdʒ wɪð]	fusionieren mit
	era [ˈɪərə]	Ära, Zeitalter
	contribution [ˌkɒntrɪˈbjuːʃn]	Beitrag
	production process [prəˌdʌkʃn ˈprəʊses]	Produktionsprozess
	deliver [dɪˈlɪvə]	liefern
	fuselage section [ˈfjuːzəlɑːʒ sekʃn]	Rumpfteil
	final assembly [ˌfaɪnl əˈsembli]	Endmontage

	take place [teɪk ˈpleɪs]	stattfinden
	so-called [ˌsəʊˈkɔːld]	so genannt
	air bridge [ˈeə brɪdʒ]	Luftbrücke
	serve [sɜːv]	bedienen
	fleet [fliːt]	Flotte
	transport aircraft [ˌtrænspɔːt ˈeəkrɑːft]	Transportflugzeug
	funny-looking [ˈfʌni lʊkɪŋ]	komisch aussehend
	concern [kənˈsɜːn]	Konzern
	worldwide [ˈwɜːldwaɪd]	weltweit
8	**on average** [ɒn ˈævərɪdʒ]	im Durchschnitt, durchschnittlich
	add up to [ˌæd ˈʌp tə]	sich addieren zu
	to date [tə ˈeɪt]	bis dato
	worth [wɜːθ]	wert, im Wert von
	competitor [kəmˈpetɪtə]	Konkurrent/in
	the following [ˈðə ˈfɒləʊɪŋ]	die folgenden
	equivalent [ɪˈkwɪvələnt]	Entsprechung
9	**first-name terms** [ˌfɜːst neɪm ˈtɜːmz]	mit Vornamen anreden
	on meeting [ɒn ˈmiːtɪŋ]	beim Treffen
	period of time [ˈpɪəriəd əv taɪm]	Zeitraum, -spanne
	on parting [ˈpɑːtɪŋ]	beim Verabschieden
	business associate [ˈbɪznəs əsəʊʃiət]	Geschäftspartner/in, -freund/in
	appropriate [əˈprəʊpriət]	angemessen, passend
	allow me to [əˈlaʊ mi tə]	gestatten Sie mir
	accountant [əˈkaʊntənt]	Buchhalter/in
	respond [rɪˈspɒnd]	reagieren (auf), antworten
10	**brochure** [ˈbrəʊʃə]	Prospekt
	attract sb's interest [əˌtrækt ˈɪntrəst]	jds Interesse wecken
	prediction [prɪˈdɪkʃn]	Vorhersage
	air travel [ˈeə trævl]	Luftfahrt
	air traffic [ˈeə træfɪk]	Luftverkehr
	infrastructure [ˈɪnfrəstrʌktʃə]	Infrastruktur
	keep up with [ˌkiːp ˈʌp wɪð]	Schritt halten mit
	overcrowding [ˌəʊvəˈkraʊdɪŋ]	Überfüllung
	approximately [əˈprɒksɪmətli]	ungefähr, etwa
	current [ˈkʌrənt]	aktuell, gegenwärtig
	obviously [ˈɒbviəsli]	offensichtlich
	solve [sɒlv]	lösen
	solution [səˈluːʃn]	Lösung
	jetliner [ˈdʒetlaɪnə]	Düsenflugzeug
	capacity [kəˈpæsəti]	Kapazität, Fassungsvermögen
	in order to [ɪn ˈɔːdə tə]	um zu
	growth [grəʊθ]	Wachstum, Zunahme

	passenger numbers [ˌpæsɪndʒə ˈnʌmbəz]	Fluggastzahlen
	at present [ət ˈpreznt]	momentan, derzeit
	passenger capacity [ˌpæsɪndʒə kəˈpæsəti]	Platz für Passagiere
	maximum [ˈmæksɪməm]	höchste/r/s, maximal
	flight range [ˈflaɪt reɪndʒ]	Reichweite
	correspond to [ˌkɒrɪˈspɒnd tə]	entsprechen
	distance [ˈdɪstəns]	Entfernung, Strecke
	extend [ɪkˈstend]	vergrößern, ausdehnen
	freighter [ˈfreɪtə]	Frachtflugzeug
	payload [ˈpeɪləʊd]	Nutzlast
	range [reɪndʒ]	Reichweite
	freight [freɪt]	Fracht
	prestige project [preˌstiːʒ ˈprɒdʒekt]	Prestigeprojekt
	roll off [ˌrəʊl ˈɒf]	rollen vom
	production line [prəˈdʌkʃn laɪn]	Fließ-, Fertigungsband
	refer to [rɪˈfɜː tə]	sich beziehen auf
11	**predict** [prɪˈdɪkt]	vorhersagen
	expectation [ˌekspekˈteɪʃn]	Erwartung
	response [rɪˈspɒns]	Reaktion, Antwort
	compete [kəmˈpiːt]	konkurrieren
	development [dɪˈveləpmənt]	Entwicklung
	unlike [ˌʌnˈlaɪk]	anders als, im Gegensatz zu
	decimal [ˈdesɪml]	Dezimalzahl
	separate [ˈsepəreɪt]	trennen
	block [blɒk]	Block, Zahlengruppe
	digit [ˈdɪdʒɪt]	einstellige Zahl
	swap [swɒp]	tauschen
	overall [ˌəʊvərˈɔːl]	Gesamt-, total
	wingspan [ˈwɪŋ spæn]	(Flügel-)Spannweite
	engine [ˈendʒɪn]	Motor, Triebwerk
	passenger load [ˈpæsɪndʒə ləʊd]	Passagierzahl
	cruising speed [ˈkruːzɪŋ spiːd]	Reisegeschwindigkeit
	fuel capacity [ˌfjuːəl kəˈpæsəti]	Treibstofffassungs-vermögen
	max. [ˈmæksɪməm]	maximal, Maximum
	takeoff weight [ˈteɪkɒf weɪt]	Startgewicht
	delivery [dɪˈlɪvəri]	Auslieferung
12	**make a comparison** [meɪk ə kəmˈpærɪsn]	einen Vergleich anstellen
	refuel [ˌriːˈfjuːəl]	auftanken
	get to know [get tə ˈnəʊ]	kennen lernen
	at last [ət ˈlɑːst]	endlich, schließlich
	rush in [ˌrʌʃ ˈɪn]	hereinstürmen
	take the leading role [teɪk ðə ˌliːdɪŋ ˈrəʊl]	die Führung übernehmen
	row [rəʊ]	Reihe
	take notes [teɪk ˈnəʊts]	(sich) Notizen machen
	excuse [ɪkˈskjuːz]	entschuldigen
	delay [dɪˈleɪ]	Verspätung
12t	**overview** [ˈəʊvəvjuː]	Überblick
	consortium [kənˈsɔːtiəm]	Konsortium
	annual turnover [ˌænjuəl ˈtɜːnəʊvə]	Jahresumsatz
	subsidiary [səbˈsɪdiəri]	Tochtergesellschaft
	supplier [səˈplaɪə]	Zulieferer
	involved in [ɪnˈvɒlvd ɪn]	beteiligt an
	transmitter [trænsˈmɪtə]	Sender
	supply [səˈplaɪ]	liefern
	quantity [ˈkwɒntəti]	Menge
	family business [ˈfæməli bɪznəs]	Familienunternehmen
	great-grandfather [ˌgrəɪtˈgrænfɑːðə]	Urgroßvater
	take over [ˌteɪk ˈəʊvə]	übernehmen
	managing director [ˌmænɪdʒɪŋ dəˈrektə]	Generaldirektor/in
	turnover [ˈtɜːnəʊvə]	Umsatz
	external duty [ɪkˌstɜːnl ˈdjuːti]	Außendienst, freie Mitarbeit
	apart from [əˈpɑːt frəm]	abgesehen von
	comprise [kəmˈpraɪz]	umfassen, bestehen aus
	switch [swɪtʃ]	Schalter
	cable [ˈkeɪbl]	Kabel
	variety [vəˈraɪəti]	Vielfalt
12	**organization** [ˌɔːgənaɪˈzeɪʃn]	Aufbau
	up to [ˈʌp tə]	bis zu
	shareholder [ˈʃeəhəʊldə]	Aktionär/in, Anteilseigner/in
	share [ʃeə]	(Geschäfts-)Anteil, Aktie
	public [ˈpʌblɪk]	Öffentlichkeit
13	**exchange** [ɪksˈtʃeɪndʒ]	austauschen
	due to [ˈdjuː tə]	wegen, aufgrund von
	currently [ˈkʌrəntli]	momentan
14	**cost reduction** [kɒst rɪˈdʌkʃn]	Kostensenkung
	commonality method [ˌkɒməˈnæləti meθəd]	Gemeinsamkeitsprinzip
	airframe [ˈeəfreɪm]	(Flugzeug-)Zelle
	onboard-system [ˌɒnˈbɔːd sɪstəm]	Bordsystem
	training characteristics [ˌtreɪnɪŋ ˌkærəktəˈrɪstɪks]	Trainingseigenschaften
	handling characteristics [ˌhændlɪŋ ˌkærəktəˈrɪstɪks]	typische Merkmale der Handhabung
	similarity [ˌsɪməˈlærəti]	Ähnlichkeit
	maintenance [ˈmeɪntənəns]	Wartung, Instandhaltung
	operational [ˌɒpəˈreɪʃənl]	Betriebs-
	substantially [səbˈstænʃəli]	wesentlich, beträchtlich
	cabin crew [ˈkæbɪn kruː]	Kabinenbesatzung, Flugbegleiter
	transfer [trænsˈfɜː]	überweisen

	for instance [fə'rɪnstəns]	zum Beispiel
	qualification [ˌkwɒlɪfɪ'keɪʃn]	Qualifikation, Abschluss einer Ausbildung
	layout ['leɪaʊt]	Grundriss, Anordnung
	virtually ['vɜːtʃuəli]	praktisch, nahezu
	crew [kruː]	Besatzung, Mannschaft
	training course ['treɪnɪŋ kɔːs]	Lehrgang
	mobility [məʊ'bɪləti]	Mobilität
	job satisfaction ['dʒɒb sætɪsfækʃn]	Zufriedenheit im Beruf, berufliche Befriedigung
	balanced ['bælənst]	ausgeglichen, ausgewogen
	workload ['wɜːkləʊd]	Arbeitsbelastung
	range [reɪndʒ]	Reihe, Auswahl
	savings ['seɪvɪŋz]	Ersparnisse
	achieve [ə'tʃiːv]	erreichen, erlangen
	enhance [ɪn'hɑːns]	erhöhen, steigern
	productivity [ˌprɒdʌk'tɪvəti]	Produktivität
	route [ruːt]	Route, Strecke
	scheduling ['ʃedjuːlɪŋ]	Zeitplanung
	significant [sɪg'nɪfɪkənt]	erheblich, spürbar
	stock [stɒk]	Vorrat, Lager(bestand)
	spare parts [ˌspeə 'pɑːts]	Ersatzteile
	account for [ə'kaʊnt fə]	ausmachen, betragen
	single-aisled [ˌsɪŋgl 'aɪld]	mit einem Gang
	discussion [dɪ'skʌʃn]	Diskussion
	fellow ['feləʊ]	Mit-
	benefit from ['benɪfɪt frəm]	profitieren von
	approach [ə'prəʊtʃ]	Methode, Ansatz
	strategy ['strætədʒi]	Strategie
	graph [grɑːf]	Kurve, grafische Darstellung
	diagram ['daɪəgræm]	Diagramm, Grafik

Unit 2

16	**medium-sized** ['miːdiəmsaɪzd]	mittelgroß
	distribute [dɪ'strɪbjuːt]	vertreiben, ausliefern
	device [dɪ'vaɪs]	Technik, Gerät
	partnership ['pɑːtnəʃɪp]	Partnerschaft
	unique [ju'niːk]	einzigartig
	cardiology diagnostics [ˌkɑːdi'ɒlədʒi ˌdaɪəg'nɒstɪks]	Herzdiagnostik
16t	**receptionist** [rɪ'sepʃənɪst]	Empfangsdame, -chef
	archives ['ɑːkaɪvz]	Archiv, Registratur
16	**manufacturing** [ˌmænju'fæktʃərɪŋ]	Fertigung, Produktion
	workshop ['wɜːkʃɒp]	Werkstatt, Workshop
	stock room ['stɒk ruːm]	Lager(raum)
	goods [gʊdz]	Ware(n), Güter
	inventory control [ˌɪnvəntri kən'trəʊl]	Inventur
	purchasing ['pɜːtʃəsɪŋ]	Einkauf
	canteen [kæn'tiːn]	Kantine
	order processing [ˌɔːdə 'prəʊsesɪŋ]	Auftragsabwicklung
	after-sales service ['ɑːftəseɪlz sɜːvɪs]	Kundendienst
	reception desk [rɪ'sepʃn desk]	Rezeption, Empfang
	distribution [ˌdɪstrɪ'bjuːʃn]	Vertrieb
	accounting [ə'kaʊntɪŋ]	Rechnungswesen, Buchhaltung
	sales [seɪlz]	Verkauf
	sales director ['seɪlz dərektə]	Verkaufsleiter/in
	product management [ˌprɒdʌkt 'mænɪdʒmənt]	Produktmanagement
	technical department [ˌteknɪkl dɪ'pɑːtmənt]	technische Abteilung
	conference room ['kɒnfərəns ruːm]	Besprechungszimmer, Konferenzraum
17	**give directions** [gɪv də'rekʃnz]	Anweisungen geben, den Weg beschreiben
	corridor ['kɒrɪdɔː]	Gang, Korridor
	rough [rʌf]	Roh(skizze)
	sketch [sketʃ]	Skizze
	sheet (of paper) [ʃiːt əv 'peɪpə]	Blatt (Papier)
	product launch ['prɒdʌkt lɔːntʃ]	Produkteinführung
18	**run smoothly** [rʌn 'smuːðli]	glatt verlaufen
	proceed [prə'siːd]	verfahren, vorgehen
	carry out [ˌkæri 'aʊt]	durchführen
	market analysis [ˌmɑːkɪt ə'næləsɪs]	Marktanalyse
	evaluate [ɪ'væljueɪt]	bewerten, abschätzen
	demand [dɪ'mɑːnd]	Nachfrage, Bedarf
	assume [ə'sjuːm]	annehmen
	existing [ɪg'zɪstɪŋ]	bestehend
	inform [ɪn'fɔːm]	informieren, unterrichten
	sales literature ['seɪlz ˌlɪtrətʃə]	(Verkaufs-)Prospekt(e), Kataloge
	arrange [ə'reɪndʒ]	arrangieren, vereinbaren
	translation [træns'leɪʃn]	Übersetzung
	advertising campaign ['ædvətaɪzɪŋ kæmpeɪn]	Werbekampagne
	advertisement [əd'vɜːtɪsmənt]	Werbung, Anzeige
	journal ['dʒɜːnl]	Zeitschrift
	send out [ˌsend 'aʊt]	verschicken, versenden
	mailing ['meɪlɪŋ]	Werbesendung
	promote [prə'məʊt]	anpreisen, bewerben
	via ['vaɪə]	über, durch, per
	sales representative ['seɪlz reprɪzentətɪv]	(Handels-)Vertreter/in
	demonstrate ['demənstreɪt]	vorstellen, vorführen
	potential [pə'tenʃl]	möglich, potenziell

	field sales force [fi:ld 'seɪlz fɔ:s]	Außenmitarbeiter
	experienced [ɪk'spɪəriənst]	erfahren
	highly skilled [ˌhaɪli 'skɪld]	gut ausgebildet
	negotiator [nɪ'gəʊʃieɪtə]	Verhandler
	hopefully ['həʊpfli]	hoffentlich
	keep sb busy [ki:p 'bɪzi]	jdn beschäftigen
	dispatch [dɪ'spætʃ]	(ab)senden
	install [ɪn'stɔ:l]	installieren, einbauen
	technician [tek'nɪʃn]	Techniker/in
	settle ['setl]	erledigen, behandeln
19	**for the moment** [fə ðə 'məʊmənt]	für den Augenblick
	go into detail [gəʊ ɪntə 'di:teɪl]	ins Detail gehen
	organization chart [ˌɔ:gənaɪ'zeɪʃn tʃɑ:t]	Organisationsstruktur
20	**department** [dɪ'pɑ:tmənt]	Ministerium, Ressort, Abteilung
21	**accommodation** [əˌkɒmə'deɪʃn]	Unterkunft, Zimmer
	far out [ˌfɑ:r 'aʊt]	weit draußen
	neighbourhood ['neɪbəhʊd]	(Wohn-)Gegend, Nachbarschaft
	personal ['pɜ:sənl]	persönlich
	impression [ɪm'preʃn]	Eindruck
	operate ['ɒpəreɪt]	operieren, arbeiten
	avoid [ə'vɔɪd]	vermeiden
	such as ['sʌtʃ əz]	wie zum Beispiel
	salary ['sæləri]	Gehalt
	suitable ['su:təbl]	geeignet, passend
	indifferent [ɪn'dɪfrənt]	gleichgültig
	definite ['defɪnət]	bestimmt, fest
	mention ['menʃn]	erwähnen
	contradict [ˌkɒntrə'dɪkt]	widersprechen
	rude [ru:d]	unhöflich, rücksichtslos
	likely ['laɪkli]	wahrscheinlich
	offended [ə'fendɪd]	beleidigt
	react [ri'ækt]	reagieren
22	**various** ['veəriəs]	verschiedene
	involve [ɪn'vɒlv]	umfassen, mit sich bringen
	written correspondence [ˌrɪtn ˌkɒrɪ'spɒndəns]	schriftliche Korrespondenz
	responsible [rɪ'spɒnsəbl]	verantwortlich, zuständig
	update [ˌʌp'deɪt]	aktualisieren, auf den neuesten Stand bringen, letzter Stand
	database ['deɪtəbeɪs]	Datenbank
	ensure [ɪn'ʃʊə]	sicherstellen, gewährleisten
	coordinate [kəʊ'ɔ:dɪneɪt]	aufeinander abstimmen, koordinieren
	inspection [ɪn'spekʃn]	Kontrolle, Prüfung
	incoming ['ɪnkʌmɪŋ]	eingehend, ankommend
	make sure [ˌmeɪk 'ʃʊə]	sicherstellen, sich vergewissern
	label ['leɪbl]	beschriften, etikettieren
	item ['aɪtəm]	Artikel
	approve [ə'pru:v]	gutheißen, genehmigen
	delivery note [dɪ'lɪvəri nəʊt]	Lieferschein
	invoice ['ɪnvɔɪs]	Rechnung
	shipping document ['ʃɪpɪŋ dɒkjumənt]	Versand-, Frachtpapier
	address label [ə'dres leɪbl]	Adressaufkleber
	requirement [rɪ'kwaɪəmənt]	Anforderung
	forwarding agent ['fɔ:wədɪŋ eɪdʒənt]	Spediteur/in
	senior ['si:niə]	vorgesetzt, leitend
	troubleshooter ['trʌblʃu:tə]	Störungssucher/in, Vermittler/in
	up to, be ~ sb ['ʌp tə]	dafür verantwortlich sein
	deal with ['di:l wɪð]	sich befassen mit
	genuine ['dʒenjuɪn]	echt
	malfunction [ˌmæl'fʌŋkʃn]	Fehlfunktion
	repair [rɪ'peə]	reparieren
	on site [ɒn 'saɪt]	vor Ort
	replace [rɪ'pleɪs]	ersetzen, austauschen
	take seriously [teɪk 'sɪəriəsli]	ernst nehmen
	conduct [kən'dʌkt]	(durch)führen
	properly ['prɒpəli]	richtig, korrekt
	user manual [ju:zə 'mænjuəl]	Benutzerhandbuch
	in charge of [ɪn 'tʃɑ:dʒ əv]	verantwortlich für
	sufficient [sə'fɪʃnt]	ausreichend, genügend
	register ['redʒɪstə]	registrieren, aufnehmen
	liaise with [li'eɪz wɪð]	sich in Verbindung setzen mit
23	**monitoring system** ['mɒnɪtərɪŋ sɪstəm]	Überwachungssystem
	apprentice [ə'prentɪs]	Auszubildende/r
	apprenticeship [ə'prentɪʃɪp]	Lehre, Ausbildung
23t	**assign so to** [ə'saɪn tə]	jdn zuteilen
	routine task [ru:'ti:n tɑ:sk]	Routinearbeit
	as well as [əz 'wel əz]	ebenso wie
	process ['prəʊses]	bearbeiten
	complaint [kəm'pleɪnt]	Beschwerde, Beanstandung, Reklamation
	cancellation [ˌkænsə'leɪʃn]	Stornierung, Absage
	credit rating ['kredɪt reɪtɪŋ]	Kreditwürdigkeit
	make out [ˌmeɪk 'aʊt]	ausstellen
	collection [kə'lekʃn]	Abholung
	personnel department [ˌpɜ:sə'nel dɪpɑ:tmənt]	Personalabteilung
	accounts department [ə'kaʊnts dɪpɑ:tmənt]	Buchhaltung
	personnel file [ˌpɜ:sə'nel faɪl]	Personalakte

	contract of employment [ˌkɒntrækt əv ɪm'plɔɪmənt]	Arbeitsvertrag
	holiday pay ['hɒlədeɪ peɪ]	Urlaubsgeld
	social security payment [ˌsəʊʃl sɪ'kjʊərəti peɪmənt]	Sozialabgabe(n)
	reminder [rɪ'maɪndə]	Mahnung
	payment ['peɪmənt]	Zahlung, Auszahlung
	tax form ['tæks fɔːm]	Steuerformular
	balance sheet ['bæləns ʃiːt]	Bilanz, Kassenbericht
	familiar with [fə'mɪliə wɪð]	vertraut mit, bekannt mit
	warehousing system ['weəhaʊzɪŋ sɪstəm]	Lagerhaltungssystem
	sort [sɔːt]	sortieren
	reorder [ˌriː'ɔːdə]	nachbestellen
	tool [tuːl]	Werkzeug
	solder ['səʊldə]	löten
	examine [ɪg'zæmɪn]	untersuchen, prüfen
	unfinished [ʌn'fɪnɪʃt]	unfertig
	issue ['ɪʃuː]	ausstellen, versehen
	serial number ['sɪəriəl nʌmbə]	Seriennummer
	archive ['ɑːkaɪv]	archivieren
	data ['deɪtə]	Daten
	exhibition [ˌeksɪ'bɪʃn]	Ausstellung
	trade fair ['treɪd feə]	Handelsmesse
	promotional material [prəˌməʊʃənl mə'tɪeriəl]	Werbematerial
23	**duty** ['djuːti]	Aufgabe, Pflicht
	summarize ['sʌməraɪz]	zusammenfassen
24	**term** [tɜːm]	Ausdruck
	concept ['kɒnsept]	Konzept
	continuous [kən'tɪnjuəs]	ständig
	improvement [ɪm'pruːvmənt]	Verbesserung
	adopt [ə'dɒpt]	adoptieren, übernehmen
	pace [peɪs]	Tempo
	constantly ['kɒnstəntli]	ständig
	evolve [ɪ'vɒlv]	(sich) entwickeln
	varied ['veərid]	unterschiedlich, vielfältig
	complex ['kɒmpleks]	kompliziert
	diversified [daɪ'vɜːsɪfaɪd]	diversifiziert
	independently [ˌɪndɪ'pendəntli]	unabhängig
	conventional [kən'venʃənl]	herkömmlich, konventionell
	hierarchical [ˌhaɪə'rɑːkɪkl]	hierarchisch
	outdated [ˌaʊt'deɪtɪd]	überholt, veraltet
	implement ['ɪmplɪmənt]	einführen, -setzen
	make a decision [ˌmeɪk ə dɪ'sɪʒn]	eine Entscheidung treffen
	leadership ['liːdəʃɪp]	Führung
	from the top [frəm ðə 'tɒp]	von oben
	bottom-up [ˌbɒtəm 'ʌp]	von unten nach oben
	instead of [ɪn'sted əv]	(an)statt
	pyramidal hierarchy [pɪˌræmɪdl 'haɪərɑːki]	pyramidenförmige Hierarchie
	horizontal [ˌhɒrɪ'zɒntl]	horizontal
	network ['netwɜːk]	Netz(werk)
	build up [ˌbɪld 'ʌp]	aufbauen
	specialized ['speʃəlaɪzd]	spezialisiert
	input ['ɪnpʊt]	Einsatz
	merit ['merɪt]	Verdienst(e)
	promotion [prə'məʊʃn]	Beförderung
	seniority [ˌsiːni'ɒrəti]	Dienstalter
	decentralized [ˌdiː'sentrəlaɪzd]	dezentralisiert
	flexible ['fleksəbl]	flexibel
	spread [spred]	verteilen
	customer satisfaction [ˌkʌstəmə ˌsætɪs'fækʃn]	Zufriedenheit der Verbraucher
	criteria [kraɪ'tɪəriə]	Kriterien, Kennzeichen
	consequently ['kɒnsɪkwəntli]	dementsprechend, infolgedessen
	innovation [ˌɪnə'veɪʃn]	Neuerung, Innovation
	traditional [trə'dɪʃənl]	traditionell
	focus on ['fəʊkəs ɒn]	Konzentration auf
	output ['aʊtpʊt]	Produktion(smenge), Ausstoß
	mass [mæs]	Masse
	versus ['vɜːsəs]	gegen(über)
	pros and cons [ˌprəʊz ənd 'kɒnz]	Für und Wider
	questionnaire [ˌkwestʃə'neə]	Fragebogen
	incorporate [ɪn'kɔːpəreɪt]	enthalten, umfassen
	according to [ə'kɔːdɪŋ tə]	nach, entsprechend
	principle ['prɪnsəpl]	Grundsatz, Prinzip

Unit 3

25	**dial** ['daɪəl]	wählen
	identify [aɪ'dentɪfaɪ]	identifizieren
	code [kəʊd]	Vorwahl
	emergency service [ɪ'mɜːdʒənsi sɜːvɪs]	Notruf
	co-operative [kəʊ'ɒpərətɪv]	Kooperative
	timber ['tɪmbə]	(Bau-)Holz
	hectare ['hekteə]	Hektar
	nail [neɪl]	Nagel
	summer house ['sʌmə haʊs]	Sommerhaus
	interesting ['ɪntrəstɪŋ]	interessant
	enquiry [ɪn'kwaɪəri]	Anfrage
26	**bulk order** [ˌbʌlk 'ɔːdə]	Großauftrag, -bestellung
	fence [fens]	Zaun
	in that case [ɪn 'ðæt keɪs]	in diesem Fall
	put sb through [ˌpʊt 'θruː]	jdn verbinden, durchstellen
	engaged [ɪn'geɪdʒd]	besetzt
	hold the line [həʊld ðə 'laɪn]	am Apparat bleiben
	go ahead [ˌgəʊ ə'hed]	anfangen
	catch [kætʃ]	verstehen

	extension [ɪk'stenʃn]	Nebenanschluss
	urgent ['ɜ:dʒənt]	dringend, eilig
	appreciate [ə'pri:ʃieɪt]	zu schätzen wissen
	manage ['mænɪdʒ]	(es) schaffen
27	**convenient** [kən'vi:niənt]	passend, angenehm
	interrupt [ˌɪntə'rʌpt]	unterbrechen
	shortly ['ʃɔ:tli]	in Kürze
	receiver [rɪ'si:və]	(Telefon-)Hörer
	answerphone ['ɑ:nsəfəʊn]	Anrufbeantworter
27t	**carton** ['kɑ:tn]	Karton, Paket
	upon inspection [əpɒn ɪn'spekʃn]	nach Prüfung
	discover [dɪ'skʌvə]	entdecken, feststellen
	window frame ['wɪndəʊ freɪm]	Fensterrahmen
	damaged ['dæmɪdʒd]	beschädigt
	sort out [ˌsɔ:t 'aʊt]	klären, lösen
	in regard to [ɪn rɪ'gɑ:d tə]	hinsichtlich, wegen
	refuse [rɪ'fju:z]	ablehnen, sich weigern
	settle ['setl]	begleichen, bezahlen
	grateful ['greɪtfl]	dankbar
	in case [ɪn 'keɪs]	falls
	thunderstorm ['θʌndəstɔ:m]	Gewitter
	ferry ['feri]	Fähre
	consignment [kən'saɪnmənt]	(Waren-)Sendung, Lieferung
	warehouse ['weəhaʊs]	Lagerhalle, -haus
	hesitate ['hezɪteɪt]	zögern
28	**memo** ['meməʊ]	Notiz, Vermerk
	communicate [kə'mju:nɪkeɪt]	übermitteln, kommunizieren
	time difference ['taɪm dɪfrəns]	Zeitunterschied
	be in touch [bi ɪn 'tʌtʃ]	in Verbindung bleiben
29	**query** ['kwɪəri]	Anfrage
	extract ['ekstrækt]	Auszug
29p	**in stock** [ɪn 'stɒk]	vorrätig
	salesperson ['seɪlzpɜ:sn]	Verkäufer/in
	alternative [ɔ:l'tɜ:nətɪv]	Alternative
	grant a discount [grɑ:nt ə 'dɪskaʊnt]	einen Rabatt gewähren
	opening hours ['əʊpənɪŋ aʊəz]	Geschäfts-, Öffnungszeiten
	complain [kəm'pleɪn]	(sich) beschweren, reklamieren
	pine [paɪn]	Kiefer
	on sale [ɒn 'seɪl]	im Schlussverkauf
	sold out [ˌsəʊld 'aʊt]	ausverkauft
	convince [kən'vɪns]	überzeugen
30t	**untreated** [ˌʌn'tri:tɪd]	unbehandelt
	calculate ['kælkjuleɪt]	be-, ausrechnen
	fence panel ['fens pænl]	Zaunsegment
	add up to [ˌæd 'ʌp tu]	zusammen betragen
	total [təʊtl]	Gesamtsumme
	disconnect [ˌdɪskə'nekt]	trennen, unterbrechen
	some kind of [sʌm 'kaɪnd əv]	irgendeine/n
	bulk discount [bʌlk 'dɪskaʊnt]	Mengenrabatt
	fair enough [ˌfeər ɪ'nʌf]	vernünftig, recht und billig
	at the latest [ət ðə 'leɪtɪst]	spätestens
	delivery address [dɪˌlɪvəri ə'dres]	Lieferadresse
	acknowledgement [ək'nɒlɪdʒmənt]	(Auftrags-)Bestätigung
	look forward to [ˌlʊk 'fɔ:wəd tə]	sich freuen auf
	hear from sb ['hɪə frəm]	von jdm hören
30	**dash** [dæʃ]	Bindestrich
	colon ['kəʊlən]	Doppelpunkt
	slash [slæʃ]	Schrägstrich
	dot [dɒt]	Punkt
	underscore [ˌʌndə'skɔ:]	unterstreichen
	politeness [pə'laɪtnəs]	Höflichkeit
	particularly [pə'tɪkjələli]	besonders
	polite [pə'laɪt]	höflich
	mind [maɪnd]	etw dagegen haben
31	**rephrase** [ˌri:'freɪz]	umformulieren
	get in touch [get ɪn 'tʌtʃ]	(sich) in Verbindung setzen
	act out [ˌækt 'aʊt]	aufführen
	take one's lunch break [teɪk wʌnz 'lʌntʃ breɪk]	Mittagspause machen
	conference ['kɒnfərəns]	Konferenz, Besprechung
	be away on business [bi əˌweɪ ɒn 'bɪznəs]	geschäftlich unterwegs sein
	no longer [nəʊ 'lɒŋgə]	nicht mehr
32	**fencing** ['fensɪŋ]	Einzäunung
	pallet ['pælət]	Palette
	handling ['hændlɪŋ]	Handhabung, Beförderung
	load [ləʊd]	(ver)laden
	open-top container [ˌəʊpəntɒp kən'teɪnə]	Container ohne Dach
	combination [ˌkɒmbɪ'neɪʃn]	Kombination
	road transport [rəʊd 'trænspɔ:t]	Straßentransport
	rail transport ['reɪl trænspɔ:t]	Bahntransport
	waggon ['wægən]	Wagen
	rail terminal [reɪl 'tɜ:mɪnl]	Bahnstation
	customs ['kʌstəmz]	Zoll(kontrolle)
	premises ['premɪsɪz]	Betrieb(sgelände)
	drop-off point [ˌdrɒp'ɒf pɔɪnt]	Entladestelle
	included [ɪn'klu:dɪd]	inbegriffen
	relevant ['reləvənt]	relevant, entsprechend
	Kind regards [kaɪnd rɪ'gɑ:dz]	Mit freundlichen Grüßen
33	**essential** [ɪ'senʃl]	notwendig, wichtig, wesentlich
	modern living [ˌmɒdn 'lɪvɪŋ]	modernes Leben

	public transport [ˌpʌblɪk ˈtrænspɔːt]	öffentliche Verkehrsmittel
	get away from [ˌget əˈweɪ frəm]	entkommen
	subscriber [səbˈskraɪbə]	Abonnent/in
	health risk [ˈhelθ rɪsk]	Gesundheitsrisiko
	electromagnetic radiation [ɪlektrəʊmægˌnetɪk ˌreɪdiˈeɪʃn]	elektromagnetische Strahlung
	emit [ɪˈmɪt]	abgeben, ausstrahlen
	aerial [ˈeəriəl]	Antenne
	sleep disorder [sliːp dɪsˈɔːdə]	Schlafstörung
	allergy [ˈælədʒi]	Allergie
	Alzheimer's disease [ˈæltshaɪməz dɪdiːz]	Alzheimerkrankheit
	heart problem [ˈhɑːt prɒbləm]	Herzproblem
	cancer [ˈkænsə]	Krebs
	brain tumor [ˈbreɪn tjuːmə]	Hirntumor
	attribute [əˈtrɪbjuːt]	zuschreiben
	hand-held [ˈhændheld]	Hand-(Gerät), tragbar
	device [dɪˈvaɪs]	Apparat, Gerät
	in particular [ɪn pəˈtɪkjələ]	insbesondere
	be vulnerable to [bi ˈvʌlnərəbl tə]	ausgesetzt sein
	skull [skʌl]	Schädel
	nervous system [ˌnɜːvəs ˈsɪstəm]	Nervensystem
	absorb [əbˈsɔːb]	aufnehmen
	potentially [pəˈtenʃəli]	potentiell
	harmful [ˈhɑːmfl]	schädlich
	radiation [ˌreɪdiˈeɪʃn]	Strahlung
	scientific [ˌsaɪənˈtɪfɪk]	(natur)wissenschaftlich
	evidence [ˈevɪdəns]	Beweis(e)
	theory [ˈθɪəri]	Theorie
	wise [waɪz]	weise, klug
	take precautions [teɪk prɪˈkɔːʃnz]	Vorsichtsmaßnahmen ergreifen
	prolonged [prəˈlɒŋd]	ausgedehnt
	risk [rɪsk]	Risiko
	heart complaint [ˈhɑːt kəmpleɪnt]	Herzbeschwerden
	testicular [tesˈtɪkjələ]	Hoden-
	mobile network [ˌməʊbaɪl ˈnetwɜːk]	Mobilnetz
	exist [ɪgˈzɪst]	existieren
	population [ˌpɒpjuˈleɪʃn]	Bevölkerung
	advocate [ˈædvəkət]	Befürworter/in
	argue [ˈɑːgjuː]	behaupten, argumentieren
	detrimental [ˌdetrɪˈmentl]	nachteilig, schädlich
	detect [dɪˈtekt]	entdecken
	pose a danger [pəʊz ə ˈdeɪndʒə]	eine Gefahr darstellen
	draw a conclusion [drɔː ə kənˈkluːʒn]	einen Schluss ziehen
	on balance [ɒn ˈbæləns]	per Saldo
	nevertheless [ˌnevəðəˈles]	trotzdem, dennoch
	obvious [ˈɒbviəs]	offensichtlich
	moderate [ˈmɒdəreɪt]	einschränken
	do harm [du ˈhɑːm]	schaden
	treat [triːt]	behandeln
	justify [ˈdʒʌstɪfaɪ]	rechtfertigen, verteidigen
	be exposed to [bi ɪkˈspəʊzd tə]	ausgesetzt sein

Unit 4

34	**travel arrangements** [ˈtrævl əreɪndʒmənts]	Reisepläne
	headquarters [ˌhedˈkwɔːtəz]	Hauptsitz
	exploration [ˌekspləˈreɪʃn]	Erforschung
	drilling [ˈdrɪlɪŋ]	Bohren
	petrochemical [ˌpetrəʊˈkemɪkl]	petrochemisches Erzeugnis
	solar power generation [ˈsəʊlə ˈpaʊə ˌdʒenəˈreɪʃn]	Erzeugung von Sonnenenergie
	stamp [stæmp]	Stempel
35	**convey** [kənˈveɪ]	über-, vermitteln
	express [ɪkˈspres]	ausdrücken, zum Ausdruck bringen
	suppose [səˈpəʊz]	glauben, vermuten
	peak [piːk]	Spitze(nzeit)
	besides [bɪˈsaɪdz]	außerdem
	PA [ˌpiː ˈeɪ]	persönliche/r Assistent/in
	book a flight [bʊk ə ˈflaɪt]	einen Flug buchen
36	**South Coast** [ˌsaʊθ ˈkəʊst]	Südküste
	check in [ˌtʃek ˈɪn]	sich anmelden, einchecken
	outbound [ˈaʊtbaʊnd]	Hin-
	ring back [ˌrɪŋ ˈbæk]	zurückrufen
	refer back to sth [rɪˌfɜː ˈbæk tə]	zurückgehen zu etw
	confirm [kənˈfɜːm]	bestätigen
	booking [ˈbʊkɪŋ]	Reservierung, Buchung
36t	**have a pen handy** [həv ə pen ˈhændi]	etw zum Schreiben haben
	Fire away [ˌfaɪər əˈweɪ]	Schießen Sie los!
	absolutely [ˈæbsəluːtli]	absolut, völlig
	counter [ˈkaʊntə]	Schalter
	departure [dɪˈpɑːtʃə]	Abflug
	fully booked [ˌfʊli ˈbʊkt]	ausgebucht
	provisionally [prəˈvɪʒənəli]	provisorisch, vorläufig
	procedure [prəˈsiːdʒə]	Verfahren
	debit [ˈdebɪt]	belasten
37	**am** [ˌeɪ ˈem]	vormittags
	pm [ˌpiː ˈem]	nachmittags
	make a reservation [ˌmeɪk ə ˌrezəˈveɪʃn]	eine Reservierung vornehmen
37p	**finance** [ˈfaɪnæns]	Finanz
	otherwise [ˈʌðəwaɪz]	sonst
37	**prompt** [prɒmpt]	Stichwort

approximate [ə'prɒksɪmət] ungefähr
company discount [ˌkʌmpəni 'dɪskaʊnt] Firmenrabatt
browse for ['braʊz fə] (im Internet) suchen nach
web page ['web peɪdʒ] Webseite
feature ['fi:tʃə] Merkmal, Kennzeichen
38 **situated** ['sɪtʃueɪtɪd] gelegen
bank [bæŋk] Ufer
well-equipped [ˌwel ɪ'kwɪpt] gut ausgestattet
suite [swi:t] Suite
superb [su:'pɜ:b] hervorragend
facility [fə'sɪləti] Einrichtung
guarantee [ˌgærən'ti:] garantieren
airconditioned ['eəkəndɪʃənd] klimatisiert
lounge [laʊndʒ] Gesellschaftsraum, Salon
access ['ækses] Zugang
additional charge [ə'dɪʃənl tʃɑ:dʒ] zusätzliche Gebühr
prior ['praɪə] vorherig
arrangement [ə'reɪndʒmənt] Absprache, Vereinbarung
leisure ['leʒə] Freizeit
vibrant ['vaɪbrənt] vibrierend, aufregend
affordable [ə'fɔ:dəbl] erschwinglich
splendid ['splendɪd] ausgezeichnet
specialise in ['speʃəlaɪz ɪn] sich spezialisieren auf
brand [brænd] Marke, Typ
aim [eɪm] bestrebt sein, beabsichtigen
provide [prə'vaɪd] bieten
flexibility [ˌfleksə'bɪləti] Flexibilität
throughout [θru:'aʊt] die ganze Zeit hindurch
comfort ['kʌmfət] Komfort, Bequemlichkeit
39 **summary** ['sʌməri] Zusammenfassung
set off [ˌset 'ɒf] aufbrechen
manageress [ˌmænɪdʒə'res] Geschäftsführerin, Leiterin, Chefin
attraction [ə'trækʃn] Attraktion, Reiz
39t **head chef** [ˌhed 'ʃef] Chefkoch, Küchenchef
relaxed [rɪ'lækst] entspannt, aufgelockert
atmosphere ['ætməsfɪə] Atmosphäre, Stimmung
authentic [ɔ:'θentɪk] authentisch, echt
exclusively [ɪk'sklu:sɪvli] ausschließlich
charming ['tʃɑ:mɪŋ] reizend, bezaubernd
unlimited [ʌn'lɪmɪtɪd] unbegrenzt
free of charge [fri: əv 'tʃɑ:dʒ] kostenfrei, gebührenfrei
39 **plenty of** ['plenti ɒv] viel, reichlich
chain [tʃeɪn] Kette
tend to ['tend tə] neigen zu, tendieren zu
bland [blænd] fade

equally ['i:kwəli] gleichermaßen
range from ['reɪndʒ frəm] reichen von
modest ['mɒdɪst] bescheiden
grand [grænd] großartig, prachtvoll
inexpensive [ˌɪnɪk'spensɪv] preiswert
generally ['dʒenrəli] im Allgemeinen
on the premises [ɒn ðə 'premɪsɪz] im Haus
indeed [ɪn'di:d] tatsächlich, wirklich
rely on [rɪ'laɪ ɒn] sich verlassen auf
recommendation [ˌrekəmen'deɪʃn] Empfehlung
guidebook ['gaɪdbʊk] Reiseführer
rate [reɪt] (ein)schätzen
award [ə'wɔ:d] zuerkennen
indicate ['ɪndɪkeɪt] (an)zeigen, hinweisen auf
luxury ['lʌkʃəri] Luxus
40 **intend** [ɪn'tend] beabsichtigen
costs incurred [ˌkɒsts ɪn'kɜ:d] angefallene Kosten
service point ['sɜ:vɪs pɔɪnt] Kundendienststelle
fee [fi:] Gebühr
per [pə] pro, per
40t **have in mind** [həv ɪn 'maɪnd] denken an, sich vorstellen
reasonable ['ri:znəbl] vernünftig
mileage ['maɪlɪdʒ] zurückgelegte Strecke, Kilometerzahl
fully comprehensive [ˌfʊli ˌkɒmprɪ'hensɪv] Vollkasko-
excess ['ekses] Selbstbeteiligung
premium ['pri:miəm] Prämie
total cover [ˌtəʊtl 'kʌvə] volle Deckung
straight away [streɪt ə'weɪ] sofort, auf der Stelle
40 **gap** [gæp] Lücke
escorted ['eskɔ:tɪd] geführt
quotation [kwəʊ'teɪʃn] Angebot
proximity [prɒk'sɪməti] Nähe
selection [sɪ'lekʃn] Auswahl
based in ['beɪst ɪn] mit (Haupt-)Sitz in
pride os on [ˌpraɪd wʌnˌself 'ɒn] stolz sein auf
rental car [ˌrentl 'kɑ:] Mietwagen
vehicle ['vi:əkl] Fahrzeug
the continent [ðə 'kɒntɪnənt] der (europäische) Kontinent
resident ['rezɪdənt] Einwohner/in
join [dʒɔɪn] sich anschließen, beitreten
mailing list ['meɪlɪŋ lɪst] Verteiler, Adressenliste
special offer [ˌspeʃl 'ɒfə] Sonderangebot
41 **minimum age requirement** [ˌmɪnɪməm eɪdʒ rɪ'kwaɪəmənt] erforderliches Mindestalter
pass one's test [pɑ:s wʌnz 'test] die Fahrprüfung machen

	means of payment [ˌmiːnz əv ˈpeɪmənt]	Zahlungsmittel
	acceptable [əkˈseptəbl]	passend
	valid [ˈvælɪd]	gültig
	driver's licence [ˈdraɪvəz laɪsns]	Führerschein
	country of residence [ˌkʌntri əv ˈrezɪdəns]	Wohnsitz
	hold a licence [həʊld ə ˈlaɪsns]	eine (Fahr-)Erlaubnis besitzen
	identification [aɪˌdentɪfɪˈkeɪʃn]	Legitimation
	in addition to [ɪn əˈdɪʃn tə]	zusätzlich, neben
	form of identification [fɔːm əv aɪˌdentɪfɪˈkeɪʃn]	Ausweispapiere
42	**convenience** [kənˈviːniəns]	Bequemlichkeit, Annehmlichkeit
	make use of sth [meɪk ˈjuːs əv]	etw einsetzen, verwenden
	instant [ˈɪnstənt]	sofort
	outlet [ˈaʊtlet]	Verkaufsstelle
	credit limit [ˈkredɪt lɪmɪt]	Dispositionskredit
	take advantage of [ˌteɪk ədˈvɑːntɪdʒ əv]	ausnützen
	sale bargain [seɪl ˈbɑːgɪn]	günstiges Angebot, Sonderangebot
	purchase [ˈpɜːtʃəs]	(Ein-)Kauf
	spending [ˈspendɪŋ]	Ausgaben
	cash withdrawal [kæʃ wɪðˈdrɔːəl]	Bargeldabhebung
	cash machine [ˈkæʃ məʃiːn]	Geldautomat
	over the counter [ˌəʊvə ðə ˈkaʊntə]	am Schalter
	itemized [ˈaɪtəmaɪzd]	spezifiziert
	monthly statement [ˌmʌnθli ˈsteɪtmənt]	monatlicher (Konto-) Auszug
	annual fee [ˌænjuəl ˈfiː]	Jahresgebühr
	refund [ˈriːfʌnd]	Rückzahlung, (Rück-) Erstattung
	interest [ˈɪntrəst]	Zins(en)
	introductory [ˌɪntrəˈdʌktəri]	Einführungs-
	interest rate [ˈɪntrəst reɪt]	Zinssatz
	credit [ˈkredɪt]	Kredit
	occasional [əˈkeɪʒənl]	gelegentlich
	go over one's credit limit [gəʊ ˌəʊvə wʌnz ˈkredɪt lɪmɪt]	den Dispositionskredit überziehen
	option [ˈɒpʃn]	Option, Wahlrecht
	direct debit [dəˌrekt ˈdebɪt]	Lastschrift-, Einzugsverfahren
	redeem [rɪˈdiːm]	ab-, einlösen
	executive [ɪgˈzekjətɪv]	leitende/r Angestellte/r, Manager/in

Unit 5

43	**not necessarily** [nɒt ˌnesəˈserəli]	nicht unbedingt
	failure [ˈfeɪljə]	Misserfolg, Fehlschlag
	rank [ræŋk]	zählen zu
	leading [ˈliːdɪŋ]	führend
	negotiate [nɪˈgəʊʃieɪt]	ver-, aushandeln
	contract [ˈkɒntrækt]	Vertrag
	signware [ˈsaɪnweə]	Beschriftung, Schriftzüge
	service station [ˈsɜːvɪs steɪʃn]	Tankstelle
	Benelux countries [ˈbenɪlʌks kʌntriz]	Beneluxländer
	finalize [ˈfaɪnəlaɪz]	endgültig festlegen
	hospitable [hɒˈspɪtəbl]	gastfreundlich
	get down to business [ˌget ˈdaʊn tə ˈbɪznəs]	zur Sache kommen
44	**leave a lot to be desired** [liːv ə ˌlɒt tə bi dɪˈzaɪəd]	viel zu wünschen übrig lassen
	ask sb's advice [ˌɑːsk sʌmwʌnz ədˈvaɪs]	jdn um Rat bitten
	be due to arrive [bi djuː tu əˈraɪv]	planmäßig ankommen
	agenda [əˈdʒendə]	Tagesordnung
	minutes [ˈmɪnɪts]	Protokoll
	timetable [ˈtaɪmteɪbl]	Fahr-, Stundenplan
	propose [prəˈpəʊz]	vorschlagen
	terms and conditions [ˌtɜːmz ənd kənˈdɪʃnz]	allgemeine Geschäftsbedingungen
	production plant [prəˈdʌkʃn plɑːnt]	Produktionsstätte
	be through [bi ˈθruː]	fertig sein
	confirmation [ˌkɒnfəˈmeɪʃn]	Bestätigung
45	**postpone** [pəˈspəʊn]	verschieben
	beforehand [bɪˈfɔːhænd]	vorher, zuvor
	chair [tʃeə]	leiten
	accomplish [əˈkʌmplɪʃ]	erreichen
	final draft [faɪnl ˈdrɑːft]	Endfassung
	circulate [ˈsɜːkjəleɪt]	(an alle) verschicken, herumgehen lassen
	arise [əˈraɪz]	sich ergeben
	consult [kənˈsʌlt]	zu Rate ziehen, konsultieren
	solicitor [səˈlɪsɪtə]	Anwalt/Anwältin
	correction [kəˈrekʃn]	Korrektur
	specific [spəˈsɪfɪk]	speziell, spezifisch
	estimate [ˈestɪmət]	Schätzung, (Kosten-) Voranschlag
	revise [rɪˈvaɪz]	revidieren, überarbeiten
	in the light of [ɪn ðə ˈlaɪt əv]	im Hinblick auf
	objection [əbˈdʒekʃn]	Einwand
	substantial [səbˈstænʃl]	wesentlich
	volume [ˈvɒljuːm]	Volumen, Umfang
	circumstances [ˈsɜːkəmstənsɪz]	Umstände
	bear costs [beə ˈkɒsts]	Kosten tragen
	Free Domicile [friː ˈdɒmɪsaɪl]	frei Haus

Ex Works [eks 'wɜːks] — ab Werk
proposal [prə'pəʊzl] — Vorschlag
reach a compromise [riːtʃ ə 'kɒmprəmaɪz] — einen Kompromiss finden
representative [ˌreprɪ'zentətɪv] — Vertreter/in
46 **responsible** [rɪ'spɒnsəbl] — verantwortlich
keep order [kiːp 'ɔːdə] — für Ruhe und Ordnung sorgen
suggestion [sə'dʒestʃən] — Vorschlag
put something off [ˌpʊt 'ɒf] — etw verschieben
standpoint ['stændpɔɪnt] — Standpunkt
46t **furthermore** [ˌfɜːðə'mɔː] — ferner, überdies
point out [ˌpɔɪnt 'aʊt] — hinweisen auf, aufmerksam machen auf
extremely [ɪk'striːmli] — sehr, äußerst
high-quality [ˌhai 'kwɒləti] — von guter Qualität
completely [kəm'pliːtli] — völlig
guarantee period [ˌgærən'tiː pɪəriəd] — Garantiezeit
frank [fræŋk] — offen, aufrichtig
terms of trade [ˌtɜːmz əv 'treɪd] — Geschäfts-, Handelsbedingungen
take into account [ˌteɪk ɪntu ə'kaʊnt] — in Betracht ziehen, berücksichtigen
46 **disagreement** [ˌdɪsə'griːmənt] — Meinungsverschiedenheit
harsh [hɑːʃ] — hart
make up one's mind [ˌmeɪk 'ʌp wʌnz maɪnd] — sich entschließen
compromise ['kɒmprəmaɪz] — einen Kompromiss eingehen
47t **sum up** [ˌsʌm 'ʌp] — zusammenfassen
commence [kə'mens] — beginnen
emphasize ['emfəsaɪz] — betonen, hervorheben
announcement [ə'naʊnsmənt] — Bekanntgabe
bidding period ['bɪdɪŋ pɪəriəd] — Ausschreibungsfrist
run through [ˌrʌn 'θruː] — überfliegen, durchgehen
prototype ['prəʊtətaɪp] — Prototyp
on demand [ɒn dɪ'mɑːnd] — nach Anforderung/Bedarf
receipt [rɪ'siːt] — Empfang, Erhalt
bring to a close [brɪŋ tu ə 'kləʊz] — beenden
constructive [kən'strʌktɪv] — konstruktiv
47 **attached** [ə'tætʃt] — verbunden, beigefügt
specification [ˌspesɪfɪ'keɪʃn] — Spezifikation, Aufstellung
undertake [ˌʌndə'teɪk] — sich verpflichten
conclude [kən'kluːd] — (ab)schließen
participant [pɑː'tɪsɪpənt] — Teilnehmer/in
48 **cultural** ['kʌltʃərəl] — kulturell
knowledge ['nɒlɪdʒ] — Wissen, Kenntnis(se)
vital ['vaɪtl] — wichtig, wesentlich
spoil [spɔɪl] — verderben
invest [ɪn'vest] — investieren, anlegen
nightmare ['naɪtmeə] — Alptraum
keen on ['kiːn ɒn] — wild auf
plentiful ['plentɪfl] — reichlich
make a show of sth [meɪk ə 'ʃəʊ əv] — etw eingehend tun
carefully ['keəfəli] — sorgfältig
card case ['kɑːd keɪs] — Kartentäschchen
in accordance with [ɪn ə'kɔːdəns wɪð] — entsprechend, gemäß, in Übereinstimmung mit
be aware [bi ə'weə] — sich bewusst sein
hyperbole [haɪ'pɜːbəli] — Übertreibung
possibly ['pɒsəbli] — möglicherweise
customarily ['kʌstəmərəli] — üblicherweise
high-ranking [ˌhaɪ'ræŋkɪŋ] — hochrangig
establish [ɪ'stæblɪʃ] — herstellen
rapport [ræ'pɔː] — (enges) Verhältnis
imply [ɪm'plaɪ] — andeuten, implizieren
grave [greɪv] — ernst, schwer
insult ['ɪnsʌlt] — Beleidigung
briefing ['briːfɪŋ] — Einweisung
paragraph ['pærəgrɑːf] — Abschnitt, kurzer Artikel
university qualification [ˌjuːnɪ'vɜːsəti ˌkwɒlɪfɪ'keɪʃn] — akademischer Grad
used to ['juːs tə] — gewöhnt an
hierarchy ['haɪərɑːki] — Hierarchie
status-conscious ['steɪtəs kɒnʃəs] — statusbewusst
49 **in advance** [ɪn əd'vɑːns] — im Voraus, vorher
fail [feɪl] — scheitern (bei), versagen (in)
50 **education market** [ˌedʒu'keɪʃn mɑːkɪt] — Bildungsmarkt
classmate ['klɑːsmeɪt] — Klassenkamerad/in
annual ['ænjuəl] — jährlich
elect [ɪ'lekt] — wählen
chairperson ['tʃeəpɜːsn] — Vorsitzende/r
preparation [ˌprepə'reɪʃn] — Vorbereitung
50p **impressive** [ɪm'presɪv] — beeindruckend
magnificent [mæg'nɪfɪsnt] — prächtig, großartig
disruption [dɪs'rʌpʃn] — Unterbrechung, Störung
take sides [teɪk 'saɪdz] — Partei ergreifen
51 **switch on to sth** [ˌswɪtʃ ɒn tə] — zu etw übergehen
virtue ['vɜːtʃuː] — Tugend
global vision [ˌgləʊbl 'vɪʒn] — globale Vision
videoconferencing [ˌvɪdiəʊ 'kɒnfərənsɪŋ] — Videokonferenzen (abhalten)
increasingly [ɪn'kriːsɪŋli] — zunehmend
imagine [ɪ'mædʒɪn] — sich vorstellen
assessment [ə'sesmənt] — Einschätzung, Beurteilung
related [rɪ'leɪtɪd] — verwandt
take up [ˌteɪk 'ʌp] — übergehen zu

	enable [ɪ'neɪbl]	in die Lage versetzen
	studio system ['stju:diəʊ sɪstəm]	Studiosystem
	cut costs [kʌt 'kɒsts]	Kosten senken
	extol [ɪk'stəʊl]	loben, preisen
	banking executive [ˌbæŋkɪŋ ɪg'zekjətɪv]	Bankmanager/in
	new-found [ˌnju:'faʊnd]	neu entdeckt
	observe [əb'zɜ:v]	beachten
	eye contact ['aɪ kɒntækt]	Blickkontakt
	valuable ['væljuəbl]	wertvoll
	multinational [ˌmʌlti'næʃnəl]	multinational
	at short notice [ət ˌʃɔ:t 'nəʊtɪs]	kurzfristig
	body language ['bɒdi læŋgwɪdʒ]	Körpersprache
	consultant [kən'sʌltənt]	Berater/in, Gutachter/in
	carrier ['kæriə]	Träger
	relevant ['reləvənt]	relevant, wichtig
	decision-making [dɪ'sɪʒn meɪkɪŋ]	Entscheidungsfindung
	operate ['ɒpəreɪt]	betreiben
	reliable [rɪ'laɪəbl]	zuverlässig
	feeling ['fi:lɪŋ]	Gefühl
	virtual ['vɜ:tʃuəl]	virtuell
	community [kə'mju:nəti]	Gemeinde
	sufficient [sə'fɪʃnt]	ausreichend, genug
	familiarise [fə'mɪliəraɪz]	bekanntmachen
	intimidated [ɪn'tɪmɪdeɪtɪd]	eingeschüchtert
	get involved in sth [get ɪn'vɒlvd ɪn]	sich an etw beteiligen
	explosion [ɪk'spləʊʒn]	Explosion
	PC videophone [ˌpi: 'si: 'vɪdiəʊfəʊn]	Computerbildtelefon
	geographical [ˌdʒi:ə'græfɪkl]	geographisch
	client ['klaɪənt]	Kunde, Kundin
	look someone in the eye [lʊk ɪn ði 'aɪ]	jdm in die Augen sehen
	conferencing facility [ˌkɒnfərəsɪŋ fə'sɪləti]	Konferenzeinrichtung
	agency ['eɪdʒənsi]	Agentur
	digital layout [ˌdɪdʒɪtl 'leɪaʊt]	digitales Layout
	advertising ['ædvətaɪzɪŋ]	Werbe-
	alter ['ɔ:ltə]	(ver)ändern
	edit ['edɪt]	redigieren, bearbeiten
	PC-based [ˌpi: 'si: beɪst]	auf Computern basierend
	practical ['præktɪkl]	praktisch
	except [ɪk'sept]	außer
	quip [kwɪp]	witzeln, scherzen
52	**make a prediction** [meɪk ə prɪ'dɪkʃn]	eine Vorhersage treffen
	recently ['ri:sntli]	neulich, kürzlich
	other than ['ʌðə ðən]	außer
	face-to-face [ˌfeɪs tə 'feɪs]	direkt, von Angesicht zu Angesicht
	claim [kleɪm]	behaupten
	make a difference [meɪk ə 'dɪfrəns]	einen Unterschied machen
	negotiation [nɪˌgəʊʃi'eɪʃn]	Verhandlung
	aspect ['æspekt]	Aspekt
	efficiency [ɪ'fɪʃnsi]	Effizienz, Leistungsfähigkeit
	relationship [rɪ'leɪʃnʃɪp]	Beziehung, Verhältnis
	bargaining ['bɑ:gɪnɪŋ]	Verhandlung
	outcome ['aʊtkʌm]	Resultat, Ergebnis

Unit 6

53	**ingredients** [ɪn'gri:diənts]	Zutaten, Bestandteile
	feedback ['fi:dbæk]	Rückmeldung
	trainee [treɪ'ni:]	Auszubildende/r, Praktikant/in
	presentation skills [ˌprezn'teɪʃn skɪlz]	Vorführfertigkeiten
	trainer ['treɪnə]	Trainer/in, Ausbilder/in
	well done [ˌwel 'dʌn]	gut gemacht
	handout ['hændaʊt]	Merkblatt
	visual aid ['vɪʒuəl eɪd]	Anschauungsmaterial
	sales figures ['seɪlz fɪgəz]	Absatzzahlen
	pie chart ['paɪ tʃɑ:t]	Kreisdiagramm
54	**explanatory** [ɪk'splænətri]	erklärend
	make sense [meɪk 'sens]	sinnvoll sein
	effective [ɪ'fektɪv]	effektiv, wirkungsvoll
	attention [ə'tenʃn]	Aufmerksamkeit
	observation [ˌɒbzə'veɪʃn]	Beobachtung, Bemerkung
	tone [təʊn]	Ton
	monotonous [mə'nɒtənəs]	monoton
	vary ['veəri]	wechseln, variieren
	speech [spi:tʃ]	Rede(weise)
	intonation [ˌɪntə'neɪʃn]	Tonfall, Satzmelodie, Intonation
	impact ['ɪmpækt]	(Aus-)Wirkung, Eindruck
	pick up on sth [ˌpɪk 'ʌp ɒn]	etw aufgreifen
	time limit ['taɪm lɪmɪt]	Zeitlimit
	steal [sti:l]	stehlen
	ramble on ['ræmbl ɒn]	abschweifen
	folks [fəʊks]	Leute
	golden rule ['gəʊldən ru:l]	goldene Regel
	persuade [pə'sweɪd]	überzeugen, überreden
	argument ['ɑ:gjumənt]	Argument
	rise [raɪz]	Heben
	in fact [ɪn 'fækt]	tatsächlich
55	**projector** [prə'dʒektə]	Projektor
	cassette recorder [kə'set rɪkɔ:də]	Kassettenrekorder
	OHP (overhead projector) [ˌəʊ eɪtʃ 'pi:]	Tageslicht-, Overheadprojektor
	OHT (overhead transparency) [ˌəʊ eɪtʃ 'ti:]	Overheadfolie
	workshop session ['wɜ:kʃɒp seʃn]	Werkstattgespräch

	static ['stætɪk]	statisch
	graphics ['græfɪks]	Grafiken
	visual ['vɪʒuəl]	visuelles Medium, Bildmaterial
	animated ['ænɪmeɪtɪd]	bewegt
	statement ['steɪtmənt]	Aussage, Erklärung
	hand-drawn [ˌhænd 'drɔːn]	von Hand gezeichnet
	brainstorm ['breɪnstɔːm]	(Ideen) sammeln
	turn off [ˌtɜːn 'ɒf]	aus-, abschalten
	gather ['gæðə]	sammeln
	promotional video [prəˌməʊʃənl 'vɪdiəʊ]	Werbevideo
	jingle ['dʒɪŋgl]	Erkennungsmelodie
56	**coating** ['kəʊtɪŋ]	Beschichtung
	stage [steɪdʒ]	Phase, Abschnitt, Stadium
	professional [prə'feʃənl]	professionell
	counter-suggestion [ˌkaʊntə sə'dʒestʃən]	Gegenvorschlag
57	**background information** [ˌbækgraʊnd ˌɪnfə'meɪʃn]	Hintergrund-information(en)
	illustrate ['ɪləstreɪt]	illustrieren, veranschaulichen
	experiment with [ɪk'sperɪmənt wɪð]	experimentieren mit
	bar chart ['bɑː tʃɑːt]	Säulen-, Balkendiagramm
	line graph ['laɪn grɑːf]	(Kurven-)Diagramm
	ring chart ['rɪŋ tʃɑːt]	Ringdiagramm
	currency exchange [ˌkʌrənsi ɪks'tʃeɪndʒ]	Währungsumtausch
	per capita income [pə ˌkæpɪtə 'ɪnkʌm]	Pro-Kopf-Einkommen
	factor ['fæktə]	Faktor
	rule of thumb [ruːl əv 'θʌm]	Faustregel
	simplicity [sɪm'plɪsəti]	Einfachheit
	precision [prɪ'sɪʒn]	Genauigkeit
	case [keɪs]	Fall
58	**work-piece** ['wɜːkpiːs]	Werkstück
	feed [fiːd]	Eingabe
	discharge ['dɪstʃɑːdʒ]	Ausgabe, Entladung
	spray [spreɪ]	Spray
	chromating ['krəʊmeɪtɪŋ]	Chromatieren (chromsaures Salz auftragen)
	galvanized steel [ˌgælvənaɪzd 'stiːl]	verzinkter Stahl
	pre-treat [ˌpriː 'triːt]	vorbehandeln
	adhesion [əd'hiːʒn]	Haftung
	chromated ['krəʊmeɪtɪd]	chromatiert
	drying oven ['draɪɪŋ ʌvn]	Trockenofen
	powder coating ['paʊdə kəʊtɪŋ]	Pulverbeschichtung
	desired [dɪ'zaɪəd]	gewünscht
	shade [ʃeɪd]	(Farb-)Ton, Schattierung
	automatic [ˌɔːtə'mætɪk]	automatisch
	cabin ['kæbɪn]	Kabine
	optionally ['ɒpʃənəli]	wahlweise
	manual coating chamber [ˌmænjuəl 'kəʊtɪŋ tʃeɪmbə]	Handbeschichtungs-kammer
	stoving process [ˌstəʊvɪŋ 'prəʊses]	Trocknung (in der Trockenkammer)
	temperature ['temprətʃə]	Temperatur
58t	**in time** [ɪn 'taɪm]	rechtzeitig
	psychiatrist [saɪ'kaɪətrɪst]	Psychiater/in
	fortune ['fɔːtʃuːn]	Vermögen
	phobia ['fəʊbiə]	Phobie (Flugangst)
	eternity [ɪ'tɜːnəti]	Ewigkeit
	next door [ˌnekst 'dɔː]	nebenan
	heard of ['hɜːd əv]	gehört von
	overwhelmed [ˌəʊvə'welmd]	überwältigt
	rave about [reɪv ə'baʊt]	schwärmen von
	ladies and gentlemen ['leɪdiz ən 'dʒentlmən]	Meine Damen und Herren
	purpose ['pɜːpəs]	Zweck, Ziel
59	**slide** [slaɪd]	Dia
	transparency [træns'pærənsi]	Folie
	at least [ət 'liːst]	wenigstens, mindestens
	punctuality [ˌpʌŋktʃu'æləti]	Pünktlichkeit
	interruption [ˌɪntə'rʌpʃn]	Unterbrechung, Störung
	adventure [əd'ventʃə]	Abenteuer
	all things considered [ˌɔːl θɪŋz kən'sɪdəd]	alles in allem
	cheek [tʃiːk]	Wange
	puff out [ˌpʌf 'aʊt]	aufblasen
	aggressive [ə'gresɪv]	aggressiv
	rejection [rɪ'dʒekʃn]	Ablehnung
	stroke [strəʊk]	streicheln
	scepticism ['skeptɪsɪzəm]	Skepsis
	arrogance ['ærəgəns]	Arroganz
	raised [reɪzd]	hochgezogen
	tense [tens]	(an)gespannt
	posture ['pɒstʃə]	(Körper-)Haltung
	lacking ['lækɪŋ]	mangelnd, fehlend
	self confidence [ˌself 'kɒnfɪdəns]	Selbstvertrauen
61	**make a deal** [meɪk ə 'diːl]	einen Vertrag schließen
	keen about [kiːn ə'baʊt] [ˌself 'kɒnfɪdəns]	scharf auf, sehr interessiert an
	university degree [juːnɪ'vɜːsəti dɪgriː]	akademischer Grad
	affiliated with [ə'fɪlieɪtɪd wɪð]	verbunden mit
	unnecessary [ʌn'nesəsri]	unnötig
	reverse side [rɪ'vɜːs saɪd]	Rückseite
	initial [ɪ'nɪʃl]	erste
	counterpart ['kaʊntəpɑːt]	Gegenüber
	make an assessment of [meɪk ən ə'sesmənt əv]	einschätzen, beurteilen
	well-informed [ˌwel ɪn'fɔːmd]	gut informiert
	intense [ɪn'tens]	intensiv

	analytical [ˌænəˈlɪtɪkl]	analytisch
	unreceptive [ˌʌnrɪˈseptɪv]	unzugänglich
	spontaneity [ˌspɒntəˈneɪəti]	Spontaneität
	prominent [ˈprɒmɪnənt]	hervorstechend
	trait [treɪt]	Eigenschaft, Charakterzug
	risk-taking [ˈrɪsk teɪkɪŋ]	Risikobereitschaft
	challenge [ˈtʃælɪndʒ]	in Frage stellen
	authority [ɔːˈθɒrəti]	Autorität, Behörde
	desirable [dɪˈzaɪərəbl]	wünschenswert
	be reluctant to do [bi rɪˈlʌktənt tə duː]	ungern tun
	convincing [kənˈvɪnsɪŋ]	überzeugend
	logically [ˈlɒdʒɪkli]	logisch
	empirical [ɪmˈpɪrɪkl]	empirisch, auf Erfahrung beruhend
	exaggeration [ɪgˌzædʒəˈreɪʃn]	Übertreibung
	tolerate [ˈtɒləreɪt]	tolerieren
	unimpressed [ˌʌnɪmˈprest]	nicht beeindruckt
	glitzy [ˈglɪtsi]	glitzernd, schillernd
	memorable [ˈmemərəbl]	einprägsam
	slogan [ˈsləʊgən]	(Werbe-)Spruch
	deficiency [dɪˈfɪʃnsi]	Mangel
	live up to [ˌlɪv ˈʌp tə]	gerecht werden
	concession [kənˈseʃn]	Vergünstigung, Zugeständnis
	confrontational [ˌkɒnfrʌnˈteɪʃənl]	auf Konfrontationskurs, konfliktbetont
	counterproductive [ˌkaʊntəprəˈdʌktɪv]	kontraproduktiv
	sensitive [ˈsensətɪv]	empfindlich, sensibel
	criticism [ˈkrɪtɪsɪzəm]	Kritik
	embarrass [ɪmˈbærəs]	verlegen machen, in Verlegenheit bringen
	unintentionally [ˌʌnɪnˈtenʃnəli]	unabsichtlich, unbeabsichtigt
	occasion [əˈkeɪʒn]	Ereignis, Anlass
	lighten up [ˌlaɪtn ˈʌp]	aufheitern
	reserve for [rɪˈzɜːv fə]	reservieren für, vorbehalten
	socialize [ˈsəʊʃəlaɪz]	gesellschaftlich (miteinander) verkehren, sich unterhalten, auf Partys gehen
	refrain from [rɪˈfreɪn frəm]	unterlassen
	long-range [ˈlɒŋ reɪndʒ]	langfristig
	planning [ˈplænɪŋ]	Planung
	spontaneous [spɒnˈteɪniəs]	spontan
	protracted [prəˈtræktɪd]	langwierig
	related to [rɪˈleɪtɪd tə]	mit Bezug auf
	painstakingly [ˈpeɪnzteɪkɪŋli]	sorgfältig, gewissenhaft
	likewise [ˈlaɪkwaɪz]	ebenso, desgleichen
	compliment [ˈkɒmplɪment]	Komplimente machen
	unsolicited [ˌʌnsəˈlɪsɪtɪd]	unverlangt, unaufgefordert, ungebeten
	praise [preɪz]	Lob
	approval [əˈpruːvl]	Zustimmung, Einverständnis
	rap [ræp]	klopfen (mit)
	knuckle [ˈnʌkl]	(Finger-)Knöchel
	tabletop [ˈteɪbltɒp]	Tischplatte
	applaud [əˈplɔːd]	applaudieren
	unchangeable [ʌnˈtʃeɪndʒəbl]	unabänderlich
62	**call sth into question** [ˌkɔːl ɪntə ˈkwestʃən]	etw in Frage stellen
	opponent [əˈpəʊnənt]	Gegner/in, Gegenüber
	beyond [bɪˈjɒnd]	jenseits (von)
	willing [ˈwɪlɪŋ]	gewillt, bereit
	seek [siːk]	suchen
	unwilling [ʌnˈwɪlɪŋ]	unwillig
	readiness [ˈredinəs]	Bereitschaft
	vice versa [ˌvaɪs ˈvɜːsə]	umgekehrt
	research [rɪˈsɜːtʃ]	Nachforschung(en)

Unit 7

63	**marketing campaign** [ˌmɑːkɪtɪŋ kæmˈpeɪn]	Werbekampagne
	associate with [əˈsəʊʃieɪt wɪð]	verbinden mit
	be put off [bi ˈpʊt ˈɒf]	zurückgehalten werden
	market research [ˌmɑːkɪt rɪˈsɜːtʃ]	Marktforschung
	launch [lɔːntʃ]	einführen
	launch campaign [ˌlɔːntʃ kæmˈpeɪn]	Markteinführung
64	**brand name** [ˈbrænd neɪm]	Markenzeichen
	reputation [ˌrepjuˈteɪʃn]	Ruf
	differentiate from [ˌdɪfəˈrenʃieɪt frəm]	unterscheiden von, absetzen von
	individual [ˌɪndɪˈvɪdʒuəl]	eigen, individuell
	brand personality [ˌbrænd ˌpɜːsəˈnæləti]	Markenprofil
	competitive [kəmˈpetətɪv]	Konkurrenz-, Wettbewerbs-
	target group [ˈtɑːgɪt gruːp]	Zielgruppe
	be in one's teens/twenties [ɪn wʌnz tiːnz, twentiz]	Teenager/in den Zwanzigern sein
	fashion-conscious [ˈfæʃn kɒnʃəs]	modebewusst
	trendy [ˈtrendi]	modisch, schick
	advise [ədˈvaɪz]	raten
	survey [ˈsɜːveɪ]	(Meinungs-)Umfrage
	drugstore [ˈdrʌgstɔː]	Drogerie
	pretty much [ˌprɪti ˈmʌtʃ]	ziemlich genau
	extensive [ɪkˈstensɪv]	umfassend
	submit [səbˈmɪt]	einreichen
	in total [ɪn ˈtəʊtl]	(ins)gesamt
	image analysis [ˌɪmɪdʒ əˈnæləsɪs]	Imageanalyse

	on the other hand [ɒn ði 'ʌðə hænd]	andererseits
	focus group ['fəʊkəs gru:p]	Zielgruppe
	in more depth [ɪn mɔ: 'depθ]	intensiver, tiefer gehend
	in detail [ɪn 'di:teɪl]	im Detail
	devise [dɪ'vaɪz]	entwerfen
	get started on sth [get 'stɑ:tɪd ɒn]	mit etw anfangen
	draw up [ˌdrɔ: 'ʌp]	abfassen, konzipieren
65	**terminology** [ˌtɜ:mɪ'nɒlədʒi]	Terminologie
	interviewee [ˌɪntəvju:'i:]	Interviewpartner/in, Befragte/r
	cosmetics [kɒz'metɪks]	Kosmetik(a)
	lipstick ['lɪpstɪk]	Lippenstift
	eye shadow ['aɪ ʃædəʊ]	Lidschatten
	nail polish ['neɪl pɒlɪʃ]	Nagellack
	series ['sɪəri:z]	Serie, Reihe
	seasonal ['si:zənl]	saisonbedingt, Saison-
	trend [trend]	Trend
	take notice of sth [teɪk 'nəʊtɪs əv]	etw beachten
	billboard ['bɪlbɔ:d]	Werbeplakat
66	**commission** [kə'mɪʃn]	beauftragen
	findings ['faɪndɪŋz]	Ergebnisse
	consumer [kən'sju:mə]	Verbraucher/in, Konsument/in
	reaction [ri'ækʃn]	Reaktion
	statistical analysis [stəˌtɪstɪkl ə'næləsɪs]	statistische Analyse
	on a daily basis [ɒn ə ˌdeɪli 'beɪsɪs]	täglich
	appealing [ə'pi:lɪŋ]	ansprechend
	pronounce [prə'naʊns]	aussprechen
	try out [ˌtraɪ 'aʊt]	(aus)probieren
	resonance ['rezənəns]	Resonanz
	overlook [ˌəʊvə'lʊk]	übersehen
	conclusion [kən'klu:ʒn]	(Schluss-)Folgerung
	on the basis of [ɒn ðə 'beɪsɪs əv]	auf der Basis von, aufgrund
	despite [dɪ'spaɪt]	trotz
	vast [vɑ:st]	riesig, gewaltig
	market potential [ˌmɑ:kɪt pə'tenʃl]	Marktpotenzial
	countrywide ['kʌntriwaɪd]	landesweit
	favored ['feɪvəd] (GB: **favoured**)	favorisiert
	attach [ə'tætʃ]	beilegen, -fügen
	appendix [ə'pendɪks]	Anhang
	target ['tɑ:gɪt]	zum Ziel haben
	placement ['pleɪsmənt]	Aufstellung
	considerable [kən'sɪdərəbl]	beträchtlich, beachtlich
	press advertising [ˌpres 'ædvətaɪzɪŋ]	Werbung in der Presse
	selective [sɪ'lektɪv]	wählerisch, selektiv
	concentrate on [kɒnsəntreɪt ɒn]	sich konzentrieren auf
67	**official** [ə'fɪʃl]	offiziell, amtlich
	full-page [ˌfʊl'peɪdʒ]	ganzseitig
	shop window ['ʃɒp wɪndəʊ]	Schaufenster
	display [dɪ'spleɪ]	zeigen, ausstellen
	merchandise ['mɜ:tʃəndaɪz]	Waren(angebot)
	direct mail [dəˌrekt 'meɪl]	Postwurfsendung
	utilize ['ju:təlaɪz]	einsetzen, nutzen
	decade ['dekeɪd]	Jahrzehnt
	date from ['deɪt frəm]	stammen aus
	clue [klu:]	Hinweis, Tipp, Indiz
	dating ['deɪtɪŋ]	Datierung
68	**classical** ['klæsɪkl]	klassisch
	moisturizer ['mɔɪstʃəraɪzə]	Feuchtigkeitscreme
	transform [træns'fɔ:m]	verwandeln
	mere [mɪə]	bloß
	capture ['kæptʃə]	erobern
	spirit ['spɪrɪt]	Geist
	remain [rɪ'meɪn]	bleiben
	come up with [ˌkʌm 'ʌp wɪð]	vorschlagen
	apparently [ə'pærəntli]	offensichtlich, anscheinend
	colour psychology [ˌkʌlə saɪ'kɒlədʒi]	Farbpsychologie
	sophisticated [sə'fɪstɪkeɪtɪd]	raffiniert
	stand for ['stænd fə]	stehen für
	inner ['ɪnə]	innere
	outer ['aʊtə]	äußere
	purity ['pjʊərəti]	Reinheit
	outdoor activity [ˌaʊtdɔ: æk'tɪvəti]	Tätigkeit im Freien
	sunbathing ['sʌnbeɪðɪŋ]	Sonnenbaden
	naturalness ['nætʃrəlnəs]	Natürlichkeit
	youthfulness ['ju:θfulnəs]	Jugendlichkeit
	freshness ['freʃnəs]	Frische
	prevail [prɪ'veɪl]	(vor)herrschen
	jewellery ['dʒu:əlri]	Schmuck
	accessory [ək'sesəri]	Accessoire
	drab [dræb]	düster, farblos
	depressing [dɪ'presɪŋ]	bedrückend, deprimierend
	post-war period [ˌpəʊst 'wɔ: pɪəriəd]	Nachkriegszeit
	optimism ['ɒptɪmɪzəm]	Optimismus
	dynamic [daɪ'næmɪk]	dynamisch
	take hold of [teɪk 'həʊld əv]	ergreifen
	glamour ['glæmə]	Glanz
	romance [rəʊ'mæns]	Romantik
	boom [bu:m]	Hochkonjunktur, Boom
	endure [ɪn'djʊə]	andauern
	reflect [rɪ'flekt]	reflektieren, wiedergeben
	characteristic of [ˌkærəktə'rɪstɪk əv]	charakteristisch für
	self-confident [ˌself 'kɒnfɪdənt]	selbstsicher, -bewusst
	demanding [dɪ'mɑ:ndɪŋ]	anspruchsvoll

	depict [dɪ'pɪkt]	darstellen
	product line ['prɒdʌkt laɪn]	Produktlinie
	skin type ['skɪn taɪp]	Hauttyp
	diversify [daɪ'vɜ:sɪfaɪ]	diversifizieren, die Produktion ausweiten
	expand [ɪk'spænd]	ausdehnen, erweitern
	globalization [ˌgləʊbəlaɪ'zeɪʃn]	Globalisierung
	buzzword ['bʌzwɜ:d]	Modewort
	packaging ['pækɪdʒɪŋ]	Verpackung
	standardize ['stændədaɪz]	standardisieren, normieren
	recognition [ˌrekeg'nɪʃn]	Wiedererkennen
	melody ['melədi]	Melodie
	function as ['fʌŋkʃn əz]	dienen als
	acoustic [ə'ku:stɪk]	akustisch
	secure [sɪ'kjuə]	sichern, festigen
	typeface ['taɪpfeɪs]	Schriftbild, -zug
69	**timeline** ['taɪmlaɪn]	Zeitachse
	take into consideration [ˌteɪk ɪntə kənˌsɪdə'reɪʃn]	berücksichtigen
	theme [θi:m]	Thema
	be aimed at [bi 'eɪmd ət]	sich wenden an
	element ['elɪmənt]	Element, Bestandteil
70	**century** ['sentʃəri]	Jahrhundert
	undergo [ˌʌndə'gəʊ]	erfahren, erleben
	radical ['rædɪkl]	radikal
	determine [dɪ'tɜ:mɪn]	bestimmen, festlegen
	nowadays ['naʊədeɪz]	heutzutage
	huge [hju:dʒ]	riesig
	acquisition [ˌækwɪ'zɪʃn]	Erwerb, Zukauf
	conglomerate [kən'glɒmərət]	Großkonzern
	refrigerator [rɪ'frɪdʒəreɪtə]	Kühlschrank
	saturated ['sætʃəreɪtɪd]	gesättigt
	attempt [ə'tempt]	versuchen
	be confronted by [bi kən'frʌntɪd baɪ]	konfrontiert sein mit
	literally ['lɪtərəli]	buchstäblich
	haircare product [ˌheəkeə 'prɒdʌkt]	Haarpflegeprodukt
	shelf [ʃelf]	Regal
	flood [flʌd]	überfluten
	domestic [də'mestɪk]	Binnen-, Inlands-
	competition [ˌkɒmpə'tɪʃn]	Konkurrenz, Wettbewerb
	fierce [fɪəs]	heftig, aggressiv
	maintain [meɪn'teɪn]	aufrechterhalten, einhalten
	distinctive [dɪ'stɪŋktɪv]	kennzeichnend, charakteristisch
	moreover [mɔ:r'əʊvə]	außerdem
	critical ['krɪtɪkl]	kritisch
	function ['fʌŋkʃn]	Funktion
	pay attention to [peɪ ə'tenʃn tə]	beachten
	prestige [pre'sti:ʒ]	Prestige
	eco-friendliness [ˌi:kəʊ 'frendlinəs]	Umweltfreundlichkeit
	economical [ˌi:kə'nɒmɪkl]	sparsam, wirtschaftlich
	interchangeable [ˌɪntə'tʃeɪndʒəbl]	austauschbar
	hypercritical [ˌhaɪpə'krɪtɪkl]	hyperkritisch
	stand out from the crowd [ˌstænd 'aʊt frəm ðə 'kraʊd]	aus der Menge herausragen
	orientation [ˌɔ:riən'teɪʃn]	Orientierung
	hold on to [ˌhəʊld 'ɒn tə]	festhalten an
	for short [fə 'ʃɔ:t]	abgekürzt
	behaviour [bɪ'heɪvjə]	Verhalten
	presence ['prezns]	Anwesenheit
	sense of identity [ˌsens əv aɪ'dentəti]	Identitätsgefühl
	unified ['ju:nɪfaɪd]	einheitlich
	uniform ['ju:nɪfɔ:m]	gleichförmig
	correspondence [ˌkɒrɪ'spɒndəns]	Briefwechsel, Korrespondenz
	apply to [ə'plaɪ tə]	anwenden auf
	interior design [ɪnˌtɪəriə dɪ'zaɪn]	Innenausstattung
	newsletter ['nju:zletə]	Rundschreiben, Informationsblatt
	instruction manual [ɪn'strʌkʃn mænjuəl]	Bedienungsanleitung, Benutzerhandbuch
	coherent [kəʊ'hɪərənt]	kohärent, zusammenhängend
	consistent [kən'sɪstənt]	einheitlich
	reinforce [ˌri:ɪn'fɔ:s]	verstärken
	treatment ['tri:tmənt]	Behandlung, Umgang
	leadership ['li:dəʃɪp]	Führerschaft, Leitung
	manners ['mænəz]	Umgangsformen, Manieren
	in recognition of [ɪn ˌrekeg'nɪʃn əv]	in Anerkennung der
	productive [prə'dʌktɪv]	produktiv
71	**within arm's reach** [wɪˌðɪn ɑ:mz 'ri:tʃ]	in Reichweite
	sense of belonging [sens əv bɪ'lɒŋɪŋ]	Zugehörigkeitsgefühl
	team spirit [ˌti:m 'spɪrɪt]	Teamgeist

Unit 8

72	**core task** ['kɔ: tɑ:sk]	Kernaufgabe
	co-operation [kəʊˌɒpə'reɪʃn]	Zusammenarbeit
	mobile communications equipment [ˌməʊbaɪl kəmju:nɪ'keɪʃnz ɪkwɪpmənt]	Mobilfunkgeräte
	analyst ['ænəlɪst]	Analyst/in
	fund manager ['fʌnd mænɪdʒə]	Fondsmanager/in
73	**split** [splɪt]	aufteilen
	industrial engineering [ɪnˌdʌstriəl ˌendʒɪ'nɪərɪŋ]	Industrietechnik

mould making ['məʊld meɪkɪŋ] – Formenherstellung
tool making ['tu:l meɪkɪŋ] – Werkzeugherstellung
assembly [ə'sembli] – Zusammenbau, Montage
surface treatment ['sɜ:fɪs tri:tmənt] – Oberflächenbehandlung
essentially [ɪ'senʃəli] – im Prinzip, im Wesentlichen
medical engineering [ˌmedɪkl ˌendʒɪ'nɪərɪŋ] – Medizintechnik
loudspeaker [ˌlaʊd'spi:kə] – Lautsprecher
involvement [ɪn'vɒlvmənt] – Beteiligung, Engagement
feasibility [ˌfi:zə'bɪləti] – Machbarkeit
nurture ['nɜ:tʃə] – pflegen
costly ['kɒstli] – kostspielig
depend on [dɪ'pend ɒn] – abhängen von
market saturation [ˌmɑ:kɪt ˌsætʃə'reɪʃn] – Marktsättigung
moulding process [ˌməʊldɪŋ 'prəʊses] – Formenherstellung
computer-integrated manufacture [kəm'pju:tə ˌɪntɪgreɪtɪd ˌmænju'fæktʃə] – computergestützte Herstellung
caption ['kæpʃn] – Bildunterschrift
74 **hollow** ['hɒləʊ] – hohl
container [kən'teɪnə] – Behälter, Gefäß
liquid ['lɪkwɪd] – Flüssigkeit
pour [pɔ:] – gießen
perform [pə'fɔ:m] – durch-, ausführen
go from strength to strength [gəʊ frəm ˌstreŋθ tə 'streŋθ] – einen Erfolg nach dem anderen erzielen
press release ['pres rɪli:s] – Pressemitteilung
publication [ˌpʌblɪ'keɪʃn] – Veröffentlichung
aim at ['eɪm ət] – richten an, anstreben
on the right track [ɒn ðə raɪt 'træk] – auf dem richtigen Weg
press conference ['pres kɒnfərəns] – Pressekonferenz
chairman ['tʃeəmən] – Vorsitzender
board of management [ˌbɔ:d əv 'mænɪdʒmənt] – Vorstand, Geschäftsführung
expansion [ɪk'spænʃn] – Erweiterung, Expansion
succeed in doing sth [səkˌsi:d ɪn 'du:ɪŋ] – mit etw Erfolg haben
in this respect [ɪn ðɪs rɪ'spekt] – in dieser Hinsicht
under review [ˌʌndə rɪ'vju:] – zu besprechen
pursue [pə'sju:] – verfolgen
growth-oriented ['grəʊθ ɔ:riəntɪd] – wachstumsorientiert
production volume [prə'dʌkʃn vɒlju:m] – Produktionsumfang
systematic [ˌsɪstə'mætɪk] – systematisch
progress ['prəʊgres] – Fortschritt/e
field [fi:ld] – Bereich, Gebiet
innovative ['ɪnəveɪtɪv] – innovativ
investment [ɪn'vestmənt] – Investition
cycle ['saɪkl] – Zyklus
significantly [sɪg'nɪfɪkəntli] – erheblich, spürbar
shorten ['ʃɔ:tn] – kürzen
reorganize [ri'ɔ:gənaɪz] – umorganisieren
automation [ˌɔ:tə'meɪʃn] – Automation
mainstream ['meɪnstri:m] – Haupt-, vorherrschend
portfolio [pɔ:t'fəʊliəʊ] – Bestand
ultimate ['ʌltɪmət] – höchst, endgültig
set up [ˌset 'ʌp] – aufbauen, einrichten
processing ['prəʊsesɪŋ] – Be-, Verarbeitung
fulfill [fʊl'fɪl] – erfüllen
strategic [strə'ti:dʒɪk] – strategisch
fully fledged [ˌfʊli 'fledʒd] – voll entwickelt
75 **methodical** [mə'θɒdɪkl] – methodisch
put into practice [ˌpʊt ɪntə 'præktɪs] – in die Praxis umsetzen
outline ['aʊtlaɪn] – Überblick, Skizze
production unit [prə'dʌkʃn ju:nɪt] – Produktionseinheit
75t **build** [bɪld] – (auf)bauen, errichten
well lit [ˌwel 'lɪt] – hell erleuchtet
solid ['sɒlɪd] – fest
wood flooring ['wʊd flɔ:rɪŋ] – Holzfußboden
environment [ɪn'vaɪrənmənt] – Umgebung
recruit [rɪ'kru:t] – neue/r Angestellte/r, Personal
tool shop ['tu:l ʃɒp] – Werkzeugausgabe
flow-shop production [ˌfləʊ ʃɒp prə'dʌkʃn] – Fließbandproduktion
mass production [ˌmæs prə'dʌkʃn] – Massenproduktion
cast [kɑ:st] – gießen
retailing ['ri:teɪlɪŋ] – Einzelhandel(sverkauf)
pass through ['pɑ:s θru:] – durchlaufen
transparent [træns'pærənt] – durchsichtig
robot ['rəʊbɒt] – Roboter
assembly line [ə'sembli laɪn] – Montage-, Fließband
assure [ə'ʃʊə] – versichern
76 **job-shop system** [ˌdʒɒb ʃɒp 'sɪstəm] – Werkstattfertigung
integration [ˌɪntɪ'greɪʃn] – Eingliederung, Integration
be based on [bi 'beɪst ɒn] – beruhen auf, basieren auf
labour-intensive [ˌleɪbər ɪn'tensɪv] – arbeitsintensiv
cost-intensive [ˌkɒst ɪn'tensɪv] – kostenintensiv
capital-intensive [ˌkæpɪtl ɪn'tensɪv] – kapitalintensiv
labour ['leɪbə] – Arbeit
skilled [skɪld] – ausgebildet, Fach-
batch production ['bætʃ prədʌkʃn] – Kleinserienproduktion

78	**keyboard** ['ki:bɔ:d]	Tastatur, Keyboard
	cutting tool ['kʌtɪŋ tu:l]	Schneidwerkzeug
	arm robot [ɑ:m 'rəʊbɒt]	Armroboter
	raw part [ˌrɔ: 'pɑ:t]	Rohling
	cutting lathe ['kʌtɪŋ leɪð]	Fräsmaschine
	supply and monitoring [sə'plaɪ ənd 'mɒnɪtərɪŋ]	Lieferung und Überwachung
	milling machine ['mɪlɪŋ məʃi:n]	Fräsautomat
	milling tool ['mɪlɪŋ tu:l]	Fräswerkzeug
	driverless ['draɪvələs]	führerlos
	computer steered [kəm'pju:tə stɪəd]	computergesteuert
79	**forever** [fə'revə]	für immer, ewig
	lifespan ['laɪfspæn]	Lebenszeit, -dauer
	viewpoint ['vju:pɔɪnt]	Standpunkt
	invention [ɪn'venʃn]	Erfindung
	keypad ['ki:pæd]	Tastenfeld
	obsolete ['ɒbsəli:t]	veraltet
	play a part [ˌpleɪ ə 'pɑ:t]	eine Rolle spielen
	influence ['ɪnfluəns]	Einfluss
	crazy about sth ['kreɪzi əbaʊt]	verrückt nach etw
	fancy ['fænsi]	ausgefallen
	unbreakable [ʌn'breɪkəbl]	unzerbrechlich
	tendency ['tendənsi]	Tendenz
	economy [ɪ'kɒnəmi]	Wirtschaft
	at large [ət 'lɑ:dʒ]	insgesamt, als Ganzes
	usable ['ju:zəbl]	nützlich
	survive [sə'vaɪv]	überleben
	niche [nɪtʃ]	Nische
	sector ['sektə]	Sektor, Bereich
	profitable ['prɒfɪtəbl]	gewinnbringend, erfolgreich
	life cycle ['laɪf saɪkl]	Lebenszyklus, -erwartung
	have in common [həv ɪn 'kɒmən]	gemeinsam haben
	maturity [mə'tʃʊərəti]	Ausgereiftheit
	decline [dɪ'klaɪn]	Abschwung
	improve [ɪm'pru:v]	verbessern
	modify ['mɒdɪfaɪ]	verändern
	linked to ['lɪŋkt tə]	verbunden mit
	turn out to be [ˌtɜ:n 'aʊt tə bi]	sich herausstellen
	in the longer term [ɪn ðə lɒŋgə 'tɜ:m]	auf längere Sicht
80	**negligible** ['neglɪdʒəbl]	geringfügig
	peak-level ['pi:k levl]	Höchststand
	mass market [ˌmæs 'mɑ:kɪt]	Massenmarkt
	be familiar with [bi fə'mɪliə wɪð]	gut kennen
81	**step forward** [step 'fɔ:wəd]	vorangehen
	region ['ri:dʒən]	Gebiet, Gegend
	talented ['tæləntɪd]	begabt, talentiert
	footwear ['fʊtweə]	Schuhwerk
	artisan [ˌɑ:tɪ'zæn]	Handwerker/in
	craft [krɑ:ft]	(Kunst-)Handwerk
	shoemaking ['ʃu:meɪkɪŋ]	Schuhmacherei
	leather working ['leðə wɜ:kɪŋ]	Lederverarbeitung
	supplement ['sʌplɪment]	ergänzen
	instruction [ɪn'strʌkʃn]	Unterrichtung
	computerized [kəm'pju:təraɪzd]	computerisiert
	tradition-bound [trə'dɪʃn baʊnd]	traditionsgebunden
	profession [prə'feʃn]	Beruf
	gain [geɪn]	gewinnen, erzielen
	tax [tæks]	Steuer
	pension ['penʃn]	Rente, Pension
	social security [ˌsəʊʃl sɪ'kjʊərəti]	Sozialversicherung, -abgaben
	obligation [ˌɒblɪ'geɪʃn]	Verpflichtung
	computer-assisted design (CAD) [kəmˌpju:tər əˌsɪstɪd dɪ'zaɪn]	computergestützte Konstruktion
	computer-assisted manufacturing (CAM) [kəmˌpju:tər əˌsɪstɪd mænju'fæktʃərɪŋ]	computergestützte Fertigung
	indispensable [ˌɪndɪ'spensəbl]	unentbehrlich
	adjunct ['ædʒʌŋkt]	Hilfsmittel
	thanks to ['θæŋks tə]	dank
	advance [əd'vɑ:ns]	Fortschritt
	microelectronics [ˌmaɪkrəʊ ˌɪlek'trɒnɪks]	Mikroelektronik
	automation product [ˌɔ:təmeɪʃn 'prɒdʌkt]	Automationsprodukt
	assist [ə'sɪst]	helfen, unterstützen
	performance [pə'fɔ:məns]	Leistung(en)
	expenditure [ɪk'spendɪtʃə]	Ausgabe(n), Kosten
	paralleling ['pærəlelɪŋ]	parallel zu
	open system architecture [ˌəʊpən sɪstəm 'ɑ:kɪtektʃə]	Architektur mit offenem System
	diverse [daɪ'vɜ:s]	verschieden, unterschiedlich
	built-in [ˌbɪlt'ɪn]	eingebaut
	scalability [ˌskeɪlə'bɪləti]	Ausbaufähigkeit
	functionality [ˌfʌŋkʃə'næləti]	Funktionalität
	task [tɑ:sk]	Aufgabe
	hardly any [ˌhɑ:dli 'eni]	kaum ein(e)
	on the part of [ɒn ðə 'pɑ:t əv]	auf Seiten des
	chemical engineer [ˌkemɪkl endʒɪ'nɪə]	Industriechemiker/in, Chemieingenieur/in
	mechanical engineer [mɪˌkænɪkl ˌendʒɪ'nɪə]	Maschinen(bau)-techniker/in
	aeronautical [ˌeərə'nɔ:tɪkl]	aeronautisch, Luftfahrt-
	computing power [kəm'pju:tɪŋ paʊə]	Rechenleistung
	on screen [ɒn 'skri:n]	auf dem Bildschirm

	turbine blade ['tɜ:baɪn bleɪd]	Turbinenschaufel
	jet aircraft engine [ˌdʒet 'eəkrɑ:ft endʒɪn]	Düsentriebwerk
82	**all-inclusive** [ˌɔ:l ɪn'klu:sɪv]	allumfassend
	maximize ['mæksɪmaɪz]	maximieren
	profitability [ˌprɒfɪtə'bɪləti]	Profitabilität

Unit 9

83	**trading partner** ['treɪdɪŋ pɑ:tnə]	Handelspartner
	order acknowledgement [ˌɔ:dər ək'nɒlɪdʒmənt]	Auftragsbestätigung
	sales enquiry [ˌseɪlz ɪn'kwaɪəri]	Verkaufsanfrage
	purchase order ['pɜ:tʃəs ɔ:də]	Bestellung
	remittance advice [rɪˌmɪtns əd'vaɪs]	Überweisungsbenachrichtigung
	chronological order [krɒnəˌlɒdʒɪkl 'ɔ:də]	zeitliche Abfolge
84	**facsimile** [fæk'sɪməli]	Fax
	ref [ref]	(Akten-)Zeichen
	for the attention of [fə ði ə'tenʃn əv]	zu Händen von
	concerning [kən'sɜ:nɪŋ]	bezüglich, betreffend
	work station ['wɜ:k steɪʃn]	Computer-Arbeitsplatz
	deep drawer chest [ˌdi:p ˌdrɔ: 'tʃest]	Schubfach
	pull-out ['pʊl aʊt]	herausziehbar
	shelf unit ['ʃelf ju:nɪt]	Regalelement
	have pleasure in doing sth ['həv 'pleʒər ɪn du:ɪŋ]	etw sehr gern tun
	enclose [ɪn'kləʊz]	beilegen, beifügen
	settlement ['setlmənt]	(Be-)Zahlung, Begleichung
	be of assistance [bi əv ə'sɪstəns]	behilflich sein
	yours sincerely [jɔ:z sɪn'sɪəli]	Mit freundlichen Grüßen
	enclosure (enc) [ɪn'kləʊʒə]	Anlage
85	**unclear** [ˌʌn'klɪə]	unklar
	switchboard ['swɪtʃbɔ:d]	(Telefon-)Zentrale
	dimensions [dɪ'menʃnz]	Abmessungen, Maße, Ausmaße
	by express courier [baɪ ɪkˌspres 'kʊriə]	mit Expressboten
	delivery date [dɪ'lɪvəri deɪt]	Liefertermin
	introductory offer [ˌɪntrə'dʌktəri ɒfə]	Einführungsangebot
	trade terms ['treɪd tɜ:mz]	Lieferbedingungen
	exceed [ɪk'si:d]	übersteigen, hinausgehen
	company policy [ˌkʌmpəni 'pɒləsi]	Firmenpolitik
	deal [di:l]	Geschäft, Abkommen
	in effect [ɪn ɪ'fekt]	tatsächlich
	fifty-fifty [ˌfɪfti'fɪfti]	fünfzig zu fünfzig, halb und halb
	decision [dɪ'sɪʒn]	Entscheidung
86	**business dealings** ['bɪznəs di:lɪŋz]	geschäftliche Verhandlungen
	inappropriate [ˌɪnə'prəʊpriət]	unpassend, unangemessen
	unprofessional [ˌʌnprə'feʃənl]	unprofessionell
	attitude ['ætɪtju:d]	Einstellung, Haltung
	want some money off [wɒnt sʌm ˌmʌni 'ɒf]	einen Rabatt/Nachlass verlangen
87	**discrepancy** [dɪs'krepənsi]	Diskrepanz, Unstimmigkeit
	order form ['ɔ:də fɔ:m]	Auftrags-, Bestellformular
	apologize [ə'pɒlədʒaɪz]	sich entschuldigen
	rectify ['rektɪfaɪ]	richtigstellen
88	**acknowledge** [ək'nɒlɪdʒ]	bestätigen
	unambiguous [ˌʌnæm'bɪgjuəs]	unzweideutig, eindeutig
	timing ['taɪmɪŋ]	(Festlegung der) Lieferzeit
	documentation [ˌdɒkjumen'teɪʃn]	Dokumentation, Papiere
	circular saw ['sɜ:kjələ sɔ:]	Kreissäge
	packing ['pækɪŋ]	Verpackung
	crate [kreɪt]	(Holz-)Kiste
	bank transfer ['bæŋk trænsfɜ:]	Banküberweisung
	rest assured [rest ə'ʃʊəd]	versichert sein
	execute ['eksɪkju:t]	ausführen
	entire [ɪn'taɪə]	vollständig
	satisfaction [ˌsætɪs'fækʃn]	Zufriedenheit
89	**exporter** [ɪk'spɔ:tə]	Exporteur/in
	importer [ɪm'pɔ:tə]	Importeur/in
	precisely [prɪ'saɪsli]	genau
	respective [rɪ'spektɪv]	jeweilig
	on board [ɒn 'bɔ:d]	an Bord
	irrevocable [ɪ'revəkəbl]	unwiderruflich
91	**provider** [prə'vaɪdə]	Lieferant, Anbieter
92	**undertaking** [ˌʌndə'teɪkɪŋ]	Verpflichtung
	liability [ˌlaɪə'bɪləti]	Haftung
	on behalf of [ɒn bɪ'hɑ:f əv]	im Namen von
	provided that [prə'vaɪdɪd ðət]	vorausgesetzt, dass
	strictly ['strɪktli]	strikt, genau
	lay down [ˌleɪ 'daʊn]	festsetzen, -legen
	political [pə'lɪtɪkl]	politisch
	economic [ˌi:kə'nɒmɪk]	wirtschaftlich
	security [sɪ'kjʊərəti]	Sicherheit
	legal ['li:gl]	gesetzlich, juristisch, legal
	binding ['baɪndɪŋ]	verbindlich
	applicant ['æplɪkənt]	Antragsteller/in
	issuing bank ['ɪʃu:ɪŋ bæŋk]	akkreditivstellende Bank

	traders bank ['treɪdəz bæŋk]	Handelsbank
	beneficiary [ˌbenɪ'fɪʃəri]	Begünstigte/r, Zahlungsempfänger/in
	debit an account [ˌdebɪt ən ə'kaʊnt]	ein Konto belasten
93	**cancel** ['kænsl]	stornieren, rückgängig machen
	charge money to [tʃɑːdʒ 'mʌni tə]	in Rechnung stellen
	transport [træn'spɔːt]	befördern, transportieren
	sequence ['siːkwəns]	Reihenfolge

Unit 10

94	**select** [sɪ'lekt]	auswählen
	in transit [ɪn 'trænzɪt]	auf dem Transport
	error ['erə]	Fehler, Irrtum
	faulty ['fɔːlti]	fehlerhaft, defekt
	incomplete [ˌɪnkəm'pliːt]	unvollständig
95	**environmental technology** [ɪnvaɪrənˌmentl tek'nɒlədʒi]	Umwelttechnik
	waste product [weɪst 'prɒdʌkt]	Abfallprodukt
	reintegrate [ˌriː'ɪntɪgreɪt]	wieder integrieren
	economic cycle [ˌiːkə'nɒmɪk saɪkl]	wirtschaftlicher Kreislauf
	organic [ɔː'gænɪk]	organisch
	industrial waste [ɪn'dʌstriəl weɪst]	Industrieabfall
	reuse [ˌriː'juːz]	wieder verwenden
	sewage works ['suːɪdʒ wɜːks]	Klärwerk
	construction site [kən'strʌkʃn saɪt]	Baustelle
	construction company [kən'strʌkʃn kʌmpəni]	Baufirma
	gravel ['grævl]	Kies
	of inferior quality [əv ɪnˌfɪəriə 'kwɒləti]	minderwertiger Qualität
	contaminated [kən'tæmɪneɪtɪd]	verunreinigt
	recycle [ˌriː'saɪkl]	recyceln, (wieder) aufbereiten
	cost-effectively [ˌkɒst ɪ'fektɪvli]	kostengünstig
	replacement [rɪ'pleɪsmənt]	Ersatz, Austausch
	at sb's expense [ət ˌsʌmwʌnz ɪk'spens]	auf jds Kosten
	see to sth ['siː tə]	sich um etw kümmern
	clear up sth [ˌklɪər 'ʌp]	etw aufklären
	never mind [ˌnevə 'maɪnd]	macht nichts
	look into sth [ˌlʊk 'ɪntə]	etw untersuchen, etw prüfen
96	**dependable** [dɪ'pendəbl]	zuverlässig
	substitute ['sʌbstɪtjuːt]	Ersatz
	investigate [ɪn'vestɪgeɪt]	untersuchen
	superior [suː'pɪəriə]	Vorgesetzte/r
	shipment ['ʃɪpmənt]	Ladung, Lieferung
	unsaleable [ʌn'seɪləbl]	unverkäuflich
	unpack [ˌʌn'pæk]	auspacken
	splintered ['splɪntəd]	gesplittert
	cupboard ['kʌbəd]	Schrank
	destined for ['destɪnd fə]	bestimmt für
97	**first-grade** [ˌfɜːst 'greɪd]	erstklassig
	Best wishes [best 'wɪʃɪz]	Mit freundlichen Grüßen
	concerned [kən'sɜːnd]	betroffen
	sincere [sɪn'sɪə]	aufrichtig
	inconvenience [ˌɪnkən'viːniəns]	Umstände
	result from [rɪ'zʌlt frəm]	sich ergeben aus
	reassurance [ˌriːə'ʃʊərəns]	Versicherung
98	**clear an account** [klɪər ən ə'kaʊnt]	eine Rechnung begleichen, abrechnen
	promptly ['prɒmptli]	unverzüglich, prompt
	ignore [ɪg'nɔː]	ignorieren, nicht beachten
	draw sb's attention to [ˌdrɔː ˌsʌmwʌnz ə'tenʃn tə]	jdn aufmerksam machen auf
	outstanding [aʊt'stændɪŋ]	ausstehend
	instruct [ɪn'strʌkt]	anweisen
	start legal proceedings [stɑːt ˌliːgl prə'siːdɪŋz]	gerichtliche Schritte einleiten
	unforeseen circumstances [ˌʌnfɔːsiːn 'sɜːkəmstənsɪz]	unvorhergesehene Umstände
100	**eventually** [ɪ'ventʃuəli]	schließlich, zum Schluss
	digging machinery [ˌdɪgɪŋ mə'ʃiːnəri]	Schürfmaschinen
	warning ['wɔːnɪŋ]	(Vor-)Warnung
	arrears [ə'rɪəz]	Rückstand, Verzug
	bear with sb [beə]	mit jdm Geduld haben
	credible ['kredəbl]	glaubwürdig
	consequence ['kɒnsɪkwəns]	Folge, Konsequenz
101	**inquire** [ɪn'kwaɪə]	sich erkundigen nach, fragen nach
	legislation [ˌledʒɪs'leɪʃn]	Gesetzgebung, gesetzliche Regelung(en)
102p	**occur** [ə'kɜː]	geschehen, vorkommen
	encounter [ɪn'kaʊntə]	stoßen auf, begegnen, Begegnung
	compost ['kɒmpɒst]	Kompost
	roughly ['rʌfli]	ungefähr
	clinker brick [ˌklɪŋkə brɪk]	Klinkerstein
	cement [sɪ'ment]	Zement
	amount to [ə'maʊnt tə]	betragen
103	**assemble** [ə'sembl]	zusammensetzen, -bauen, montieren
	subassemble [ˌsʌb ə'sembl]	vormontieren
	weld [weld]	schweißen
	machine [mə'ʃiːn]	maschinell herstellen/bearbeiten

eliminate [ɪ'lɪmɪneɪt]	beseitigen
be inherent within [bi ɪn'hɪərənt wɪðɪn]	innewohnen, gehören zu
stored [stɔ:d]	gelagert
manifestation [ˌmænɪfe'steɪʃn]	Kennzeichen
break down [ˌbreɪk 'daʊn]	aufteilen
category ['kætəgəri]	Kategorie
downstream process [ˌdaʊnstri:m 'prəʊses]	nach unten gerichteter (Produktions-)Prozess
upstream process [ˌʌpstri:m 'prəʊses]	nach oben gerichteter (Produktions-)Prozess
subcomponent [ˌsʌbkəm'pəʊnənt]	Unterteil
inventory ['ɪnvəntri]	Inventar, Bestand, Lagerbestände
storage space ['stɔ:rɪdʒ speɪs]	Lagerraum
overproduction [ˌəʊvəprə'dʌkʃn]	Überproduktion
takt time ['tækt taɪm]	Taktzeit
operational time [ˌɒpə'reɪʃənl taɪm]	Betriebszeit
shift [ʃɪft]	Schicht
single piece flow ['sɪŋgl pi:s fləʊ]	Einzelstückproduktion
manufacturing space [ˌmænju'fæktʃərɪŋ speɪs]	Produktionsfläche
inter process inventory [ˌɪntə ˌprəʊses 'ɪnvəntri]	Zwischenlagerung
lead-time ['li:d taɪm]	Laufzeit
material flow [mə'tɪəriəl fləʊ]	Materialfluss

A–Z WORD LIST

Diese Liste enthält alle Wörter in alphabetischer Reihenfolge. Hier sind jedoch die Wörter, die zum Grundwortschatz gehören, nicht aufgeführt. Die Zahl nach dem Stichwort bezieht sich auf die Seite, auf der das Wort zum ersten Mal erscheint.
p = das Wort befindet sich im *Pairwork File*.
t = das Wort befindet sich im *Transcript*.

A

absolutely 36t *absolut, völlig*
absorb 33 *aufnehmen*
acceptable 41 *passend*
access 38 *Zugang*
accessory 68 *Accessoire*
accommodation 21 *Unterkunft, Zimmer*
accomplish 45 *erreichen*
according to 24 *nach, entsprechend*
account for 14 *ausmachen, betragen*
accountant 9 *Buchhalter/in*
accounting 16 *Rechnungswesen, Buchhaltung*
accounts department 23t *Buchhaltung*
achieve 14 *erreichen, erlangen*
acknowledge 88 *bestätigen*
acknowledgement 30t *(Auftrags-)Bestätigung*
acoustic 68 *akustisch*
acquisition 70 *Erwerb, Zukauf*
act out 31 *aufführen*
actually 7 *eigentlich, tatsächlich*
add up to 8 *sich addieren zu, zusammen betragen*
additional charge 38 *zusätzliche Gebühr*
address label 22 *Adressaufkleber*
adhesion 58 *Haftung*
adjunct 81 *Hilfsmittel*
adopt 24 *adoptieren, übernehmen*
advance 81 *Fortschritt*
adventure 59 *Abenteuer*
advertisement 18 *Werbung, Anzeige*
advertising 51 *Werbe-*
advertising campaign 18 *Werbekampagne*
advise 64 *raten*
advocate 33 *Befürworter/in*
aerial 33 *Antenne*
aeronautical 81 *aeronautisch, Luftfahrt-*
affiliated with 61 *verbunden mit*
affordable 38 *erschwinglich*
after-sales service 16 *Kundendienst*
agency 51 *Agentur*
agenda 44 *Tagesordnung*
aggressive 59 *aggressiv*
aim 38 *bestrebt sein, beabsichtigen*
aim at 69 *richten an, anstreben*
air bridge 7 *Luftbrücke*
air traffic 10 *Luftverkehr*
air travel 10 *Luftfahrt*
airconditioned 38 *klimatisiert*
aircraft 7 *Flugzeug*
airframe 14 *(Flugzeug-)Zelle*
all things considered 59 *alles in allem*
allergy 33 *Allergie*
all-inclusive 82 *allumfassend*
allow me to 9 *gestatten Sie mir*
alter 51 *(ver)ändern*
alternative 29p *Alternative*
Alzheimer's disease 33 *Alzheimerkrankheit*
am 37 *vormittags*
amount to 102p *betragen*
analyst 72 *Analyst/in*
analytical 61 *analytisch*
animated 55 *bewegt*
announcement 47t *Bekanntgabe*
annual 50 *jährlich*
annual fee 42 *Jahresgebühr*
annual turnover 12t *Jahresumsatz*
answerphone 27 *Anrufbeantworter*
apart from 12t *abgesehen von*
apologize 87 *sich entschuldigen*
apparently 68 *offensichtlich, anscheinend*
appealing 66 *ansprechend*
appendix 66 *Anhang*
applaud 61 *applaudieren*
applicant 92 *Antragsteller/in*
apply to 70 *anwenden auf*
appreciate 26 *zu schätzen wissen*
apprentice 23 *Auszubildende/r*
apprenticeship 23 *Lehre, Ausbildung*
approach 14 *Methode, Ansatz*
appropriate 9 *angemessen, passend*
approval 61 *Zustimmung, Einverständnis*
approve 22 *gutheißen, genehmigen*
approximate 37 *ungefähr*
approximately 10 *ungefähr, etwa*
archive 23t *archivieren*
archives 16t *Archiv, Registratur*
argue 33 *behaupten, argumentieren*
argument 54 *Argument*
arise 45 *sich ergeben*
arm robot 78 *Armroboter*
arrange 18 *arrangieren, vereinbaren*
arrangement 38 *Absprache, Vereinbarung*
arrears 100 *Rückstand, Verzug*
arrogance 59 *Arroganz*
artisan 81 *Handwerker/in*
as well as 23t *ebenso wie*
ask sb's advice 44 *jdn um Rat bitten*

aspect **52** *Aspekt*
assemble **103** *zusammensetzen, -bauen, montieren*
assembly **73** *Zusammenbau, Montage*
assembly line **75t** *Montage-, Fließband*
assessment **51** *Einschätzung, Beurteilung*
assign sb to **23t** *jdn zuteilen*
assist **81** *helfen, unterstützen*
assistance, be of **84** *behilflich sein*
associate with **63** *verbinden mit*
assume **18** *annehmen*
assure **75t** *versichern*
at large **79** *insgesamt, als Ganzes*
at last **12** *endlich, schließlich*
at least **59** *wenigstens, mindestens*
at present **10** *momentan, derzeit*
at short notice **51** *kurzfristig*
at sb's expense **95** *auf jds Kosten*
at that time **7** *zu jener Zeit*
at the latest **30t** *spätestens*
atmosphere **39t** *Atmosphäre, Stimmung*
attach **66** *beilegen, -fügen*
attached **47** *verbunden, beigefügt*
attempt **70** *versuchen*
attention **54** *Aufmerksamkeit*
attitude **86** *Einstellung, Haltung*
attract sb's interest **10** *jds Interesse wecken*
attraction **39** *Attraktion, Reiz*
attribute **33** *zuschreiben*
authentic **39t** *authentisch, echt*
authority **61** *Autorität, Behörde*
automatic **58** *automatisch*
automation **74** *Automation*
automation product **81** *Automationsprodukt*
aviation industry **6** *Luftfahrtindustrie*
avoid **21** *vermeiden*
award **39** *zuerkennen*
aware, be ~ **48** *sich bewusst sein*
away, be ~ on business **31** *geschäftlich unterwegs sein*

B

background information **57** *Hintergrund-information(en)*
balance sheet **23t** *Bilanz, Kassenbericht*
balanced **14** *ausgeglichen, ausgewogen*
bank **38** *Ufer*
bank transfer **88** *Banküberweisung*
banking executive **51** *Bankmanager/in*
bar chart **57** *Säulen-, Balkendiagramm*
bargaining **52** *Verhandlung*
based, be ~ in **6** *seinen Sitz haben in*
based, be ~ on **76** *beruhen auf, basieren auf*
batch production **76** *Kleinserienproduktion*
bear costs **45** *Kosten tragen*
bear with sb **100** *mit jdm Geduld haben*
beforehand **45** *vorher, zuvor*
behaviour **70** *Verhalten*
beneficiary **92** *Begünstigte/r, Zahlungsempfänger/in*
benefit from **14** *profitieren von*
Benelux countries **43** *Beneluxländer*
besides **34** *außerdem*
Best wishes **97** *Mit freundlichen Grüßen*
beyond **62** *jenseits (von)*
bidding period **47t** *Ausschreibungsfrist*
billboard **65** *Werbeplakat*
binding **92** *verbindlich*
bland **39** *fade*
block **11** *Block, Zahlengruppe*
board of management **74** *Vorstand, Geschäftsführung*
body language **51** *Körpersprache*
book a flight **34** *einen Flug buchen*
booking **36** *Reservierung, Buchung*
boom **68** *Hochkonjunktur, Boom*
bottom-up **24** *von unten nach oben*
brain tumor **33** *Hirntumor*
brainstorm **55** *(Ideen) sammeln*
brand **38** *Marke, Typ*
brand name **64** *Markenzeichen*
brand personality **64** *Markenprofil*
break down **103** *aufteilen*
briefing **48** *Einweisung*
bring to a close **47t** *beenden*
brochure **10** *Prospekt*
browse for **37** *(im Internet) suchen nach*
build **75t** *(auf)bauen, errichten*
build up **24** *aufbauen*
built-in **81** *eingebaut*
bulk discount **30t** *Mengenrabatt*
bulk order **26** *Großauftrag, -bestellung*
business associate **9** *Geschäftspartner/in, -freund/in*
business dealings **86** *geschäftliche Verhandlungen*
buzzword **68** *Modewort*
by express courier **85** *mit Expressboten*

C

cabin **58** *Kabine*
cabin crew **14** *Kabinenbesatzung, Flugbegleiter*
cable **12t** *Kabel*
calculate **30t** *be-, ausrechnen*
call sth into question **62** *etw in Frage stellen*
cancel **93** *stornieren, rückgängig machen*
cancellation **23t** *Stornierung, Absage*
cancer **33** *Krebs*
canteen **16** *Kantine*
capacity **10** *Kapazität, Fassungsvermögen*
capital-intensive **76** *kapitalintensiv*
caption **73** *Bildunterschrift*
capture **68** *erobern*
card case **48** *Kartentäschchen*
cardiology diagnostics **16** *Herzdiagnostik*
carefully **48** *sorgfältig*
carrier **51** *Träger*
carry out **18** *durchführen*
carton **27t** *Karton, Paket*

case 57 *Fall*
cash machine 42 *Geldautomat*
cash withdrawal 42 *Bargeldabhebung*
cassette recorder 55 *Kassettenrekorder*
cast 75t *gießen*
catch 26 *verstehen*
category 103 *Kategorie*
cement 102p *Zement*
century 70 *Jahrhundert*
chain 39 *Kette*
chair 45 *leiten*
chairman 74 *Vorsitzender*
chairperson 50 *Vorsitzende/r*
challenge 61 *in Frage stellen*
characteristic of 68 *charakteristisch für*
charge money to 93 *in Rechnung stellen*
charming 39t *reizend, bezaubernd*
check in 36 *sich anmelden, einchecken*
cheek 59 *Wange*
chemical engineer 81 *Industriechemiker/in, Chemieingenieur/in*
chromated 58 *chromatiert*
chromating 58 *Chromatieren (chromsaures Salz auftragen)*
chronological order 83 *zeitliche Abfolge*
circular saw 88 *Kreissäge*
circulate 45 *(an alle) verschicken, herumgehen lassen*
circumstances 45 *Umstände*
claim 52 *behaupten*
classical 68 *klassisch*
classmate 50 *Klassenkamerad/in*
clear an account 98 *eine Rechnung begleichen, abrechnen*
clear up sth 95 *etw aufklären*
client 51 *Kunde, Kundin*
clinker brick 102p *Klinkerstein*
clue 67 *Hinweis, Tip, Indiz*
coating 56 *Beschichtung*
code 25 *Vorwahl*
coherent 70 *kohärent, zusammenhängend*
collection 23t *Abholung*
colon 30 *Doppelpunkt*
colour psychology 68 *Farbpsychologie*
combination 32 *Kombination*
come up with 68 *vorschlagen*
comfort 38 *Komfort, Bequemlichkeit*
commence 47t *beginnen*
commission 66 *beauftragen*
commonality method 14 *Gemeinsamkeitsprinzip*
communicate 28 *übermitteln, kommunizieren*
community 51 *Gemeinde*
company discount 37 *Firmenrabatt*
company policy 85 *Firmenpolitik*
compete 11 *konkurrieren*
competition 70 *Konkurrenz, Wettbewerb*
competitive 64 *Konkurrenz-, Wettbewerbs-*
competitor 8 *Konkurrent/in*
complain 29p *(sich) beschweren, reklamieren*
complaint 23t *Beschwerde, Beanstandung, Reklamation*
completely 46t *völlig*
complex 24 *kompliziert*
compliment 61 *Komplimente machen*
component 7 *(Bau-)Element, Bauteil*
compost 102p *Kompost*
comprise 12t *umfassen, bestehen aus*
compromise 46 *einen Kompromiss eingehen*
computer steered 78 *computergesteuert*
computer-assisted design (CAD) 81 *computergestützte Konstruktion*
computer-assisted manufacturing (CAM) 81 *computergestützte Fertigung*
computer-integrated manufacture 73 *computergestützte Herstellung*
computerized 81 *computerisiert*
computing power 81 *Rechenleistung*
concentrate on 66 *sich konzentrieren auf*
concept 24 *Konzept*
concern 7 *Konzern*
concerned 97 *betroffen*
concerning 84 *bezüglich, betreffend*
concession 61 *Vergünstigung, Zugeständnis*
conclude 47 *(ab)schließen*
conclusion 66 *(Schluss-)Folgerung*
conduct 22 *(durch)führen*
conference 31 *Konferenz, Besprechung*
conference room 16 *Besprechungszimmer, Konferenzraum*
conferencing facility 51 *Konferenzeinrichtung*
confirm 36 *bestätigen*
confirmation 44 *Bestätigung*
confrontational 61 *auf Konfrontationskurs, konfliktbetont*
confronted, be ~ by 70 *konfrontiert sein mit*
conglomerate 70 *Großkonzern*
consequence 100 *Folge, Konsequenz*
consequently 24 *dementsprechend, infolgedessen*
considerable 66 *beträchtlich, beachtlich*
consignment 27t *(Waren-)Sendung, Lieferung*
consistent 70 *einheitlich*
consortium 12t *Konsortium*
constantly 24 *ständig*
construction company 95 *Baufirma*
construction site 95 *Baustelle*
constructive 47t *konstruktiv*
consult 45 *zu Rate ziehen, konsultieren*
consultant 51 *Berater/in, Gutachter/in*
consumer 66 *Verbraucher/in, Konsument/in*
container 74 *Behälter, Gefäß*
contaminated 95 *verunreinigt*
continuous 24 *ständig*
contract 43 *Vertrag*
contract of employment 23t *Arbeitsvertrag*

contradict 21 *widersprechen*
contribution 7 *Beitrag*
convenience 42 *Bequemlichkeit, Annehmlichkeit*
convenient 27 *passend, angenehm*
conventional 24 *herkömmlich, konventionell*
convey 34 *über-, vermitteln*
convince 29p *überzeugen*
convincing 61 *überzeugend*
co-operation 72 *Zusammenarbeit*
co-operative 25 *Kooperative*
coordinate 22 *aufeinander abstimmen, koordinieren*
core task 72 *Kernaufgabe*
correction 45 *Korrektur*
correlation 6 *Korrelation, Wechselbeziehung*
correspond to 10 *entsprechen*
correspond with 22 *entsprechen*
correspondence 70 *Briefwechsel, Korrespondenz*
corridor 17 *Gang, Korridor*
cosmetics 65 *Kosmetik(a)*
cost reduction 14 *Kostensenkung*
cost-effectively 95 *kostengünstig*
cost-intensive 76 *kostenintensiv*
costly 73 *kostspielig*
costs incurred 40 *angefallene Kosten*
counter 36t *Schalter*
counterpart 61 *Gegenüber*
counterproductive 61 *kontraproduktiv*
counter-suggestion 56 *Gegenvorschlag*
country of residence 41 *Wohnsitz*
countrywide 66 *landesweit*
craft 81 *(Kunst-)Handwerk*
crate 88 *(Holz-)Kiste*
crazy about sth 79 *verrückt nach etw*
credible 100 *glaubwürdig*
credit 42 *Kredit*
credit limit 42 *Dispositionskredit*
credit rating 23t *Kreditwürdigkeit*
crew 14 *Besatzung, Mannschaft*
criteria 24 *Kriterien, Kennzeichen*
critical 70 *kritisch*
criticism 61 *Kritik*
cruising speed 11 *Reisegeschwindigkeit*
cultural 48 *kulturell*
cupboard 96 *Schrank*
currency exchange 57 *Währungsumtausch*
current 10 *aktuell, gegenwärtig*
currently 13 *momentan*
customarily 48 *üblicherweise*
customer satisfaction 24 *Zufriedenheit der Verbraucher*
customs 32 *Zoll(kontrolle)*
cut costs 51 *Kosten senken*
cutting lathe 78 *Fräsmaschine*
cutting tool 78 *Schneidwerkzeug*
cycle 74 *Zyklus*

D

damaged 27t *beschädigt*
dash 30 *Bindestrich*
data 23t *Daten*
database 22 *Datenbank*
date from 67 *stammen aus*
dating 67 *Datierung*
deal 85 *Geschäft, Abkommen*
deal with 22 *sich befassen mit*
debit 36t *belasten*
debit an account 92 *ein Konto belasten*
decade 67 *Jahrzehnt*
decentralized 24 *dezentralisiert*
decimal 11 *Dezimalzahl*
decision 85 *Entscheidung*
decision-making 51 *Entscheidungsfindung*
decline 79 *Abschwung*
deep drawer chest 84 *Schubfach*
deficiency 61 *Mangel*
definite 21 *bestimmt, fest*
delay 12 *Verspätung*
delayed 7 *verspätet*
deliver 7 *liefern*
delivery 11 *Auslieferung*
delivery address 30t *Lieferadresse*
delivery date 85 *Liefertermin*
delivery note 22 *Lieferschein*
demand 18 *Nachfrage, Bedarf*
demanding 68 *anspruchsvoll*
demonstrate 18 *vorstellen, vorführen*
department 20 *Ministerium, Ressort, Abteilung*
departure 36t *Abflug*
depend on 73 *abhängen von*
dependable 96 *zuverlässig*
depict 68 *darstellen*
depressing 68 *bedrückend, deprimierend*
desirable 61 *wünschenswert*
desired 58 *gewünscht*
despite 66 *trotz*
destined for 96 *bestimmt für*
detect 33 *entdecken*
determine 70 *bestimmen, festlegen*
detrimental 33 *nachteilig, schädlich*
development 11 *Entwicklung*
device 16 *Technik, Gerät, Apparat*
devise 64 *entwerfen*
diagram 14 *Diagramm, Grafik*
dial 25 *wählen*
differentiate from 64 *unterscheiden von, absetzen von*
digging machinery 100 *Schürfmaschinen*
digit 11 *einstellige Zahl*
digital layout 51 *digitales Layout*
dimensions 85 *Abmessungen, Maße, Ausmaße*
direct debit 42 *Lastschrift-, Einzugsverfahren*
direct mail 67 *Postwurfsendung*

directions, to give ~ 17 *Anweisungen geben, den Weg beschreiben*
disagreement 46 *Meinungsverschiedenheit*
discharge 58 *Ausgabe, Entladung*
disconnect 30t *trennen, unterbrechen*
discover 27t *entdecken, feststellen*
discrepancy 87 *Diskrepanz, Unstimmigkeit*
discussion 14 *Diskussion*
dispatch 18 *(ab)senden*
display 67 *zeigen, ausstellen*
disruption 50p *Störung*
distance 10 *Entfernung, Strecke*
distinctive 70 *kennzeichnend, charakteristisch*
distribute 16 *vertreiben, ausliefern*
distribution 16 *Vertrieb*
diverse 81 *verschieden, unterschiedlich*
diversified 24 *diversifiziert*
diversify 7 *ausweiten, diversifizieren*
do business with 7 *Geschäfte machen mit*
do harm 33 *schaden*
documentation 88 *Dokumentation, Papiere*
domestic 70 *Binnen-, Inlands-*
dot 30 *Punkt*
downstream process 103 *nach unten gerichteter (Produktions-)Prozess*
drab 68 *düster, farblos*
draw a conclusion 33 *einen Schluss ziehen*
draw sb's attention to 98 *jdn aufmerksam machen auf*
draw up 64 *abfassen, konzipieren*
drilling 34 *Bohren*
driver's licence 41 *Führerschein*
driverless 78 *führerlos*
drop-off point 32 *Entladestelle*
drugstore 64 *Drogerie*
drying oven 58 *Trockenofen*
due, be ~ to arrive 44 *planmäßig ankommen*
due to 13 *wegen, aufgrund von*
duty 23 *Aufgabe, Pflicht*
dynamic 68 *dynamisch*

E

eco-friendliness 70 *Umweltfreundlichkeit*
economic 92 *wirtschaftlich*
economic cycle 95 *wirtschaftlicher Kreislauf*
economical 70 *sparsam, wirtschaftlich*
economy 79 *Wirtschaft*
edit 51 *redigieren, bearbeiten*
education market 50 *Bildungsmarkt*
effective 54 *effektiv, wirkungsvoll*
efficiency 52 *Effizienz, Leistungsfähigkeit*
elect 50 *wählen*
electromagnetic radiation 33 *elektromagnetische Strahlung*
electronic 7 *elektronisch*
electronics 6 *Elektronik*
element 69 *Element, Bestandteil*
eliminate 103 *beseitigen*
embarrass 61 *verlegen machen, in Verlegenheit bringen*
emergency service 25 *Notruf*
emit 33 *abgeben, ausstrahlen*
emphasize 47t *betonen, hervorheben*
empirical 61 *empirisch, auf Erfahrung beruhend*
enable 51 *in die Lage versetzen*
enclose 84 *beilegen, beifügen*
enclosure (enc) 84 *Anlage*
encounter 102p *stoßen auf, begegnen, Begegnung*
endure 68 *andauern*
engaged 26 *besetzt*
engine 11 *Motor, Triebwerk*
enhance 14 *erhöhen, steigern*
enquiry 25 *Anfrage*
ensure 22 *sicherstellen, gewährleisten*
entire 88 *vollständig*
environment 75t *Umgebung*
environmental technology 95 *Umwelttechnik*
equally 39 *gleichermaßen*
equivalent 8 *Entsprechung*
era 7 *Ära, Zeitalter*
error 94 *Fehler, Irrtum*
escorted 40 *geführt*
essential 33 *notwendig, wichtig, wesentlich*
essentially 73 *im Prinzip, im Wesentlichen*
establish 48 *herstellen*
estimate 45 *Schätzung, (Kosten-)Voranschlag*
eternity 58t *Ewigkeit*
evaluate 18 *bewerten, abschätzen*
eventually 100 *schließlich, zum Schluss*
evidence 33 *Beweis(e)*
evolve 24 *(sich) entwickeln*
Ex Works 45 *ab Werk*
exaggeration 61 *Übertreibung*
examine 23t *untersuchen, prüfen*
exceed 85 *übersteigen, hinausgehen*
except 51 *außer*
excess 40t *Selbstbeteiligung*
exchange 13 *austauschen*
exclusively 39t *ausschließlich*
excuse 12 *entschuldigen*
execute 88 *ausführen*
executive 42 *leitende/r Angestellte/r, Manager/in*
exhibition 23t *Ausstellung*
exist 33 *existieren*
existing 18 *bestehend*
expand 68 *ausdehnen, erweitern*
expansion 74 *Erweiterung, Expansion*
expectation 11 *Erwartung*
expenditure 81 *Ausgabe(n), Kosten*
experienced 18 *erfahren*
experiment with 57 *experimentieren mit*
explanatory 54 *erklärend*
exploration 34 *Erforschung*
explosion 51 *Explosion*

exporter 89 *Exporteur/in*
exposed, be ~ to 33 *ausgesetzt sein*
express 34 *ausdrücken, zum Ausdruck bringen*
extend 10 *vergrößern, ausdehnen*
extension 26 *Nebenanschluss*
extensive 64 *umfassend*
external duty 12t *Außendienst, freie Mitarbeit*
extol 51 *loben, preisen*
extract 29 *Auszug*
extremely 46t *sehr, äußerst*
eye contact 51 *Blickkontakt*
eye shadow 65 *Lidschatten*

F

face-to-face 52 *direkt, von Angesicht zu Angesicht*
facility 38 *Einrichtung*
facsimile 84 *Fax*
factory 12t *Fabrik*
fail 49 *scheitern (bei), versagen (in)*
failure 43 *Misserfolg, Fehlschlag*
fair enough 30t *vernünftig, recht und billig*
familiar with 23t *vertraut mit, bekannt mit*
familiarise 51 *bekanntmachen*
family business 12t *Familienunternehmen*
fancy 79 *ausgefallen*
far out 21 *weit draußen*
fashion-conscious 64 *modebewusst*
faulty 94 *fehlerhaft, defekt*
favo(u)red 66 *favorisiert*
feasibility 73 *Machbarkeit*
feature 37 *Merkmal, Kennzeichen*
federal state 6 *Bundesland*
fee 40 *Gebühr*
feed 58 *Eingabe*
feedback 53 *Rückmeldung*
feel at ease 7 *sich wohl fühlen*
feeling 51 *Gefühl*
fellow 14 *Mit-*
fence 26 *Zaun*
fence panel 30t *Zaunsegment*
fencing 32 *Einzäunung*
ferry 27t *Fähre*
field sales force 18 *Außenmitarbeiter*
field 74 *Bereich, Gebiet*
fierce 70 *heftig, aggressiv*
fifty-fifty 85 *fünfzig zu fünfzig, halb und halb*
final assembly 7 *Endmontage*
final draft 45 *Endfassung*
finalize 43 *endgültig festlegen*
finance 37p *Finanz*
findings 66 *Ergebnisse*
fire away 36t *Schießen Sie los!*
first-grade 97 *erstklassig*
first-name terms, be on ~ 9 *mit Vornamen anreden*
fleet 7 *Flotte*
flexibility 38 *Flexibilität*
flexible 24 *flexibel*
flight range 10 *Reichweite*
flood 70 *überfluten*
flow-shop production 75t *Fließbandproduktion*
focus group 64 *Zielgruppe*
focus on 24 *Konzentration auf*
folks 54 *Leute*
footwear 81 *Schuhwerk*
for instance 14 *zum Beispiel*
for short 70 *abgekürzt*
for the attention of 84 *zu Händen von*
for the moment 19 *für den Augenblick*
forever 79 *für immer, ewig*
form of identification 41 *Ausweispapiere*
fortune 58t *Vermögen*
forwarding agent 22 *Spediteur/in*
found 7 *gründen*
frank 46t *offen, aufrichtig*
Free Domicile 45 *frei Haus*
free of charge 39t *kostenfrei, gebührenfrei*
freight 10 *Fracht*
freighter 10 *Frachtflugzeug*
freshness 68 *Frische*
from the top 24 *von oben*
fuel capacity 11 *Treibstofffassungsvermögen*
fulfill 74 *erfüllen*
full-page 67 *ganzseitig*
fully booked 36t *ausgebucht*
fully comprehensive 40t *Vollkasko-*
fully fledged 74 *voll entwickelt*
function as 68 *dienen als*
function 70 *Funktion*
functionality 81 *Funktionalität*
fund manager 72 *Fondsmanager/in*
funny-looking 7 *komisch aussehend*
furthermore 46t *ferner, überdies*
fuselage section 7 *Rumpfteil*

G

gain 81 *gewinnen, erzielen*
galvanized steel 58 *verzinkter Stahl*
gap 40 *Lücke*
gather 55 *sammeln*
generally 39 *im Allgemeinen*
genuine 22 *echt*
geographical 51 *geographisch*
get away from 33 *entkommen*
get down to business 43 *zur Sache kommen*
get in touch 31 *(sich) in Verbindung setzen*
get involved in sth 51 *sich an etw beteiligen*
get started on sth 64 *mit etw anfangen*
get to know 12 *kennen lernen*
glamour 68 *Glanz*
glitzy 61 *glitzernd, schillernd*
global vision 51 *globale Vision*
globalization 68 *Globalisierung*
go ahead 26 *anfangen*

go from strength to strength 74 *einen Erfolg nach dem anderen erzielen*
go into detail 19 *ins Detail gehen*
go over one's credit limit 42 *den Dispositionskredit überziehen*
golden rule 54 *goldene Regel*
goods 16 *Ware(n), Güter*
grand 39 *großartig, prachtvoll*
grant a discount 29p *einen Rabatt gewähren*
graph 14 *Kurve, grafische Darstellung*
graphics 55 *Grafiken*
grateful 27t *dankbar*
grave 48 *ernst, schwer*
gravel 95 *Kies*
great-grandfather 12t *Urgroßvater*
growth 10 *Wachstum, Zunahme*
growth-oriented 74 *wachstumsorientiert*
guarantee 38 *garantieren*
guarantee period 46t *Garantiezeit*
guidebook 39 *Reiseführer*

H

haircare product 70 *Haarpflegeprodukt*
hand-drawn 55 *von Hand gezeichnet*
hand-held 33 *Hand-(Gerät), tragbar*
handling characteristics 14 *typische Merkmale der Handhabung*
handling 32 *Handhabung, Beförderung*
handout 53 *Merkblatt*
hardly any 81 *kaum ein(e)*
harmful 33 *schädlich*
harsh 46 *hart*
have a pen handy 36t *etw zum Schreiben haben*
have in mind 40t *denken an, sich vorstellen*
have pleasure in doing sth 84 *etw sehr gern tun*
have sth in common 34 *etw gemeinsam haben*
head chef 39t *Chefkoch, Küchenchef*
headquarters 34 *Hauptsitz*
health risk 33 *Gesundheitsrisiko*
hear from sb 30t *von jdm hören*
heard of 58t *gehört von*
heart complaint 33 *Herzbeschwerden*
heart problem 33 *Herzproblem*
hectare 25 *Hektar*
hesitate 27t *zögern*
hierarchical 24 *hierarchisch*
hierarchy 48 *Hierarchie*
highly skilled 18 *gut ausgebildet*
high-quality 46t *von guter Qualität*
high-ranking 48 *hochrangig*
hold a licence 41 *eine (Fahr-)Erlaubnis besitzen*
hold on to 70 *festhalten an*
hold the line 26 *am Apparat bleiben*
holiday pay 23t *Urlaubsgeld*
hollow 74 *hohl*
hopefully 18 *hoffentlich*
horizontal 24 *horizontal*
hospitable 43 *gastfreundlich*
how do you do 9 *Guten Tag/Abend!*
huge 70 *riesig*
hyperbole 48 *Übertreibung*
hypercritical 70 *hyperkritisch*

I

identification 41 *Legitimation*
identify with 70 *sich identifizieren mit*
ignore 98 *ignorieren, nicht beachten*
illustrate 57 *illustrieren, veranschaulichen*
image analysis 64 *Imageanalyse*
imagine 51 *sich vorstellen*
immigration stamp 34 *Einwanderungsstempel*
impact 54 *(Aus-)Wirkung, Eindruck*
implement 24 *einführen, -setzen*
imply 48 *andeuten, implizieren*
importer 89 *Importeur/in*
impression 21 *Eindruck*
impressive 50p *beeindruckend*
improve 79 *verbessern*
improvement 24 *Verbesserung*
in accordance with 48 *entsprechend, gemäß, in Übereinstimmung mit*
in addition to 41 *zusätzlich, neben*
in advance 49 *im Voraus, vorher*
in case 27t *falls*
in charge of 22 *verantwortlich für*
in detail 64 *im Detail*
in effect 85 *tatsächlich*
in fact 54 *tatsächlich*
in more depth 64 *intensiver, tiefer gehend*
in order to 10 *um zu*
in particular 33 *insbesondere*
in recognition of 70 *in Anerkennung der*
in regard to 27t *hinsichtlich, wegen*
in stock 29p *vorrätig*
in that case 26 *in diesem Fall*
in the light of 45 *im Hinblick auf*
in the longer term 79 *auf längere Sicht*
in this respect 74 *in dieser Hinsicht*
in time 58t *rechtzeitig*
in total 64 *(ins)gesamt*
in transit 94 *auf dem Transport*
inappropriate 86 *unpassend, unangemessen*
included 32 *inbegriffen*
incoming 22 *eingehend, ankommend*
incomplete 94 *unvollständig*
inconvenience 97 *Umstände*
incorporate 24 *enthalten, umfassen; einbauen*
increasingly 51 *zunehmend*
indeed 39 *tatsächlich, wirklich*
independently 24 *unabhängig*
indicate 39 *(an)zeigen, hinweisen auf*
indifferent 21 *gleichgültig*
indispensable 81 *unentbehrlich*
individual 64 *eigen, individuell*

industrial engineering 73 *Industrietechnik*
industrial waste 95 *Industrieabfall*
inexpensive 39 *preiswert*
influence 79 *Einfluss*
inform 18 *informieren, unterrichten*
infrastructure 10 *Infrastruktur*
ingredients 53 *Zutaten, Bestandteile*
inherent, be ~ within 103 *innewohnen, gehören zu*
initial 61 *erste*
inner 68 *innere*
innovation 24 *Neuerung, Innovation*
innovative 74 *innovativ*
input 24 *Einsatz*
inquire 101 *sich erkundigen nach, fragen nach*
inspection 22 *Kontrolle, Prüfung*
install 18 *installieren, einbauen*
instant 42 *sofort*
instead of 24 *(an)statt*
instruct 98 *anweisen*
instruction 81 *Unterrichtung*
instruction manual 70 *Bedienungsanleitung, Benutzerhandbuch*
insult 48 *Beleidigung*
integration 76 *Eingliederung, Integration*
intend 40 *beabsichtigen*
intense 61 *intensiv*
inter process inventory 103 *Zwischenlagerung*
interchangeable 70 *austauschbar*
interest 42 *Zins(en)*
interest rate 42 *Zinssatz*
interesting 25 *interessant*
interior design 70 *Innenausstattung*
interrupt 27 *unterbrechen*
interruption 59 *Unterbrechung, Störung*
interviewee 65 *Interviewpartner/in, Befragte/r*
intimidated 51 *eingeschüchtert*
intonation 54 *Tonfall, Satzmelodie, Intonation*
introductory 42 *Einführungs-*
introductory offer 85 *Einführungsangebot*
invention 79 *Erfindung*
inventory 103 *Inventar, Bestand, Lagerbestände*
inventory control 16 *Inventur*
invest 48 *investieren, anlegen*
investigate 96 *untersuchen*
investment 74 *Investition*
invoice 22 *Rechnung*
involve 22 *umfassen, mit sich bringen*
involved in 12t *beteiligt an*
involvement 73 *Beteiligung, Engagement*
irrevocable 89 *unwiderruflich*
issue 23t *ausstellen, versehen*
issuing bank 92 *akkreditivstellende Bank*
item 22 *Artikel*
itemized 42 *spezifiziert*

J

jet aircraft engine 81 *Düsentriebwerk*
jetliner 10 *Düsenflugzeug*
jewellery 68 *Schmuck*
jingle 55 *Erkennungsmelodie*
job satisfaction 14 *Zufriedenheit im Beruf, berufliche Befriedigung*
job-shop system 76 *Werkstattfertigung*
join 40 *sich anschließen, beitreten*
journal 18 *Zeitschrift*
justify 33 *rechtfertigen, verteidigen*

K

keen about 61 *scharf auf, sehr interessiert an*
keen on 48 *wild auf*
keep order 46 *für Ruhe und Ordnung sorgen*
keep sb busy 18 *jdn beschäftigen*
keep up with 10 *Schritt halten mit*
keyboard 78 *Tastatur, Keyboard*
keypad 79 *Tastenfeld*
Kind regards 32 *Mit freundlichen Grüßen*
knowledge 48 *Wissen, Kenntnis(se)*
knuckle 61 *(Finger-)Knöchel*

L

label 22 *beschriften, etikettieren*
labour 76 *Arbeit*
labour-intensive 76 *arbeitsintensiv*
lacking 59 *mangelnd, fehlend*
ladies and gentlemen 58t *Meine Damen und Herren*
launch 63 *einführen*
launch campaign 63 *Markteinführung*
lay down 92 *festsetzen, -legen*
layout 14 *Grundriss, Anordnung*
leadership 24 *Führung, Führerschaft, Leitung*
leading 43 *führend*
lead-time 103 *Laufzeit*
leather working 81 *Lederverarbeitung*
leave a lot to be desired 44 *viel zu wünschen übrig lassen*
legal 92 *gesetzlich, juristisch, legal*
legislation 101 *Gesetzgebung, gesetzliche Regelung(en)*
leisure 38 *Freizeit*
liability 92 *Haftung*
liaise with 22 *sich in Verbindung setzen mit*
life cycle 79 *Lebenszyklus, -erwartung*
lifespan 79 *Lebenszeit, -dauer*
lighten up 61 *aufheitern*
likely 21 *wahrscheinlich*
likewise 61 *ebenso, desgleichen*
line graph 57 *(Kurven-)Diagramm*
linked to 79 *verbunden mit*
lipstick 65 *Lippenstift*
liquid 74 *Flüssigkeit*
literally 70 *buchstäblich*
live up to 61 *gerecht werden*
load 32 *(ver)laden*
located 6 *sich befinden*

logically 61 *logisch*
long-range 61 *langfristig*
look forward to 30t *sich freuen auf*
look into sth 95 *etw untersuchen, etw prüfen*
look someone in the eye 51 *jdm in die Augen sehen*
loudspeaker 73 *Lautsprecher*
lounge 38 *Gesellschaftsraum, Salon*
lovely 7 *schön, reizend*
luxury 39 *Luxus*

M

machine 103 *maschinell herstellen/bearbeiten*
magnificent 50p *prächtig, großartig*
mailing 18 *Werbesendung*
mailing list 40 *Verteiler, Adressenliste*
mainstream 74 *Haupt-, vorherrschend*
maintain 70 *aufrechterhalten, einhalten*
maintenance 14 *Wartung, Instandhaltung*
make a comparison 12 *einen Vergleich anstellen*
make a deal 61 *einen Vertrag schließen*
make a decision 24 *eine Entscheidung treffen*
make a difference 52 *einen Unterschied machen*
make a prediction 52 *eine Vorhersage treffen*
make a reservation 37 *eine Reservierung vornehmen*
make a show of sth 48 *etw eingehend tun*
make an assessment of 61 *einschätzen, beurteilen*
make out 23t *ausstellen*
make sense 54 *sinnvoll sein*
make sure 22 *sicherstellen, sich vergewissern*
make up one's mind 46 *sich entschließen*
make use of sth 42 *etw einsetzen, verwenden*
malfunction 22 *Fehlfunktion*
manage 26 *(es) schaffen*
manageress 39 *Geschäftsführerin, Leiterin, Chefin*
managing director 12t *Generaldirektor/in*
manifestation 103 *Kennzeichen*
manners 70 *Umgangsformen, Manieren*
manual coating chamber 58 *Handbeschichtungskammer*
manufacturing 16 *Fertigung, Produktion*
manufacturing space 103 *Produktionsfläche*
market analysis 18 *Marktanalyse*
market potential 66 *Marktpotenzial*
market research 63 *Marktforschung*
market saturation 73 *Marktsättigung*
marketing campaign 63 *Werbekampagne*
mass 24 *Masse*
mass market 80 *Massenmarkt*
mass production 75t *Massenproduktion*
material flow 103 *Materialfluss*
maturity 79 *Ausgereiftheit*
max. 11 *maximal, Maximum*
maximize 82 *maximieren*
maximum 10 *höchste/r/s, maximal*
means of payment 41 *Zahlungsmittel*
meanwhile 7 *inzwischen*
mechanical engineer 81 *Maschinen(bau)techniker/in*
medical engineering 73 *Medizintechnik*
medium-sized 16 *mittelgroß*
melody 68 *Melodie*
memo 28 *Notiz, Vermerk*
memorable 61 *einprägsam*
mention 21 *erwähnen*
merchandise 67 *Waren(angebot)*
mere 68 *bloß*
merge with 7 *fusionieren mit*
merit 24 *Verdienst(e)*
methodical 75 *methodisch*
microelectronics 81 *Mikroelektronik*
mileage 40t *zurückgelegte Strecke, Kilometerzahl*
milling machine 78 *Fräsautomat*
milling tool 78 *Fräswerkzeug*
mind 30 *etw dagegen haben*
minimum age requirement 41 *erforderliches Mindestalter*
minutes 44 *Protokoll*
mobile communications equipment 72 *Mobilfunkgeräte*
mobile network 33 *Mobilnetz*
mobility 14 *Mobilität*
moderate 33 *einschränken*
modern living 33 *modernes Leben*
modest 39 *bescheiden*
modify 79 *verändern*
moisturizer 68 *Feuchtigkeitscreme*
monitoring system 23 *Überwachungssystem*
monotonous 54 *monoton*
monthly statement 42 *monatlicher (Konto-)Auszug*
moreover 70 *außerdem*
mould making 73 *Formenherstellung*
moulding process 73 *Formenherstellung*

N

nail 25 *Nagel*
nail polish 65 *Nagellack*
naturalness 68 *Natürlichkeit*
negligible 80 *geringfügig*
negotiate 43 *ver-, aushandeln*
negotiation 52 *Verhandlung*
negotiator 18 *Verhandler*
neighbourhood 21 *(Wohn-)Gegend, Nachbarschaft*
nervous system 33 *Nervensystem*
net total 30t *Nettosumme*
network 24 *Netz(werk)*
never mind 95 *macht nichts*
nevertheless 33 *trotzdem, dennoch*
new-found 51 *neu entdeckt*
newsletter 70 *Rundschreiben, Informationsblatt*
next door 58t *nebenan*
niche 79 *Nische*
nightmare 48 *Alptraum*
no longer 31 *nicht mehr*
not necessarily 43 *nicht unbedingt*
nowadays 70 *heutzutage*

nurture 73 *pflegen*

O

objection 45 *Einwand*
obligation 81 *Verpflichtung*
observation 54 *Beobachtung, Bemerkung*
observe 51 *beachten*
obsolete 79 *veraltet*
obvious 33 *offensichtlich*
obviously 10 *offensichtlich*
occasion 61 *Ereignis, Anlass*
occasional 42 *gelegentlich*
occur 102p *geschehen, vorkommen*
of inferior quality 95 *minderwertiger Qualität*
offended 21 *beleidigt*
official 67 *offiziell, amtlich*
OHP (overhead projector) 55 *Tageslicht-, Overheadprojektor*
OHT (overhead transparency) 55 *Overheadfolie*
on a daily basis 66 *täglich*
on average 8 *im Durchschnitt, durchschnittlich*
on balance 33 *per Saldo*
on behalf of 92 *im Namen von*
on board 89 *an Bord*
on demand 47t *nach Anforderung/Bedarf*
on meeting 9 *beim Treffen*
on parting 9 *beim Verabschieden*
on sale 29p *im Schlussverkauf*
on screen 81 *auf dem Bildschirm*
on site 22 *vor Ort*
on the basis of 66 *auf der Basis von, aufgrund*
on the other hand 64 *andererseits*
on the part of 81 *auf Seiten des*
on the premises 39 *im Haus*
on the right track 74 *auf dem richtigen Weg*
on time 18 *pünktlich*
onboard-system 14 *Bordsystem*
open system architecture 81 *Architektur mit offenem System*
opening hours 29p *Geschäfts-, Öffnungszeiten*
open-top container 32 *Container ohne Dach*
operate 51 *betreiben*
operation 7 *Betrieb*
operational 14 *Betriebs-*
operational time 103 *Betriebszeit*
opponent 62 *Gegner/in, Gegenüber*
opportunity 7 *Gelegenheit*
optimism 68 *Optimismus*
option 42 *Option, Wahlrecht*
optionally 58 *wahlweise*
order acknowledgement 83 *Auftragsbestätigung*
order form 87 *Auftrags-, Bestellformular*
order processing 16 *Auftragsabwicklung*
organic 95 *organisch*
organization chart 19 *Organisationsstruktur*
orientation 70 *Orientierung*
other than 52 *außer*
otherwise 37p *sonst*
outbound 36 *Hin-*
outcome 52 *Resultat, Ergebnis*
outdated 24 *überholt, veraltet*
outdoor activity 68 *Tätigkeit im Freien*
outer 68 *äußere*
outlet 42 *Verkaufsstelle*
outline 75 *Überblick, Skizze*
output 24 *Produktion(smenge), Ausstoß*
outstanding 98 *ausstehend*
over the counter 42 *am Schalter*
overall 11 *Gesamt-, total*
overcrowding 10 *Überfüllung*
overlook 66 *übersehen*
overproduction 103 *Überproduktion*
overview 12t *Überblick*
overwhelmed 58t *überwältigt*

P

PA 34 *persönliche/r Assistent/in*
pace 24 *Tempo*
packaging 68 *Verpackung*
packing 88 *Verpackung*
painstakingly 61 *sorgfältig, gewissenhaft*
pallet 32 *Palette*
paragraph 48 *Abschnitt, kurzer Artikel*
paralleling 81 *parallel zu*
participant 47 *Teilnehmer/in*
particularly 30 *besonders*
partnership 16 *Partnerschaft*
pass one's test 41 *die Fahrprüfung machen*
pass through 75t *durchlaufen*
passenger capacity 10 *Platz für Passagiere*
passenger load 11 *Passagierzahl*
passenger numbers 10 *Fluggastzahlen*
pay attention to 70 *beachten*
payload 10 *Nutzlast*
payment 23t *Zahlung, Auszahlung*
PC videophone 51 *Computerbildtelefon*
PC-based 51 *auf Computern basierend*
peak 34 *Spitze(nzeit)*
peak-level 80 *Höchststand*
pension 81 *Rente, Pension*
per capita income 57 *Pro-Kopf-Einkommen*
per 40 *pro, per*
perform 74 *durch-, ausführen*
performance 81 *Leistung(en)*
period of time 9 *Zeitraum, -spanne*
personal 21 *persönlich*
personal assistant 7 *(persönliche/r) Assistent/in*
personnel department 23t *Personalabteilung*
personnel file 23t *Personalakte*
persuade 54 *überzeugen, überreden*
petrochemical 34 *petrochemisches Erzeugnis*
phobia 58t *Phobie*
pick up on sth 54 *etw aufgreifen*
pie chart 53 *Kreisdiagramm*

pine **29p** *Kiefer*
placement **66** *Aufstellung*
planning **61** *Planung*
play a part **79** *eine Rolle spielen*
pleased to meet you **7** *es freut mich, Sie kennen zu lernen*
plentiful **48** *reichlich*
plenty of **39** *viel, reichlich*
pm **37** *nachmittags/abends*
point out **46t** *hinweisen auf, aufmerksam machen auf*
polite **30** *höflich*
politeness **30** *Höflichkeit*
political **92** *politisch*
population **33** *Bevölkerung*
portfolio **74** *Bestand*
pose a danger **33** *eine Gefahr darstellen*
possibly **48** *möglicherweise*
postpone **45** *verschieben*
posture **59** *(Körper-)Haltung*
post-war period **68** *Nachkriegszeit*
potential **18** *möglich, potenziell*
potentially **33** *potentiell*
pour **74** *gießen*
powder coating **58** *Pulverbeschichtung*
practical **51** *praktisch*
praise **61** *Lob*
precisely **89** *genau*
precision **57** *Genauigkeit*
predict **11** *vorhersagen*
prediction **10** *Vorhersage*
premises **32** *Betrieb(sgelände)*
premium **40t** *Prämie*
preparation **50** *Vorbereitung*
presence **70** *Anwesenheit*
presentation skills **53** *Vorführfertigkeiten*
press advertising **66** *Werbung in der Presse*
press conference **74** *Pressekonferenz*
press release **74** *Pressemitteilung*
prestige **70** *Prestige*
prestige project **10** *Prestigeprojekt*
pre-treat **58** *vorbehandeln*
pretty much **64** *ziemlich genau*
prevail **68** *(vor)herrschen*
pride os on **40** *stolz sein auf*
principle **24** *Grundsatz, Prinzip*
prior **38** *vorherig*
procedure **36t** *Verfahren*
proceed **18** *verfahren, vorgehen*
process **23t** *bearbeiten*
processing **74** *Be-, Verarbeitung*
product launch **17** *Produkteinführung*
product line **68** *Produktlinie*
product management **16** *Produktmanagement*
production line **10** *Fließ-, Fertigungsband*
production plant **44** *Produktionsstätte*
production process **7** *Produktionsprozess*
production unit **75** *Produktionseinheit*
production volume **74** *Produktionsumfang*
productive **70** *produktiv*
productivity **14** *Produktivität*
profession **81** *Beruf*
professional **56** *professionell*
profitability **82** *Profitabilität*
profitable **79** *gewinnbringend, erfolgreich*
progress **74** *Fortschritt/e*
projector **55** *Projektor*
prolonged **33** *ausgedehnt*
prominent **61** *hervorstechend*
promote **18** *anpreisen, bewerben*
promotion **24** *Beförderung*
promotional material **23t** *Werbematerial*
promotional video **55** *Werbevideo*
prompt **37** *Stichwort*
promptly **98** *unverzüglich, prompt*
pronounce **66** *aussprechen*
properly **22** *richtig, korrekt*
proposal **45** *Vorschlag*
propose **44** *vorschlagen*
pros and cons **24** *Für und Wider*
prototype **47t** *Prototyp*
protracted **61** *langwierig*
provide **38** *bieten*
provided that **92** *vorausgesetzt, dass*
provider **91** *Lieferant, Anbieter*
provisionally **36t** *provisorisch, vorläufig*
proximity **40** *Nähe*
psychiatrist **58t** *Psychiater/in*
public **12** *Öffentlichkeit*
public relations **17** *Öffentlichkeitsarbeit*
public transport **33** *öffentliche Verkehrsmittel*
publication **74** *Veröffentlichung*
puff out **59** *aufblasen*
pull-out **84** *herausziehbar*
punctuality **59** *Pünktlichkeit*
purchase order **83** *Bestellung*
purchase **42** *(Ein-)Kauf*
purchasing **16** *Einkauf*
purity **68** *Reinheit*
purpose **58t** *Zweck, Ziel*
pursue **74** *verfolgen*
put into practice **75** *in die Praxis umsetzen*
put off **46** *verschieben, zurückhalten*
put sb through **26** *jdn verbinden, durchstellen*
pyramidal hierarchy **24** *pyramidenförmige Hierarchie*

Q

qualification **14** *Qualifikation, Abschluss einer Ausbildung*
quantity **12t** *Menge*
query **29** *Anfrage*
questionnaire **24** *Fragebogen*
quip **51** *witzeln, scherzen*
quotation **40** *Angebot*

R

radiation 33 *Strahlung*
radical 70 *radikal*
rail terminal 32 *Bahnstation*
rail transport 32 *Bahntransport*
raised 59 *hochgezogen*
ramble on 54 *abschweifen*
range from 39 *reichen von*
range 10 *Reichweite, Reihe, Auswahl*
rank 43 *zählen zu*
rap 61 *klopfen (mit)*
rapport 48 *(enges) Verhältnis*
rate 39 *(ein)schätzen*
rave about 58t *schwärmen von*
raw part 78 *Rohling*
reach a compromise 45 *einen Kompromiss finden*
react 21 *reagieren*
reaction 66 *Reaktion*
readiness 62 *Bereitschaft*
reasonable 40t *vernünftig*
reassurance 97 *Versicherung*
receipt 47t *Empfang, Erhalt*
receiver 27 *(Telefon-)Hörer*
recently 52 *neulich, kürzlich*
reception desk 16 *Rezeption, Empfang*
receptionist 16t *Empfangsdame, -chef*
recognition 68 *Wiedererkennen*
recommendation 39 *Empfehlung*
recruit 75t *neue/r Angestellte/r, Personal*
rectify 87 *richtigstellen*
recycle 95 *recyceln, (wieder) aufbereiten*
redeem 42 *ab-, einlösen*
ref 84 *(Akten-)Zeichen*
refer back to sth 36 *zurückgehen zu etw*
refer to 10 *sich beziehen auf*
reflect 68 *reflektieren, wiedergeben*
refrain from 61 *unterlassen*
refrigerator 70 *Kühlschrank*
refuel 12 *auftanken*
refund 42 *Rückzahlung, (Rück-)Erstattung*
refuse 27t *ablehnen, sich weigern*
region 81 Gebiet, Gegend
register 22 *registrieren, aufnehmen*
reinforce 70 verstärken
reintegrate 95 *wieder integrieren*
rejection 59 *Ablehnung*
related 51 *verwandt*
related to 61 *mit Bezug auf*
relationship 52 *Beziehung, Verhältnis*
relaxed 39t *entspannt, aufgelockert*
relevant 32 *relevant, entsprechend, wichtig*
reliable 51 *zuverlässig*
reluctant, be ~ to do 61 *ungern tun*
rely on 39 *sich verlassen auf*
remain 68 *bleiben*
reminder 23t *Mahnung*
remittance advice 83 *Überweisungsbenachrichtigung*
rental car 40 *Mietwagen*
reorder 23t *nachbestellen*
reorganize 74 *umorganisieren*
repair 22 *reparieren*
rephrase 31 *umformulieren*
replace 22 *ersetzen, austauschen*
replacement 95 *Ersatz, Austausch*
representative 45 *Vertreter/in*
reputation 64 *Ruf*
requirement 22 *Anforderung*
research 62 *Nachforschung(en)*
reserve for 61 *reservieren für, vorbehalten*
resident 40 *Einwohner/in*
resonance 66 *Resonanz*
respective 89 *jeweilig*
respond 9 *reagieren (auf), antworten*
response 11 *Reaktion, Antwort*
responsible 22 *verantwortlich, zuständig*
rest assured 88 *versichert sein*
result from 97 *sich ergeben aus*
retailing 75t *Einzelhandel(sverkauf)*
retain 69 *(bei)behalten*
reuse 95 *wieder verwenden*
reverse side 61 *Rückseite*
revise 45 *revidieren, überarbeiten*
ring back 36 *zurückrufen*
ring chart 57 *Ringdiagramm*
rise 54 *Heben*
risk 33 *Risiko*
risk-taking 61 *Risikobereitschaft*
road transport 32 *Straßentransport*
robot 75t *Roboter*
roll off 10 *rollen vom*
romance 68 *Romantik*
rough 17 *Roh(skizze)*
roughly 102p *ungefähr*
route 14 *Route, Strecke*
routine task 23t *Routinearbeit*
row 12 *Reihe*
rude 21 *unhöflich, rücksichtslos*
rule of thumb 57 *Faustregel*
run smoothly 18 *glatt verlaufen*
run through 47t *überfliegen, durchgehen*
rush in 12 *hereinstürmen*

S

salary 21 *Gehalt*
sale bargain 42 *günstiges Angebot, Sonderangebot*
sales 16 *Verkauf*
sales director 16 *Verkaufsleiter/in*
sales enquiry 83 *Verkaufsanfrage*
sales figures 53 *Absatzzahlen*
sales literature 18 *(Verkaufs-)Prospekt(e), Kataloge*
sales representative 18 *(Handels-)Vertreter/in*
salesperson 29p *Verkäufer/in*
satisfaction 88 *Zufriedenheit*

saturated 70 *gesättigt*
savings 14 *Ersparnisse*
scalability 81 *Ausbaufähigkeit*
scepticism 59 *Skepsis*
scheduling 14 *Zeitplanung*
scientific 33 *(natur)wissenschaftlich*
seasonal 65 *saisonbedingt, Saison-*
sector 79 *Sektor, Bereich*
secure 68 *sichern, festigen*
security 92 *Sicherheit*
see to sth 95 *sich um etw kümmern*
seek 62 *suchen*
select 94 *auswählen*
selection 40 *Auswahl*
selective 66 *wählerisch, selektiv*
self confidence 59 *Selbstvertrauen*
self-confident 68 *selbstsicher, -bewusst*
send out 18 *verschicken, versenden*
senior 22 *vorgesetzt, leitend*
seniority 24 *Dienstalter*
sense of belonging 71 *Zugehörigkeitsgefühl*
sense of identity 70 *Identitätsgefühl*
sensitive 61 *empfindlich, sensibel*
separate 11 *trennen*
sequence 93 *Reihenfolge*
serial number 23t *Seriennummer*
series 65 *Serie, Reihe*
serve 7 *bedienen*
service point 40 *Kundendienststelle*
service station 43 *Tankstelle*
set off 39 *aufbrechen*
set up 74 *aufbauen, einrichten*
settle 18 *erledigen, behandeln, begleichen*
settlement 84 *(Be-)Zahlung, Begleichung*
sewage works 95 *Klärwerk*
shade 58 *(Farb-)Ton, Schattierung*
share 12 *(Geschäfts-)Anteil, Aktie*
shareholder 12 *Aktionär/in, Anteilseigner/in*
sheet (of paper) 17 *Blatt (Papier)*
shelf 70 *Regal*
shelf unit 84 *Regalelement*
shift 103 *Schicht*
ship building 6 *Schiff(s)bau*
shipment 96 *Ladung, Lieferung*
shipping document 22 *Versand-, Frachtpapier*
shoemaking 81 *Schuhmacherei*
shop window 67 *Schaufenster*
shorten 74 *kürzen*
shortly 27 *in Kürze*
significant 14 *erheblich, spürbar*
significantly 74 *erheblich, spürbar*
signware 43 *Beschriftung, Schriftzüge*
similarity 14 *Ähnlichkeit*
simplicity 57 *Einfachheit*
sincere 97 *aufrichtig*
single piece flow 103 *Einzelstückproduktion*
single-aisled 14 *mit einem Gang*
site 6 *Stelle, Platz*
situated 38 *gelegen*
sketch 17 *Skizze*
skilled 76 *ausgebildet, Fach-*
skin type 68 *Hauttyp*
skull 33 *Schädel*
slash 30 *Schrägstrich*
sleep disorder 33 *Schlafstörung*
slide 59 *Dia*
slogan 61 *(Werbe-)Spruch*
so-called 7 *sogenannt*
social security 81 *Sozialversicherung, -abgaben*
social security payment 23t *Sozialabgabe(n)*
socialize 61 *gesellschaftlich (miteinander) verkehren, sich unterhalten, auf Parties gehen*
solar power generation 34 *Erzeugung von Sonnenenergie*
sold out 29p *ausverkauft*
solder 23t *löten*
solicitor 45 *Anwalt/Anwältin*
solid 75t *fest*
solution 10 *Lösung*
solve 10 *lösen*
some kind of 30t *irgendeine/n*
sophisticated 68 *raffiniert*
sort 23t *sortieren*
sort out 27t *klären, lösen*
South Coast 36 *Südküste*
spare parts 14 *Ersatzteile*
special offer 40 *Sonderangebot*
specialise in 38 *sich spezialisieren auf*
specialized 24 *spezialisiert*
specific 45 *speziell, spezifisch*
specification 47 *Spezifikation, Aufstellung*
speech 54 *Rede(weise)*
spending 42 *Ausgaben*
spirit 68 *Geist*
splendid 38 *ausgezeichnet*
splintered 96 *gesplittert*
split 73 *aufteilen*
spoil 48 *verderben*
spontaneity 61 *Spontaneität*
spontaneous 61 *spontan*
spray 58 *Spray*
spread 24 *verteilen*
stage 56 *Phase, Abschnitt, Stadium*
stand for 68 *stehen für*
stand out from the crowd 70 *aus der Menge herausragen*
standardize 68 *standardisieren, normieren*
standpoint 46 *Standpunkt*
start legal proceedings 98 *gerichtliche Schritte einleiten*
statement 55 *Aussage, Erklärung*
static 55 *statisch*
statistical analysis 66 *statistische Analyse*
status-conscious 48 *statusbewusst*

steal **54** *stehlen*
step forward **81** *vorangehen*
stock room **16** *Lager(raum)*
stock **14** *Vorrat, Lager(bestand)*
storage space **103** *Lagerraum*
stored **103** *gelagert*
stoving process **58** *Trocknung (in der Trockenkammer)*
straight away **40t** *sofort, auf der Stelle*
strategic **74** *strategisch*
strategy **14** *Strategie*
strictly **92** *strikt, genau*
stroke **59** *streicheln*
studio system **51** *Studiosystem*
style **38** *Stil*
subassemble **103** *vormontieren*
subcomponent **103** *Unterteil*
submit **64** *einreichen*
subscriber **33** *Abonnent/in*
subsidiary **12t** *Tochtergesellschaft*
substantial **45** *wesentlich*
substantially **14** *wesentlich, beträchtlich*
substitute **96** *Ersatz*
succeed in doing sth **74** *mit etw Erfolg haben*
such as **21** *wie zum Beispiel*
sufficient **22** *ausreichend, genügend, genug*
suggestion **46** *Vorschlag*
suitable **21** *geeignet, passend*
suite **38** *Suite*
sum up **47t** *zusammenfassen*
summarize **23** *zusammenfassen*
summary **39** *Zusammenfassung*
summer house **25** *Sommerhaus*
sunbathing **68** *Sonnenbaden*
superb **38** *hervorragend*
superior **96** *Vorgesetzte/r*
supplement **81** *ergänzen*
supplier **12t** *Zulieferer*
supply **12t** *liefern*
supply and monitoring **78** *Lieferung und Überwachung*
suppose **34** *glauben, vermuten*
surface treatment **73** *Oberflächenbehandlung*
survey **64** *(Meinungs-)Umfrage*
survive **79** *überleben*
swap **11** *tauschen*
switch **12t** *Schalter*
switch on to sth **51** *zu etw übergehen*
switchboard **85** *(Telefon-)Zentrale*
system component **73** *Systemteil*
systematic **74** *systematisch*

T

tabletop **61** *Tischplatte*
take advantage of **42** *ausnützen*
take care of **7** *sich kümmern um*
take hold of **68** *ergreifen*
take into account **46t** *in Betracht ziehen, berücksichtigen*
take into consideration **69** *berücksichtigen*
take notes **12** *(sich) Notizen machen*
take notice of sth **65** *etw beachten*
take one's lunch break **31** *Mittagspause machen*
take over **12t** *übernehmen*
take place **7** *stattfinden*
take precautions **33** *Vorsichtsmaßnahmen ergreifen*
take sides **50p** *Partei ergreifen*
take seriously **22** *ernst nehmen*
take the leading role **12** *die Führung übernehmen*
take up **51** *übergehen zu*
takeoff weight **11** *Startgewicht*
takt time **103** *Taktzeit*
talented **81** *begabt, talentiert*
target group **64** *Zielgruppe*
target **66** *zum Ziel haben*
task **81** *Aufgabe*
tax **81** *Steuer*
tax form **23t** *Steuerformular*
team spirit **71** *Teamgeist*
technical department **16** *technische Abteilung*
technician **18** *Techniker/in*
technique **46t** *Methode, Technik*
temperature **58** *Temperatur*
tend to **39** *neigen zu, tendieren zu*
tendency **79** *Tendenz*
tense **59** *(an)gespannt*
term **24** *Ausdruck*
terminology **65** *Terminologie*
terms and conditions **44** *allgemeine Geschäftsbedingungen*
terms of trade **46t** *Geschäfts-, Handelsbedingungen*
testicular **33** *Hoden-*
textiles **6** *Textilien*
thanks to **81** *dank*
the continent **40** *der (europäische) Kontinent*
the following **8** *Folgenden*
theme **69** *Thema*
theory **33** *Theorie*
through, be ~ **44** *fertig sein*
throughout **38** *die ganze Zeit hindurch*
thunderstorm **27t** *Gewitter*
timber **25** *(Bau-)Holz*
time difference **28** *Zeitunterschied*
time limit **54** *Zeitlimit*
timeline **69** *Zeitachse*
timetable **44** *Fahr-, Stundenplan*
timing **88** *(Festlegung der) Lieferzeit*
to date **8** *bis dato*
tolerate **61** *tolerieren*
tone **54** *Ton*
tool **23t** *Werkzeug*
tool making **73** *Werkzeugherstellung*
tool shop **75t** *Werkzeugausgabe*
total **30t** *Gesamtsumme*

total cover 40t *volle Deckung*
touch, be in ~ 28 *in Verbindung bleiben*
trade fair 23t *Handelsmesse*
trade terms 85 *Lieferbedingungen*
traders bank 92 *Handelsbank*
trading partner 83 *Handelspartner*
traditional 24 *traditionell*
tradition-bound 81 *traditionsgebunden*
trainee 53 *Auszubildende/r, Praktikant/in*
trainer 53 *Trainer/in, Ausbilder/in*
training characteristics 14 *Trainingseigenschaften*
training course 14 *Lehrgang*
trait 61 *Eigenschaft, Charakterzug*
transfer 14 *überweisen*
transform 68 *verwandeln*
translation 18 *Übersetzung*
transmitter 12t *Sender*
transparency 59 *Folie*
transparent 75t *durchsichtig*
transport 93 *befördern, transportieren*
transport aircraft 7 *Transportflugzeug*
travel arrangements 34 *Reisepläne*
treat 33 *behandeln*
treatment 70 *Behandlung, Umgang*
trend 65 *Trend*
trendy 64 *modisch, schick*
troubleshooter 22 *Störungssucher/in, Vermittler/in*
try out 66 *(aus)probieren*
turbine blade 81 *Turbinenschaufel*
turn off 55 *aus-, abschalten*
turn out to be 79 *sich herausstellen*
turnover 12t *Umsatz*
typeface 68 *Schriftbild, -zug*

U

ultimate 74 *höchst, endgültig*
unambiguous 88 *unzweideutig, eindeutig*
unbreakable 79 *unzerbrechlich*
unchangeable 61 *unabänderlich*
unclear 85 *unklar*
under review 74 *zu besprechen*
undergo 70 *erfahren, erleben*
underscore 30 *unterstreichen*
undertake 47 *sich verpflichten*
undertaking 92 *Verpflichtung*
unfinished 23t *unfertig*
unforeseen circumstances 98 *unvorhergesehene Umstände*
unified 70 *einheitlich*
uniform 70 *gleichförmig*
unimpressed 61 *nicht beeindruckt*
unintentionally 61 *unabsichtlich, unbeabsichtigt*
unique 16 *einzigartig*
university degree 61 *akademischer Grad*
university qualification 48 *akademischer Grad*
unlike 11 *anders als, im Gegensatz zu*
unlimited 39t *unbegrenzt*
unnecessary 61 *unnötig*
unpack 96 *auspacken*
unprofessional 86 *unprofessionell*
unreceptive 61 *unzugänglich*
unsaleable 96 *unverkäuflich*
unsolicited 61 *unverlangt, unaufgefordert, ungebeten*
untreated 30t *unbehandelt*
unwilling 62 *unwillig*
up to 12 *bis zu*
up to sb, be ~ 22 *dafür verantwortlich sein*
update 22 *aktualisieren, auf den neuesten Stand bringen, letzter Stand*
upon inspection 27t *nach Prüfung*
upstream process 103 *nach oben gerichteter (Produktions-)Prozess*
urgent 26 *dringend, eilig*
usable 79 *nützlich*
used to 48 *gewöhnt an*
user manual 22 *Benutzerhandbuch*
utilize 67 *einsetzen, nutzen*

V

valid 41 *gültig*
valuable 51 *wertvoll*
varied 24 *unterschiedlich, vielfältig*
variety 12t *Vielfalt*
various 22 *verschiedene*
vary 54 *wechseln, variieren*
vast 66 *riesig, gewaltig*
vehicle 40 *Fahrzeug*
vehicle manufacturing 6 *Fahrzeugproduktion*
versus 24 *gegen(über)*
via 18 *über, durch, per*
vibrant 38 *vibrierend, aufregend*
vice versa 62 *umgekehrt*
videoconferencing 51 *Videokonferenzen (abhalten)*
viewpoint 79 *Standpunkt*
virtual 51 *virtuell*
virtually 14 *praktisch, nahezu*
virtue 51 *Tugend*
visual 55 *visuelles Medium, Bildmaterial*
visual aid 53 *Anschauungsmaterial*
vital 48 *wichtig, wesentlich*
volume 45 *Volumen, Umfang*
vulnerable, to be ~ 33 *ausgesetzt sein*

W

waggon 32 *Wagen*
want some money off 86 *einen Rabatt/Nachlass verlangen*
warehouse 27t *Lagerhalle, -haus*
warehousing system 23t *Lagerhaltungssystem*
warning 100 *(Vor-)Warnung*
waste product 95 *Abfallprodukt*
web page 37 *Webseite*
weld 103 *schweißen*
well done 53 *gut gemacht*

well lit 75t *hell erleuchtet*
well-equipped 38 *gut ausgestattet*
well-informed 61 *gut informiert*
willing 62 *gewillt, bereit*
window frame 27t *Fensterrahmen*
wingspan 11 *(Flügel-)Spannweite*
wise 33 *weise, klug*
within arm's reach 71 *in Reichweite*
wood flooring 75t *Holzfußboden*
work station 84 *Computer-Arbeitsplatz*
workload 14 *Arbeitsbelastung*
work-piece 58 *Werkstück*
workshop 16 *Werkstatt, Workshop*
workshop session 55 *Werkstattgespräch*
worldwide 7 *weltweit*
worth 8 *wert, im Wert von*
written correspondence 22 *schriftliche Korrespondenz*

Y

yours sincerely 84 *Mit freundlichen Grüßen*
youthfulness 68 *Jugendlichkeit*

BASIC WORD LIST

Diese Liste enthält ca. 850 Grundwörter, die in *Industry Matters* als bekannt vorausgesetzt werden.
Nicht aufgeführt, jedoch vorausgesetzt, sind einige elementare Wörter, wie Pronomen, Zahlen, Wochentage sowie Wörter, die im Englischen und Deutschen die gleiche Bedeutung haben, wie z. B. *monitor*, *restaurant* und *hotel*.

a bit ein wenig, etwas
a lot of viel, sehr
ability Fähigkeit, Können
able to fähig zu, in der Lage zu
about über, etwa, um
above über, oben
abroad im/ins Ausland
across (hin)über, durch
action Aktion, Handlung
active aktiv, tätig
additional zusätzlich
address Adresse, adressieren
advantage Vorteil, -zug
ad(vert) Inserat, Anzeige
advice (guter) Rat
Africa Afrika
after nach, nachdem
afternoon Nachmittag
afterwards nachher, danach
again wieder
age Zeitalter, Alter
ago vor
agree zustimmen, sich einigen
ahead vorne, voraus
air Luft
airline Fluggesellschaft
airport Flughafen
alarm Alarm(anlage)
all alle, alles
almost fast, beinahe
alone allein(e)
already schon, bereits
alright in Ordnung
also auch, außerdem
American amerikanisch
among in(mitten), zwischen
amongst unter
angry zornig, ärgerlich
another noch eine/r/s, ein/e andere/r/s
answer Antwort, (be)antworten
anybody jemand, jeder
anyone jemand, jede/r
anything etwas, alles
anyway jedenfalls, sowieso
apart getrennt, entfernt
apartment Wohnung
appear erscheinen, auftreten
Arabic arabisch
architecture Architektur
area Fläche, Gebiet, Bereich
Argentine argentinisch
around herum, ungefähr
arrive ankommen
article Artikel, Gegenstand
Asia Asien
Asian asiatisch
ask fragen, bitten
assistant Assistent/in
at the moment im Augenblick
attempt Versuch, versuchen
attend teilnehmen an
audience Publikum, Zuhörer
Australia Australien
Australian australisch
automobile Auto(mobil)
autumn Herbst
available erhältlich, lieferbar
back Rücken, zurück
basis Basis, Grundlage
be sein
beach Strand
beauty Schönheit
because weil
become werden
bedroom Schlafzimmer
beer Bier
before vor(her), bevor
begin anfangen
behind hinter, hinten
Belgian belgisch
believe glauben
belong to (dazu) gehören
below unter, unten
between zwischen
beverage Getränk
biro Kugelschreiber
biscuit Keks
black schwarz
blue blau
border Grenze
boss Chef/in
both beide
bottle Flasche
box Kiste, Schachtel, Karton
Brazil Brasilien
break Pause, (zer)brechen
breakfast Frühstück
breast Brust
brief kurz
Britain Großbritannien
British britisch
Briton Brite/Britin
build (auf)bauen
building Gebäude
business card (Visiten-)Karte
business class Businessklasse
business letter Geschäftsbrief
business person Geschäftsperson
business travel Geschäftsreisen
busy beschäftigt, besetzt
but aber, sondern
buy kaufen
buyer Käufer/in, Einkäufer/in
call Anruf, (an)rufen
can dürfen, können
cancel streichen
capital Hauptstadt
car Auto
car park Parkplatz, -haus
car parking Parkplätze
card Karte
carry tragen
cartoon Karikatur
cash Bargeld
catalogue Katalog
cause Ursache, Grund, verursachen
CD player CD-Spieler
celebrate feiern
cell(ular) phone Mobiltelefon
centre Mitte, Zentrum
certain bestimmt
certainly sicherlich, gewiss
chair Stuhl
chance Gelegenheit
change (sich) ändern
chapter Kapitel
chat sich unterhalten
cheap billig
check (über)prüfen
chemicals Chemikalien
cheque Scheck
child, children Kind, Kinder
chin Kinn
Chinese chinesisch, Chinesisch
choice Wahl, Auswahl
choose (aus)wählen, (sich) aussuchen

circle Kreis
city (Groß-)Stadt
class (Schul-)Klasse
clear klar, deutlich, abfertigen
close eng, nah(e)
close (ab)schließen
closed geschlossen
clothes Kleidung, Kleider
coal Kohle
coffee Kaffee
coffee break Kaffeepause
colleague Kollege, Kollegin
collect abholen
colour Farbe
come kommen
come in hereinkommen
comfortable bequem
comma Komma
comment Kommentar
common gemeinsam
company Unternehmen, Firma
complete vollständig
consider ansehen
contact sich wenden an
content Inhalt
context Kontext
continue (sich) fortsetzen
control kontrollieren, beherrschen
conversation Unterhaltung
Copenhagen Kopenhagen
copy Kopie, kopieren
correct berichtigen
cost Kosten
country Land, Staat
couple Paar
course Kurs, Lehrgang
cover Abdeckung
create (er)schaffen
credit card Kreditkarte
criticize kritisieren
culture Kultur
customer Kunde, Kundin
cut schneiden
daily täglich
dangerous gefährlich
Danish dänisch, Dänisch
date Datum, Termin
dear liebe/r
decrease abnehmen
define definieren
definitely bestimmt
describe beschreiben
description Beschreibung
design Entwurf, Konstruktion
desk (Schreib-)Tisch
detail Einzelheit, Detail
develop (sich) entwickeln
dialogue Dialog
dictionary Wörterbuch
difference Unterschied
different verschieden
difficult schwer, schwierig
difficulty Schwierigkeit
digital digital
dining Speisen
dinner (Abend-)Essen
direct gerade, unmittelbar
director Direktor/in, Leiter/in
disadvantage Nachteil
disagree widersprechen
discuss besprechen
do tun, machen
document Dokument, Papier
door Tür
double doppelt
doubt Zweifel, (be)zweifeln
draw ziehen, zeichnen
drink Getränk, trinken
drive fahren
dry trocken
during während
each jede/r/s
each other einander
earn verdienen
east Osten, Ost-
easy einfach, leicht
economy class Touristenklasse
effect (Aus-)Wirkung
eg z.B.
Egypt Ägypten
Egyptian ägyptisch
either ... or entweder ... oder
email E-Mail
email address E-Mail-Adresse
employee Angestellte/r
end Ende, Schluss
engineer Ingenieur/in, Techniker/in
English englisch, Englisch
enjoy genießen
enough genug
enter betreten, eingeben
equipment Geräte, Einrichtung
especially besonders
Europe Europa
European Europäer/in, europäisch
even sogar
evening Abend
every jede/r/s
everyday alltäglich
everyone jede/r/s, alle
everything alles
exactly exakt, genau
excellent ausgezeichnet
exciting aufregend
exercise Übung
exercise book (Schul-)Heft
expect erwarten
expensive teuer
experience Erfahrung
expert Fachmann/frau
explain erklären
expression Ausdruck
extra zusätzlich
eyebrow Augenbraue
factory Fabrik
fair Messe
fall (hin)fallen
famous berühmt
fashion Mode
fashionable modisch, modern
father Vater
feel (sich) fühlen
few wenige
fill in ausfüllen
final endgültig
find finden, suchen
find out herausfinden
fine gut, Geldstrafe
finished fertig
Finnish finnisch, Finnisch
firm Firma, fest
first floor erste Etage
first name Vorname
first of all zu(aller)erst, zunächst
fit passen (zu), installieren
flat flach, Wohnung
floor Etage, (Fuß-)Boden
fly fliegen
food Essen, Nahrung
for für
for example zum Beispiel
forget vergessen
form Form, Formular
formal formell, förmlich
fountain pen Füllfederhalter
France Frankreich
free frei, gratis
French französisch, Französisch
frequent häufig
frequently oft, häufig
friend Freund/in
friendly freundlich
from von, aus
fuel Treibstoff
full voll
further weitere
future Zukunft, (zu)künftig
garden Garten
general allgemein
gently leicht, sanft
German deutsch, Deutsch
Germany Deutschland
get holen, bekommen
get bored sich langweilen
gift Geschenk
give geben
glad froh
globally global
globe Erdball
go gehen

goal Tor, Ziel
good morning guten Morgen
good gut
great groß(artig)
green grün
greet (be)grüßen
ground Boden, Erde
ground floor Erdgeschoss
group Gruppe
grow wachsen
guess (er)raten
gym Turnhalle
half Hälfte, halb
hand Hand
happen geschehen
happy glücklich
hard schwer, hart
hate hassen
have haben, nehmen, essen, einladen
head Kopf
health Gesundheit
hear hören
heavy schwer
height Höhe, Größe
hello Hallo
help oneself to sth sich mit etw bedienen
help Hilfe, helfen
helpful hilfreich, nützlich
here hier
high hoch
hint Hinweis
hire mieten, leihen
history Geschichte
hold halten (für)
holiday Ferien, Urlaub
holiday season Urlaubszeit
home Heim, Haus
honest ehrlich
hope hoffen
hour Stunde
house Haus
how wie
however jedoch, aber
Hungary Ungarn
husband (Ehe-)Mann
ice cream Eis(krem)
idea Idee, Gedanke
identical identisch
identify with sich identifizieren mit
image Image, Bild
immediate unmittelbar
immediately sofort, umgehend
in front of vor
in other words anders ausgedrückt
increase Erhöhung, erhöhen
industrial Industrie-, industriell
industry Industrie, Gewerbe, Branche
informal informell
information Auskunft, Information(en)
information technology (IT) Informationstechnologie
insurance Versicherung
interview Interview, befragen
introduce (oneself) (sich) vorstellen
introduction Vorstellung
invite einladen
Ireland Irland
iron Eisen
Italian italienisch, Italienisch
Italy Italien
Japanese japanisch, Japanisch
jaw Kiefer, Backe
joke scherzen
journey Reise, Fahrt
just nur, gerade, genau
keep (be)halten
key Schlüssel, Taste
kid Kind
kind nett, Art, Sorte
know kennen, wissen
large groß
last letzte/r/s, dauern
late spät
later on später
lead (to) führen (zu)
leave (ver)lassen
left links
left, on the ~ auf der linken Seite
length Länge
let erlauben, (zu)lassen
letter Buchstabe, Brief
life Leben
light Licht, hell, leicht
like mögen, gern haben
list Liste, auflisten
listen to an-, zuhören
listener Zuhörer/in
little klein, wenig
live wohnen, leben
location (Stand-)Ort, Lage
long lang
look (at) (an)sehen, betrachten
look up nachschlagen
lorry Lastwagen, Lkw
loud laut
lovely schön, reizend
low niedrig, leise
lunch (Mittag-)Essen
machine Maschine, Gerät
magazine Zeitschrift
mail Post
main Haupt-
major Haupt-
make machen
management Führung
manufacture Herstellung
manufacturer Hersteller/in
many viele
market Markt
married verheiratet
match Spiel, zuordnen
material Material, Stoff
matter Sache, etw ausmachen
may dürfen, können
mean bedeuten, meinen
meaning Bedeutung, Sinn
media Medien
medical medizinisch, Medizin-
meet treffen
meeting Versammlung, Besprechung, Treffen
member Mitglied
message Nachricht
method Methode
microphone Mikrophon
mid- Mitte der
milk Milch
minimum Minimum, Mindest-
mirror Spiegel, (wider)spiegeln
missing fehlend
mistake Fehler
mobile phone Mobiltelefon
mobile Mobilfunk-, Handy-
model Modell
moment Moment, Augenblick
money Geld
month Monat
more mehr
motivated motiviert
mountain (größerer) Berg
mouth Mund, Mündung
move (sich) bewegen, umziehen
movie (Spiel-)Film
must müssen
name Name
nearby nahe gelegen
necessary nötig, notwendig
need brauchen
neighbour Nachbar/in
neither ... nor weder ... noch
never nie(mals)
new neu
newspaper Zeitung
next nächste/r/s, danach
next to (direkt) neben
nice schön, nett
none keine/r/s
normal üblich, gewöhnlich
north Norden, Nord-
North American nordamerikanisch
nose Nase
notice Bekanntmachung
now nun, jetzt

number Nummer, Zahl
objective Ziel, Zweck
of course selbstverständlich
offer Angebot, (an)bieten
office Büro
office equipment Büroeinrichtung
often oft, häufig
oil Öl
old alt
on holiday auf Urlaub
on time pünktlich
on vacation auf Urlaub
oneself sich (selbst)
only nur, einzig
open offen, (sich) öffnen
opinion Meinung
opposite Gegenteil, gegenüber (von)
ordinary gewöhnlich
organization Organisation
organize organisieren
original ursprünglich, Original
other andere/r/s
over über, zu Ende, vorbei
own besitzen
pack (ver)packen
package Paket, Pauschale
page Seite
paint lackieren, (an)streichen
pair Paar
paper Papier, Zeitung
parent Elternteil, Mutter(gesellschaft)
part Teil, Rolle
partner Partner/in
party Party, Partei
passport Reisepass
past Vergangenheit
pay (be)zahlen
pen Füller, Kuli
per cent Prozent
person, people Mensch(en), Leute
personally persönlich
philosophy Philosophie
phone Telefon, anrufen
phone, over the ~ telefonisch, per Telefon
phrase Redewendung
pick up aufheben, nehmen
picture Bild, Gemälde
piece Stück, Teil
pilot Pilot/in
pineapple Ananas
place Stelle, Platz, Ort
plan Plan, planen
plane Flugzeug
plant Werk, Pflanze
plastic Plastik, Kunststoff
pleasant angenehm, nett
please bitte
pleasure Vergnügen, Freude
pocket Tasche
point Punkt, Spitze
politics (die) Politik
poor arm, schlecht
popular beliebt
position Stelle, Stellung
positive positiv
possible möglich
postcard Postkarte
power Kraft, Strom, Leistung, Macht
powerful stark
practice Praxis, Übung
prefer vorziehen
prepare vorbereiten
present Gegenwart, Geschenk, präsentieren
presentation Vorstellung
press pressen
price (Kauf-)Preis
print drucken
printer Drucker/in
private privat, persönlich
probably wahrscheinlich
problem Problem
produce produzieren, herstellen
product Produkt, Erzeugnis
production Produktion
profit Profit, Gewinn
program (Computer-)Programm
programme Programm
project Projekt
promise Versprechen, versprechen
prove beweisen
public öffentlich, Öffentlichkeit, Publikum
pull ziehen
quality Qualität
quarter of an hour Viertelstunde
question Frage
quiet still, ruhig, leise
quite ziemlich, ganz
rather ziemlich
reach erreichen
read lesen
ready fertig, bereit
really wirklich, tatsächlich
reason Vernunft, Grund
receive erhalten
recognise erkennen
recommend empfehlen
record Beleg, Rekord, aufzeichnen
red rot
reduce reduzieren
regular regelmäßig
remember sich erinnern
repeat wiederholen
reply Antwort, antworten
report Bericht, berichten
represent darstellen
request erbitten, bitten (um)
require benötigen
responsibility Verantwortung
result Resultat
return zurückkehren
right rechts, richtig, Recht
right, on the ~ auf der rechten Seite
right away sofort
right now zurzeit
role Rolle
room Zimmer, Raum, Platz
rule Vorschrift, Regel
safety Sicherheit
salad Salat
sale (Schluss-)Verkauf
same der-, die-, dasselbe
sandwich belegtes Brot
save sparen, sichern
say sagen
Scandinavia Skandinavien
scene Szene
schedule Zeitplan
school Schule
seat (Sitz-)Platz
secretary Sekretär/in
see sehen
seem (er)scheinen
sell (sich) verkaufen
seller Verkäufer/in
send senden, schicken
sensible vernünftig
serious ernst(haft)
several einige, mehrere
shake hands sich die Hand geben
shall sollen, werden
share Anteil, teilen
ship Schiff
shoe Schuh
shop Laden, Geschäft
short kurz, klein
show Show, zeigen
sign Zeichen, (Verkehrs-)Schild
signal Signal, Zeichen, zeigen
similar ähnlich
simple einfach
since da, weil, seit
single ledig, einzeln
sir mein Herr
sit (down) sich setzen
situation Lage
sky Himmel
slow langsam
small klein
smell Geruch, riechen
smile lächeln
snack Imbiss
so deshalb, so
some einige, etwas

somebody else jemand anders
something etwas
sometimes manchmal
soon bald
sorry traurig, Es tut mir leid
sound klingen
South African südafrikanisch
South America Südamerika
south Süden, Süd-
Spain Spanien
speaker Sprecher/in
special besondere/r/s
specialist Spezialist/in, Fachmann/frau
speed Geschwindigkeit
spell buchstabieren
spend ausgeben, verbringen
sport Sport(art)
spring Frühling
stand stehen
standard Niveau, Standard
start Anfang, Start, starten
state Zustand, Staat
States, the ~ die (Vereinigten) Staaten
station Bahnhof
stay bleiben
steel Stahl
step treten
straight ahead geradeaus
street Straße
stress Betonung, Stress
strike Streik
strong stark, kräftig
structure Aufbau
student Student/in, Lernende/r
study Studie, lernen, studieren
style Stil
success Erfolg
such solche/r/s
sugar Zucker
suggest vorschlagen
summer Sommer
supermarket Supermarkt
support (unter)stützen
sure sicher(lich)
surname Nach-, Familienname
surprise Überraschung
sweater Pullover
Swedish schwedisch, Schwedisch
symbol Symbol, Zeichen
table Tisch, Tabelle
take nehmen, dauern
take a seat Platz nehmen
talk (about) sprechen, reden (über)
team Mannschaft
technical technisch
technological technologisch
telephone Telefon
tell sagen, erzählen
terrible furchtbar
test Prüfung, prüfen
textbook Lehrbuch
thank danken
thank you danke
that das, dass, jene/r/s
there da, dort
therefore deshalb
thin dünn
think denken
this dies, diese/r/s
thorough gründlich
though jedoch
thought Gedanke
through durch
thus so, somit, daher
tight eng, knapp
time Zeit
tip Trinkgeld, Hinweis
title Titel
today heute
together zusammen
toilet Toilette
tomorrow morgen
too zu, auch
topic Thema
total Summe, (ins)gesamt
tour eine Rundreise machen
traffic (Straßen-)Verkehr
train Zug, ausbilden, trainieren
translate übersetzen
transportation Transport, Beförderung
travel Reisen, reisen
trouble Ärger, Problem/e
trousers Hose
truck Last(kraft)wagen
true richtig, wahr
truth Wahrheit
try versuchen
turn to zuwenden, gehen zu
turn (sich) drehen
TV Fernsehen, -seher
type Art, Typ
typical typisch
unchanged unverändert
under unter
understand verstehen
unfortunately leider
unless wenn nicht, es sei denn
unmarried unverheiratet
unsure unsicher
until bis
up oben, hinauf
use Verwendung, Gebrauch, benutzen, verwenden
useful nützlich
user-friendly benutzerfreundlich
usual gewöhnlich
usually meistens
very sehr
view Sicht, Ausblick
visit Besuch, besuchen
visitor Besucher/in
voice Stimme
wait for warten auf
walk (zu Fuß) gehen
warn warnen
waste Abfall, verschwenden
water Wasser
way Weg, Art (und Weise)
wear tragen
week Woche
weekend Wochenende
weekly wöchentlich
weigh wiegen
welcome begrüßen
well gut
west Westen, West-
what was, welche/r/s
where wo, wohin
whether ob
which welche/r/s
while während
whilst während
white board weiße Tafel
white weiß
whole ganze/r/s
why warum
wide breit, weit
wife (Ehe-)Frau
will werde(n)
wish wünschen
with mit, bei
within innerhalb (von)
without ohne
wood Holz
word Wort
work Arbeit, funktionieren, arbeiten
worker Arbeiter/in
world Welt
worried beunruhigt
would würde/n
write schreiben
wrong falsch
year Jahr
yellow gelb
yes ja
yet schon, doch
you're welcome bitte (schön)

IRREGULAR VERB LIST

arise	**arose**	**arisen**	*entstehen*
be	**was/were**	**been**	*sein*
bear	**bore**	**born(e)**	*(er)tragen*
become	**became**	**become**	*werden*
begin	**began**	**begun**	*starten, anfangen*
bind	**bound**	**bound**	*fesseln, binden*
break	**broke**	**broken**	*brechen, kaputtmachen*
bring	**brought**	**brought**	*bringen*
build	**built**	**built**	*bauen*
buy	**bought**	**bought**	*kaufen*
catch	**caught**	**caught**	*fangen*
choose	**chose**	**chosen**	*wählen*
come	**came**	**come**	*kommen*
cost	**cost**	**cost**	*kosten*
cut	**cut**	**cut**	*schneiden*
do	**did**	**done**	*tun, machen*
draw	**drew**	**drawn**	*zeichnen, ziehen*
drink	**drank**	**drunk**	*trinken*
drive	**drove**	**driven**	*fahren*
fall	**fell**	**fallen**	*fallen*
feel	**felt**	**felt**	*fühlen*
find	**found**	**found**	*finden*
fly	**flew**	**flown**	*fliegen*
forget	**forgot**	**forgotten**	*vergessen*
get	**got**	**got**	*bekommen*
give	**gave**	**given**	*geben*
go	**went**	**gone**	*gehen*
grow	**grew**	**grown**	*wachsen*
have	**had**	**had**	*haben*
hear	**heard**	**heard**	*hören*
hide	**hid**	**hidden**	*(sich) verstecken*
hit	**hit**	**hit**	*schlagen*
hold	**held**	**held**	*halten*
keep	**kept**	**kept**	*behalten*
know	**knew**	**known**	*wissen, kennen*
lay	**laid**	**laid**	*legen*
lead	**led**	**led**	*führen*
learn	**learnt**	**learnt (learned)**	*lernen*
leave	**left**	**left**	*(weg)gehen, (ver)lassen*
let	**let**	**let**	*lassen, erlauben*
lose	**lost**	**lost**	*verlieren*
make	**made**	**made**	*machen, tun*
mean	**meant**	**meant**	*bedeuten*
meet	**met**	**met**	*treffen*
pay	**paid**	**paid**	*bezahlen*

put	**put**	**put**	*legen, stellen*
read	**read**	**read**	*lesen*
ring	**rang**	**rung**	*klingeln*
rise	**rose**	**risen**	*steigen, sich erheben*
run	**ran**	**run**	*laufen, verwalten*
say	**said**	**said**	*sagen*
see	**saw**	**seen**	*sehen*
seek	**sought**	**sought**	*suchen*
sell	**sold**	**sold**	*verkaufen*
send	**sent**	**sent**	*senden*
set	**set**	**set**	*setzen, stellen, legen*
shake	**shook**	**shaken**	*schütteln*
show	**showed**	**shown (showed)**	*zeigen*
shut	**shut**	**shut**	*schließen*
sink	**sank**	**sunk**	*(ver)senken*
sit	**sat**	**sat**	*sitzen*
smell	**smelt**	**smelt (smelled)**	*riechen*
speak	**spoke**	**spoken**	*sprechen*
spell	**spelt**	**spelt (spelled)**	*buchstabieren*
spend	**spent**	**spent**	*ausgeben*
split	**split**	**split**	*aufteilen*
spoil	**spoilt**	**spoilt (spoiled)**	*verderben*
stand	**stood**	**stood**	*stehen*
steal	**stole**	**stolen**	*stehlen*
take	**took**	**taken**	*nehmen*
tell	**told**	**told**	*erzählen*
think	**thought**	**thought**	*denken*
wear	**wore**	**worn**	*tragen*
write	**wrote**	**written**	*schreiben*

ACKNOWLEDGEMENTS

DANKSAGUNG

Wir danken folgenden Firmen für die freundliche Unterstützung:

Balda AG, Bad Oeynhausen
Beiersdorf AG, Hamburg
Chevron
Daimler Chrysler Aerospace Airbus, Hamburg
ETH Umwelttechnik GmbH, Hamburg
Flughafen Frankfurt/Main
Holzland Wulf, Ahrensburg
Kubald AG, Neustadt am Rübenberge
Lloyd's of London
Medset Medizintechnik GmbH, Hamburg
Thistle Tower Hotel, London
UPS United Parcel Service

QUELLENVERZEICHNIS

Grafiken

Oxford Designers & Illustrators

Fotos

Balda AG, Bad Oeynhausen: *S. 5, 72, 73, 79;* **Beiersdorf AG**, Hamburg: *S. 5, 63, 68;* **Car Rental London**: *S. 40;* **COMSTOCK**, Luxemburg: *S. 22 (3), 25, 83;* **Corbis Stockmarket**, Düsseldorf: *Titel/J. Madere, S.17/M. Panci, S. 51/J. Feingersh;* **Daimler Chrysler Aerospace Airbus**, Hamburg: *S. 4, 8, 14;* **English Tourism Council**: *S. 39;* **ETH Umwelttechnik GmbH**, Hamburg: *S. 5, 95;* **Executive Planet**: *S. 61;* **Flughafen Frankfurt/Main**: *S. 10;* **Heritage Hotels**: *S. 50;* **Holzland Wulf**, Ahrensburg: *S. 4, 26, 28, 29, 30;* **HSBC**: *S. 42;* **Getty Images**, München: *S. 81/Stone/B. De Hogues, S. 89/Stone/S. Beer;* **The IMAGE BANK**, Berlin: *S. 7/Color Day, S. 15/G. Cralle/H. Sims (2)/D. Pizzi, S. 22/Infocus Int'l/B. Erlanson/N. Russell, S. 53/B. Erlanson;* **Kubald AG**, Neustadt: *S. 43, 56, 58;* **Medset Medizintechnik GmbH**, Hamburg: *S. 4, 16;* **Research Machines plc**: *S. 50;* **SIEMENS AG**, München: *S. 79;* **Thistle Tower Hotel**, London: *S. 38;* **UPS United Parcel Service**: *S. 91;* **The Wren's Hotel Group**: *S. 37*

Texte

Balda AG, Bad Oeynhausen: *S.74;* **Beiersdorf AG**, Hamburg: *S. 68;* **Car Rental London**: *S. 40;* **Daimler Chrysler Aerospace Airbus**, Hamburg: *S. 10, S. 14;* **executiveplanet.com**: *S. 61;* **HSBC**: *S. 42;* **Lloyd's of London**: *S. 113–118;* **Thistle Tower Hotel**, London: *S. 38;* **UPS United Parcel Service**: *S. 91;* **Weekly Telegraph**: *S. 51*

Nicht alle Copyright-Inhaber konnten ermittelt werden, deren Urheberrechte werden hiermit vorsorglich und ausdrücklich anerkannt.